THE
PRIEST
HUNTERS

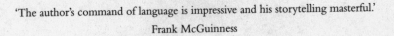

'The author's command of language is impressive and his storytelling masterful.'
Frank McGuinness

Praise for *Boycott*

'A hugely ambitious debut novel, Murphy astutely backs up his narrative with minute
research and well-drawn characters. Some of the famine scenes he conjures are
unforgettably harrowing, and he has produced an engaging labour of
love novel that deserves a wide readership.'
Dermot Bolger, *Irish Independent*

'*Boycott* has all the marks of a mature novelist and one with many more novels to come.
There is a great sense of urgency that motivates the book, which is perfectly
paced and beautifully written. Its achievement is impressive.'
Frank McGuinness

'A stirring and deeply researched story, it is a rattling yarn, with action racing along,
brilliant twists, flawed heroes and evil villains. *Boycott* is a powerful story, and I look forward
to the next novel from this muscular writer.'
Books Ireland

'Beautifully written. A skilful blend of fact and fiction.'
Sue Leonard, *Irish Examiner*

Praise for *The Most Famous Irish People You've Never Heard Of*
'A reminder of all that is good and great about our fine little island.'
Clare People

'A fascinating read.'
Sunday World

COLIN C. MURPHY was the Creative Director of one of Ireland's leading advertising agencies for over a decade, but left the advertising business in 2009 to pursue a full-time career in writing.

In 2012 his first novel, *Boycott*, about the notorious nineteenth-century land agent, was published to widespread critical acclaim. He is also the author of *The Most Famous Irish People You've Never Heard Of*.

Colin happened upon the subject of 'priest hunting' a number of times in the course of his general research and was soon fascinated by these eighteenth-century bounty hunters. As he began to dig deeper, he was surprised to find a large number of accounts of the activities of these men still survived, despite the fact that the events pre-dated most newspapers and that many of the records pertaining to priest hunting were destroyed in the civil war. He subsequently spent over a year researching and writing *The Priest Hunters*.

THE
PRIEST
HUNTERS

COLIN C. MURPHY

THE O'BRIEN PRESS
DUBLIN

First published 2013 by The O'Brien Press Ltd,

12 Terenure Road East, Rathgar, Dublin 6, Ireland.

Tel: +353 1 4923333; Fax: +353 1 4922777

E-mail: books@obrien.ie

Website: www.obrien.ie

ISBN: 978-1-84717-311-9

1 2 3 4 5 6 7 8 9 10
13 14 15 16 17

Layout and design: The O'Brien Press Ltd.

Cover design by Tanya Ross

Printed and bound by CPI Group (UK) Ltd, Croydon, CR0 4YY

The paper in this book is produced using pulp from managed forests.

DEDICATION

To my father, John.

ACKNOWLEDGEMENTS

I would like to thank the staff at The O'Brien Press for their help in producing this book, particularly the publisher, Michael O'Brien; my editor, Helen Carr; designer, Emma Byrne, for the book layout and design and Tanya Ross for the front cover design.

CONTENTS

INTRODUCTION

In the aftermath the Cromwellian Invasion of Ireland (1649-53) and half a century later, the Battle of the Boyne, Catholicism became increasingly linked to politics and political alliances and Catholics – Irish Catholics in particular – came to be viewed by the English monarchy in much the same way as they would view any other foreign enemy power. To counter this threat they introduced a series of repressive Penal Laws designed to essentially 'Protestantise' Ireland. The huge undertaking this presented put the authorities in Ireland under intense pressure to rid the country of Catholic clergymen – they simply didn't have the resources to control the overwhelmingly Catholic population. To assist them in their task, a new statute was issued in 1709 granting rewards of twenty pounds for any person apprehending a priest, or fifty pounds for the capture of a bishop – extremely large sums of money at the time. Within months a new breed of men had emerged from the shadows.

The age of the priest hunter had dawned.

Note: The use of the term [sic], denoting that spelling and grammatical errors are not in transcription but are reproduced from the original material, has been avoided due to the overwhelming number of errors in the original eighteenth century documentation and because certain words have evolved with different spelling in the intervening centuries, e.g. 'severall'. Other words such as 'sheweth' meaning 'shows that' or 'tells us that …' have disappeared from modern usage. A full listing of the sources from which all of this material was derived is presented at the back of the book.

Eager for blood money, with some Orange magistrate or landlord whose creed was hatred of papists as their master, accompanied by bands of soldiers, the priest-hounds hunted God's ministers night and day. A race of men whose love of money and hatred of Christianity peculiarly fitted them for the work, were employed to chase priests out of their hiding places, and drag them from their lurking holes. These agents of persecution assumed the garb of priests and went through the ceremonies of the Catholic religion. They thus wormed themselves into the confidence of the unwary, from whom they learned the names and haunts of concealed priests. Thus the clergy were tracked to their most secret retreats, and dragged sometimes from the very altar, robed in their sacred vestments, before tribunals, which sentenced them to perpetual banishment.
Thomas de Burgo, Hibernia Dominicana, 1762

Part One

A History of Violence

THE SPOILS OF WAR

T he dead almost outnumbered the living.

Those who lived did not breathe free air, but survived on the margins of existence, disenfranchised, poverty-stricken and robbed even of the right to seek solace from the God of their choosing. This was the situation in which the vast majority of Irish men and women found themselves in the immediate aftermath of the Cromwellian conquest of Ireland, when much of the land was seized and granted as rewards to the invading generals and their troops, who were awarded large allotments in lieu of wages. Protestant settlers who had been in Ireland before the war also took advantage of the it to increase their holdings. As a result of these events, the ownership of land by Irish Catholics plummeted from sixty per cent to less than ten per cent in just over a decade, and what they did own was mostly the infertile, mountainous land of Connaught. It is this time that provides the cradle of the later society that would condone and encourage the generous rewarding of men who hunted down clergy like

15

animals. It is here that the genesis of the age of the priest hunters can be found.

During the Irish rebellion of 1641 the Catholic rebels massacred about four thousand Protestant settlers in Ulster, with double that number perishing through exposure after being evicted from their homes and lands. But truth, it is often said, is the first casualty of war and by the time word of the massacre reached London popular pamphlets had exaggerated the figure to two hundred thousand. Revenge for this atrocity provided a principal motivation for Cromwell's invasion eight years later and his infamous massacres of the inhabitants of Wexford and Drogheda, women and children included. Cromwell left Ireland after just nine months, passing the baton of conquest to his generals and his son, Henry, and the four years of subsequent warfare were said to have claimed over six hundred thousand lives through battle and the disease that tended to accompany conflict in those times. It is likely that this number is also an exaggeration, but nonetheless, Ireland's population was reduced by anything from a quarter to three-quarters in just a few short years. One could travel for days on end without encountering a soul and those you might meet would most likely be reduced to starvation or possibly even cannibalism. As historian John P. Prendergast, writing in 1870 described it:

> ... *the plague and famine had swept away whole counties, that a man might travel twenty or thirty miles and*

*not see a living creature. Man, beast, and bird were
all dead, or had quit those desolate places. The troopers
would tell stories of the place where they saw a smoke, it
was so rare to see either smoke by day, or fire or candle by
night. They were seen to pluck stinking carrion out of a
ditch, black and rotten; and were said to have even taken
corpses out of the grave to eat. A party of horse, hunting
for Tories on a dark night, discovered a light; drawing near, they found it a ruined cabin, and, besetting it
round, some alighted and peeped in at the window. There
they saw a great fire of wood, and sitting round about it
a company of miserable old women and children,
and betwixt them and the fire a dead corpse lay
broiling, which as the fire roasted, they cut off collops
and ate.*

  Printed Declaration of the Council, 12th of May 1658.

The other factor that played a key role in decimating the population was the slave trade. Early in the conquest, in the immediate aftermath of the massacre at Drogheda, Cromwell himself
said,

> *I do not think thirty of their whole number escaped with
> their lives. Those that did are in safe custody in the
> Barbados.*

Britain had been involved in the lucrative trading of slaves for

17

almost a century and Cromwell and his generals recognised the opportunity to reward his foot soldiers by granting them free rein to seize and sell the people of Ireland into bondage. In the eyes of the English Parliament the Irish Catholic peasant was reduced to the level of a mere commodity, no more worthy of rights than a cow or a sheep. Here was an early precursor of the trade in clergymen that would follow in later decades as bands of soldiers roamed Ireland year after year in search of easy profit. They fell upon entire communities during the night, tearing families from their beds of straw and spiriting them away – men, women and children bound for the slave ships and life as chattels in the emerging colonies of the Caribbean. The practice of arbitrarily seizing Irish peasants, particularly the young, continued throughout the war and for a decade after, and was often accompanied by the burning of whole villages, the murder of the older men and raping of the women. In response to a request by Admiral Penn of Jamaica, Henry Cromwell had a thousand 'Irish wenches' rounded up for sale as slaves and suggested that between fifteen hundred and two thousand Irish boys of twelve to fourteen years of age could also be supplied with ease. Such had been the success of his round-ups that he found himself in essence 'over-stocked' and commented in his reply to the Admiral:

> *We could well spare them and they might be of use to you. Who knows, but it might be a means to make them Englishmen.*

Because of the nature of these 'slave hunts', no detailed records have survived, or were even kept, of the number of peasants seized, but estimates put the figure at anything between one hundred and three hundred thousand people sold into slavery. Besides enriching his men, it also cleared the land of its inhabitants and left much of it ripe for further plantation by Cromwell's officers.

By the time Cromwell and his forces had wrested control of Ireland from the Irish Catholic Confederation, who had governed most of Ireland since the 1641 rebellion, the population had been utterly devastated by war, disease and famine. And in the decade after the war, things didn't get much easier, as a new series of laws designed to generally disenfranchise Catholics would further oppress the ravaged population. Some sense of how brutally these laws were enforced may be gleaned from the fact that seventeen of the Catholic martyrs beatified in 1992 were from this period.

What's more, even those Catholic landowners who had played no part in the fighting had their lands confiscated and were granted the infamous option of 'To hell or to Connaught' – in other words they could re-settle in the largely infertile province of Connaught (and Clare) or else they would be executed. This was largely a means of confining any remaining Irish resistance within the boundaries of the Atlantic Ocean and the River Shannon.

This period saw the first phase of serious repression of the Catholic religion. The practice of Catholicism was criminalised and gangs of soldiers roamed the countryside in search of illicit masses often held in remote areas atop 'Mass Rocks'. (See Panel). Those found participating in these ceremonies were often butchered or sold into slavery. Catholics were also banished from Ireland's towns as a means of further reducing them to penury. An inscription on Bandon gates, in County Cork, famously declared:

> *Jew, Turk, or atheist*
> *May enter here, but not a papist.*

Typifying the defiance of the now hunted Irish Catholic clergy, a local priest by the name of O'Leary reputedly added:

> *Who wrote these lines, he wrote them well,*
> *For the same are writ on the gates of hell.*

A MASS OF MASS ROCKS

Mass rocks were in use for over a century in Ireland, serving principally as makeshift altars, but also on occasion as a screen behind which the priest would conceal himself to hide his identity. They were usually large boulders, roughly the size of a car, with a flattish top into which a cross was often carved. Despite the fact that they were usually located in remote areas far from the prying eyes of the authorities such as mountainsides or in dense woodland, many mass rocks were the scene of terrible atrocities, particularly in the aftermath of the

Cromwellian invasion. Their fellow Irish often betrayed the locations of the illegal masses for a reward, and on some occasions men, women and children alike were brutally massacred by the troops. There are literally thousands of mass rocks throughout Ireland, some of which were located in remote countryside at the time, but are now enveloped in a city, such as that at Shantalla in Galway, now called 'Emancipation Rock' as, appropriately, Daniel O'Connell gave an oration there in the nineteenth century. His subsequent efforts would forever consign the need for the mass rock to history.

It is important to note that the wave of anti-Catholicism that swept over Ireland (and England) during this time was not purely sectarian in nature. Although many Protestants, particularly in Cromwell's time, did view Catholics as heretics, since Henry VIII's Act of Supremacy (1534) and Elizabeth I's Oath of Supremacy (1559) had made the English sovereign the head of the Church of England, Catholics were considered to be allied to the Church of Rome, which was viewed as a foreign power. So the repression of Catholics was, in many ways, no different to the repression of a people on the basis of their nationality. Not only were Catholics viewed as heretical, but also as potential usurpers of the state. What's more, events such as the Gunpowder Plot half a century before, when a group of Catholics tried to blow up the House of Lords, and the so-called Popish Plot in

1678, which was a fake conspiracy to assassinate King Charles II devised by a Catholic-hating charlatan called Titus Oates, had fuelled an atmosphere of anti-Catholic hysteria throughout England.

Writing in 1914, the Reverend William P. Burke described the situation at the time:

> ... *if the outlook of these statesmen be duly considered and the circumstances of the time taken into account the task to which they set themselves will not seem so extravagant nor the means so inadequate. In our day religion and politics are regarded as two spheres hardly touching, in fact almost mutually exclusive; the axiom a free church in a free state is in practice almost universally acted on. But [then] the secularist ideal was still unknown; religion was believed to be a matter of vital politics; people were as convinced of the necessity of a state church as of a state police and could no more conceive a nation without an established religion than a man without a blood circulation. And further if there was one principle more than another settled and acknowledged by statesmen it was that all Catholics were rebels in posse if not actually, that loyalty to Rome was alike incompatible with civil allegiance and with individual liberty, and that therefore the first duty of a Protestant government to the Catholic religion was to uproot it.*

Reverend Burke's comment about 'religion and politics are two spheres hardly touching' was written at a time when Ireland was still part of Britain and so was essentially true. He was not to know that in the future Irish state, politics and religion would become entwined with the complexity of a double helix of DNA, yet his observation on the mindset of the politicians of the time is accurate. Ironically it would be the oppression of Catholicism during that bleak age that would forge the initial bond between religion and government. During the seventeenth century Ireland was overwhelmingly Catholic and one of the consequences of their persecution by England was that nationalism, more so than in any other country in Europe, became inextricably entwined with Catholicism in ways that nowadays one would more associate with the linking of Islam to the national identity of Arab states.

The practice of one's religion became also a statement of rebellion against an oppressor and the hunted priests and bishops became symbols of resistance, heroes to the beleaguered masses who would literally risk life and limb to protect them.

THE MERRIE MONARCH

Oliver Cromwell – possibly Ireland's greatest figure of hatred – went to his heavenly (or hellish) reward in September 1658, leading to a restoration of the monarchy in England and the reign of Charles II. There could be no greater contrast between the two men: one a puritanical, intolerant oppressor, the other a colourful, complaisant, even hedonistic, ruler. The rule of Charles II would also see a respite in the reign of terror being inflicted on Ireland's and Britain's Catholics. But in historical terms it would be but a brief calm before another gathering storm.

Charles II rescinded a lot of the anti-Catholic legislation that had marked the previous years and personally favoured religious tolerance. This may have been partly due to his having promised his ally Louis XIV of France to convert to Catholicism at some point in the future. Ultimately his conversion would not take place until he was lying on his deathbed, but during his twenty-five year reign he was in frequent conflict with the English Parliament as he tried to introduce greater religious freedom not just for Catholics, but for Protestant dissenters and Presbyterians, another of the religious groups persecuted under Cromwell.

Charles' tolerance may equally have been motivated by his somewhat licentious attitude to life and his blithe nature – he was known as the 'Merrie Monarch' and he devoted as much time to courting his mistresses as he did to matters of state. Although married, his philandering was public knowledge and he is known to have bedded at least seven mistresses who bore him twelve illegitimate children. The fact that his wife was childless and illegitimate offspring could not succeed to the throne was ultimately to have a profound effect on Ireland's future.

Interestingly, one of Charles' mistresses, Louise de Kérouaille, a Catholic, was an ancestress of Diana, Princess of Wales, Camilla, Duchess of Cornwall and Sarah, Duchess of York. Another was Nell Gwyn, an illiterate actress and a Protestant who is the ancestress of Samantha Cameron, the wife of the British Prime Minister, David Cameron. A comment attributed to Nell dramatises the ill will and distrust felt towards Catholicism at the time. Once, when travelling through Oxford the crowd mistook her for Louise and began yelling insults at her. Nell nonchalantly leaned out the coach window and called out 'Pray good people be civil, I am the *Protestant* whore.'

In Ireland the hunting down of priests or simply of people in the act of practising their faith had been relaxed. Many of the land-owning Protestant Irish were equally relieved at the easing of tensions. The peasant Irish now farmed their land, cooked their meals and tended to their horses and having them routinely butchered didn't make Protestant lives any easier, besides which, a great number of them found the whole practice immoral. Although the incident below comes from some twenty years later, it serves to illustrate the tolerant attitudes some Protestants felt towards the oppressed. It concerns the pursuit of an aged Catholic priest called Rev. Phelim O'Hamill, of County Antrim, and the Protestant magistrate, Mr McCartney, who accepted his surrender:

> ... [O'Hamill] hath this day surrendered himself to me. I have put him into our town gaol, and desire you would communicate this account to their Excellencies, the Lords Justices, where I intend to keep him till I know their further pleasure. But I must state that the behaviour of Phelim O'Hamill had been so exemplary since the revolution, and he hath, during the disturbances, shown such kindness to Protestants, protecting their property from injury, that the leading Protestants of the country now come forward to offer bail and to solicit his release.

Yet a grim cloud would soon blot out the brief glimpse Catholics had been given of a brighter world or instances of harmony such as described above.

As Charles' bed-hopping days drew to an end, it became apparent to the English establishment that despite his famed libido, he had failed to provide a Protestant heir to the throne. Several events during Charles' reign had also contributed to growing anti-Catholic fervour. In 1666 the Great Fire of London had destroyed much of the city, the tragedy being quickly and wrongly blamed on Popish conspirators. Because it had destroyed the livelihoods and homes of so many ordinary people it lasted long in the memory, the imagined Catholic arsonists never being forgiven. In 1676, it emerged that the presumptive heir, Charles' brother James, had converted to Catholicism. Then in 1685, the year of Charles' death, Louis XIV expelled the Huguenots from France causing a ripple of Protestant foreboding to spread across Europe.

Charles and James had a stroke of luck in more ways than one in 1683 when circumstances forced them to change their travelling plans, which saved them from an assassination attempt known as the Rye House Plot. The anti-Catholic conspirators were either executed or forced to flee abroad, several of them escaping to the sanctuary of Holland and the sympathetic court of William III, or William of Orange as he is more commonly known. Yet the attempt on the royals' lives had the effect of swinging public favour behind them and when Charles died, James succeeded to the throne with great public celebration.

His reign would be short-lived.

GREEN, WHITE
AND ORANGE

As a young man, James had spent much time in the Spanish royal court; it was here that he became on friendly terms with two Irishmen, Peter and Richard Talbot. Peter was the Catholic Archbishop of Dublin and Richard had survived Cromwell's massacre at Drogheda, and the pair undoubtedly influenced James' later decision to convert to Catholicism, which he was forced to keep secret for seven years.

Lechery seemed to run in the family, as James, like Charles, had an eye for the ladies and was reputed to have openly ogled the wives of other members of the court. The diarist Samuel Pepys recorded that James 'did eye my wife mightily' and the monarch is known to have indulged himself with a number of mistresses. While still single, James seduced Anne Hyde resulting in a pregnancy and decided to marry her. She would be pregnant a total of eight times in her lifetime, but only two daughters would survive, Mary and Anne; their uncle, Charles, who was King at the time of their birth, insisted for political reasons that they be raised as Protestants. Both women would play a subsequent and influential role in the forthcoming renewed suppression of Catholicism in Ireland.

When Mary was fifteen, in an attempt to assuage fears about his own religious leanings, her uncle, King Charles, arranged her marriage to William of Orange; her father, James, gave his consent only reluctantly. (James' own first wife having died some years beforehand, he also decided to take a fifteen-year-old bride. The fact that she was a Catholic Italian princess, Mary of Modena, didn't help to ease fears about a creeping papal influence.)

But if the Protestant establishment was worried then, James' brief three-year reign struck terror into their hearts. In 1687 he introduced the Declaration of Indulgence, which sought to suspend all the earlier penal laws introduced by the likes of Elizabeth I and Cromwell. He granted all Christian denominations the right to practise their faith, which made the Anglican Church fearful it would lose its position at the centre of British political power. James also began a process of granting Catholics positions of high office and also officially received the Papal Nuncio at court, an act that was viewed by many as tantamount to treason.

The following letter from Bishop John Brennan of Waterford and Lismore makes clear reference to Irish Catholics' delight at James' accession and also his placing of Catholics into positions of importance. It also contains a reference to his belief that the dark penal days are at an end.

> *To the Sacred Congregation of the Propagation of the*
> *Faith,*
> *At last this fierce and long tempest of persecution came*
> *to an end and the Divine Goodness is pleased to console*
> *His afflicted ones by placing on the royal throne our most*
> *pious King James who publicly professes the Catholic and*
> *Apostolic Faith and practises Christian virtue in a rare*
> *manner. Soon after his coronation he deputed as Viceroy*
> *of this Kingdom his Lordship the Count of Tyrconnell, a*
> *native of the country and brother of the Archbishop of*
> *Dublin, Talbot of blessed memory. He is a sincere and*
> *zealous Catholic much inclined to promote the glory of*
> *God and the splendour of the holy faith and to advance*
> *the Catholic Lords and nobility of the Kingdom in posi-*
> *tion and in fortune.*
> *Bishop John Brennan, November 1687*

Bishop Brennan's optimism would be sadly misplaced.

Conscious that his manoeuvrings were causing alarm James took the very unusual step of going on a speaking tour around England in an attempt to allay his enemies' fears. In one speech made in Chester, he actually demonstrated a level of religious tolerance that was in many ways ahead of its time.

Suppose there should be a law made that all black men should be imprisoned, it would be unreasonable and we had as little reason to quarrel with other men for being of different [religious] opinions as for being of different complexions.

But it was all to no avail. When his wife bore him a son and potential Catholic heir in the summer of 1688, it was to prove the birth of a new era in British politics as the Protestant establishment now recognised the possibility of a Popish dynasty.

This proved a Catholic too far for a great number of prominent English politicians and Protestant churchmen. They petitioned William of Orange to come to their help and restore the Protestant faith to the heart of Britain's power structures – in essence to de-throne James. William was only too happy to comply and in November of that year he invaded England. Unfortunately James had upset too many Protestants in his own ranks and several of his most senior generals deserted him and offered their services to William. Then his own daughter, Anne, who like her sister Mary (William's wife) had been raised a Protestant, did likewise. James realised his throne was crumbling beneath him and tried to flee to France. He was first captured but then released by William, keen not to make a martyr of the king, and his old ally Louis XIV granted him sanctuary.

James was deemed to have effectively abdicated and his daughter Mary was declared the rightful heir. William would serve alongside his wife; he as King and she as Queen. This would be England's only co-regency in history. Among the first of their acts was to pass a law that forbade a Catholic ascending the English throne or a monarch to marry a Catholic, a law that persists to this day, and a pointer to a rough road ahead for Ireland's Catholics.

SEAMUS AN CHACA

Two years after James' flight to France he attempted to regain the throne by confronting a Williamite army at the Battle of the Boyne. Despite the addition of six thousand French soldiers (see panel) to his ranks, supplied by Louis of France, his Jacobite forces still found themselves greatly outnumbered. (The term 'Jacobite' comes from the Latin for 'James', '*Jacobus*'). To make matters worse, many of his foot soldiers were untrained Irish peasants whose only weapons were farm implements. Although commemorated by the Orange Order on 12 July 1690, the battle actually took place on 1 July, the discrepancy due to the later adoption of the Gregorian calendar. It was a day that saw James' army routed and was, at the time, headline news across Europe, particularly as it was viewed as finally curtailing France's ever-expanding influence across the continent, and because of the alliance of the Protestant William with Catholic Rome.

In the aftermath James made a hasty retreat south to Wexford and boarded a ship for France. His abandonment of his Irish forces earned him the eternal sobriquet *'Seamus an chaca'*, literally 'James the shit'.

RELIGION AND THE BATTLE OF THE BOYNE

Although it has always been widely propagandised as a great Protestant victory over Catholics, it was anything but. One of William's key allies was Pope Alexander VIII (Papacy: 1689-1692) whose enemy, the Catholic James II, had the support of France's Louis XIV who in turn was in conflict with the Pope and with Catholic Spain. William's elite infantry troops, called the Dutch Blue Guards, charged into battle that day carrying a papal banner, and many of those troops were Dutch Catholics. On James' side, many of the French regiments were composed of German Protestants and James also had the support of a small number of English and Scottish Protestants who believed in the monarchy above religion and felt James had been illegally dethroned. In reality the battle was about political control in Europe and both Protestants and Catholics fought on both sides.

Although William offered a pardon to the regular soldiers in the Jacobite army, his generosity didn't extend to the officers or the Catholic landed classes, who were then left with no alternative but to continue the war. Most of the forces retreated to Limerick where a siege ensued in late 1690, which they successfully defended, forcing the Williamite army to retreat. But determined to finally overcome Catholic resistance, during the following year the Williamite army inflicted huge losses on the Irish forces in a number of battles, particularly the Battle of Aughrim, where the Jacobites lost four thousand men with the same number deserting in the aftermath. Despite the prominence given by history to The Battle of the Boyne, this battle was far more significant in the Williamite war and, in fact, up until the early nineteenth century, it was Aughrim that was the scene of annual Protestant celebrations, not the Boyne.

With the Jacobites routed, the Williamite army returned to Limerick and laid siege to the city for the second time in a year, this time successfully. Realising the battle was lost, Patrick Sarsfield took command of the city from the French leaders and negotiated a surrender under the Treaty of Limerick.

Under the terms of the treaty, fourteen thousand officers and men were permitted to leave Ireland in what became known as The Flight of the Wild Geese. It is believed that ten thousand women and children accompanied them. Those who remained had to swear an oath of loyalty to William and Mary in return for which toleration would be shown for their Catholic faith. Article 1 of the treaty stated:

> *The Roman Catholics of this kingdom shall enjoy such*

> *privileges in the exercise of their religion as are consistent*
> *with the laws of Ireland, or as they did enjoy in the reign*
> *of King Charles the second: and their majesties, as soon as*
> *their affairs will permit them to summon a parliament in*
> *this kingdom, will endeavour to procure the said Roman*
> *Catholics such farther security in that particular, as may*
> *preserve them from any disturbance upon the account of*
> *their said religion.*

In the context of the times, the treaty seemed truly generous and merciful, but ironically, thanks largely to the Pope, the Jacobites' enjoyment of William's apparent toleration would be short-lived.

ON THE WRONG SIDE
OF THE LAW

Recently discovered documents have revealed that prior to William's Boyne victory, Pope Innocent XI secretly paid him the equivalent of about four million euro in today's terms to help William's war effort. Researchers Rita Monaldi and Francesco Sorti uncovered documents from a papal envoy discussing large sums that William apparently owed Innocent, and also papers from Innocent's family records that reveal that the Holy See sent 150,000 *scudi* (the then Italian currency) to William via a secret intermediary. This seemed to confirm claims made by other historians down the centuries. And at the time, Innocent XI had good reason to support William, as his enemy Louis XIV had been severely restricting papal authority in France for almost a decade.

Yet just two short years after the end of the war, the then Pope, Innocent XII, decided it would *now* serve the Vatican's interests better to switch allegiance from William and Mary to Louis XIV, and when the Pope decided to recognise James II, and subsequently his son James Francis Edward (who would become known as 'The Old Pretender') as the legitimate heirs to the English throne, William and Mary's attitude to all Catholics hardened, as once again they were seen as potential usurpers of the state. And isolated on a small island far from the protective arm of Louis or the Vatican, Ireland's Catholics found themselves once more facing the prospect of suppression.

Although the phrase wouldn't be coined for some eighty years, this in effect marked the beginning of the 'Protestant Ascendancy' in Ireland, which would endure for almost two centuries. The phrase is actually misleading in many ways as it gives the impression of Protestant ascendancy over Catholicism, but the ruling classes also sought to repress Presbyterians and all non-Christians.

Over the coming decades King William and Queen Mary, and subsequently Queen Anne, Mary's sister, would put their royal seal of approval on a multitude of laws designed to essentially 'Protestantise' Ireland.

Beginning in 1695 a new set of Penal Laws was introduced that bit by bit would strip Irish Catholics of almost all their basic human rights, including the right to practise their religion. The new laws would also leave them socially excluded, scraping an existence on the fringes of society. Professor William Lecky, a Protestant nineteenth-century historian who was sympathetic to the plight of the Irish Catholic (Lecky's statue can be seen in the grounds of Trinity College), described the object of the new penal laws thus:

> To deprive Catholics of all civil life, to reduce them to
> a condition of extreme, brutal ignorance, to disassociate
> them from the soil … and to expatriate the race.

The new laws, which were originally written in legalese that would have been near incomprehensible for the average peasant, were defined in simpler terms by the respected professor:

- The Catholic Church was forbidden to keep church registers.
- The Irish Catholic was forbidden the exercise of his religion.
- He was forbidden to receive education.
- He was forbidden to enter a profession.
- He was forbidden to hold public office.
- He was forbidden to engage in trade or commerce.
- He was forbidden to live in a corporate town or within five miles thereof.
- He was forbidden to own a horse of greater value than five pounds.
- He was forbidden to own land.
- He was forbidden to lease land.
- He was forbidden to accept a mortgage on land in security

for a loan.

- He was forbidden to vote.
- He was forbidden to keep any arms for his protection.
- He was forbidden to hold a life annuity.
- He was forbidden to buy land from a Protestant.
- He was forbidden to receive a gift of land from a Protestant.
- He was forbidden to inherit land from a Protestant.
- He was forbidden to inherit anything from a Protestant.
- He was forbidden to rent any land that was worth more than thirty shillings a year.
- He was forbidden to reap from his land any profit exceeding a third of the rent.
- He could not be guardian to a child.
- He could not, when dying, leave his infant children under Catholic guardianship.
- He could not attend Catholic worship.
- He was compelled by law to attend Protestant worship.
- He could not himself educate his child.
- He could not send his child to a Catholic teacher.
- He could not employ a Catholic teacher to come to his child.
- He could not send his child abroad to receive education.

In terms of this book, the laws that principally concern us are the first two, and also the banning of people attending Catholic worship. King William would go further in 1697, when he issued a decree ordering that all Catholic clergy must actually vacate Ireland by a given date. In fact the law sought to legally link Catholicism with sedition and rebellion:

> *Whereas it is notoriously known, that the late rebellions*
> *in this kingdom have been promoted by popish bishops*
> *and other ecclesiastical persons of the popish religion …*
> *all popish archbishops, bishops, vicars-general, deans,*
> *Jesuits, monks, friars, and all other regular popish clergy*
> *shall depart out of this kingdom before the 1st day of*
> *May, 1698.*

The law went on to threaten imprisonment and exile for failing to leave Ireland, and should a clergyman decide to return, he would be guilty of high treason, an offence punishable by death.

The laws also outlined extremely severe penalties for harbouring a member of the 'popish clergy' including fines amounting to roughly a year's earnings or double that sum for a second offence or for a third, the confiscation of all his worldly possessions for life.

Possibly conscious that their new penal laws might be viewed as excessive by their own magistrates and justices of the peace and that these men who lived and worked among the Catholic peasants might have some sympathy for their plight, William decided they needed to incentivise them. They included in their laws a section instructing their officers of the law to regularly issue warrants for the apprehension of clergy with the threat that should they fail to do their duty, they would be fined one hundred pounds for every 'act of neglect' in this regard and lose their job for life.

The officials had little or no choice but to set about their task with gusto. Countless priests, friars and nuns were rounded up by soldiers and hauled before the courts and before long hundreds of men and women of the cloth were being loaded in chains aboard ships and condemned to permanent banishment from their native soil.

Yet it was soon apparent to the authorities that they had only scratched the surface. Through the hated informers they learned that for every priest they had seized, five more were at large, practising mass in remote places far from their eyes, living as hermits or seeking shelter within their flock, disguising themselves as the peasants they sought to serve.

Queen Mary had died in 1694 and William III had continued to rule alone until his death in 1702. His successor was Mary's sister, Anne. Both of the women had been estranged from their father, James II, and raised as Protestants and Anne would continue the policy of repression during her reign. In fact the acts she introduced between 1703 and 1709 actually made matters worse for Catholicism as they sought to undermine what they saw as a giant conspiracy of priest and peasant on the island of Ireland. It would be a specific clause in Anne's new penal laws that would give rise to the new profession of priest-hunting.

THE DAWN OF THE HUNTER

The humble petition of William Montgomery.
Sheweth That at the Assizes for the County of Antrim
held on the 28th day of March 1716, John McDonald a
popish priest not registered was tried and found guilty for
exercising the function of a popish priest and not being
registered at your Petitioner's prosecution. That your Peti-
tioner was at great trouble and expense in apprehending
and prosecuting the said McDonald. He therefore prays
for a grant of the reward set forth in the proclamation.
Enclosed is certificate of the Clerk of the Crown.

The 'humble petitioner' above would officially have been labelled as 'an Agent of the Crown'. To the general public he was the loathsome 'priest hunter'. Although his sentence is not known, the most likely fate of Fr McDonald is that he faced imprisonment for what might be months, or in some cases, years, followed by permanent banishment to Europe. William Montgomery would be handsomely rewarded for hunting down the priest. It is recorded that six months later he was granted thirty pounds for his efforts. (It seems the mechanisms of the state in the eighteenth century moved with comparable slowness to our present day bureaucracy).

Innumerable such petitions still exist, some colourful, detailing countless captures of clergymen and testifying to the effectiveness of the new statute that had appeared in Britain's law books early in the reign of Queen Anne.

King William's Banishment Act had succeeded in removing hundreds of priests from Ireland's shores, but to the authorities' consternation many of them secretly returned, despite the threat of the death penalty. With their policy clearly failing, Queen Anne decided on a new approach. (To her credit, she was reportedly troubled that the rigorous implementation of this and subsequent acts might infringe the Treaty of Limerick, which had promised to preserve certain rights for Catholics. However she was not sufficiently bothered to prevent their implementation.) So her ministers and lawmakers conceived the Act for Registering the Popish Clergy in 1704, which they hoped would give them greater control over the influence of 'Popery' and while not eliminating Catholicism utterly, would continue to stigmatise Catholics and marginalise them in terms of wealth and influence.

The act required all priests and bishops to register at their local court by a set date, providing their name, age, parish, when and by whom they were ordained. They were also required to provide the enormous surety of one hundred pounds, to be forfeited if they engaged in non-peaceable behaviour, which could be very loosely interpreted. They were also barred from practising their religion outside of their designated parish and they could not have a curate, elements that would severely limit the spread and continuance of Catholicism. Priests were also offered the opportunity to convert to the Church of Ireland, for which act they would be rewarded with an annual payment of twenty pounds to be raised through levies on the impoverished parishioners. It is hardly surprising that very few took up this offer, as it would have engendered such loathing of them within the community that their lives might be at risk.

At the time many of the clergy weren't too troubled by the registration act. It seemed the least bad option, as they believed that it gave them a legal standing and that they would be allowed to openly practise their faith in a limited manner. Besides, most secretly intended to breach the laws restricting them to their parishes, aware that enforcing such a law would be difficult, especially in remote, rural parishes. Accordingly the majority of priests registered, numbering one thousand and eighty-nine. The penalties for not registering were as before – transportation, prison or even death.

Within a few years it was apparent that most of the registered priests were in breach of the rules and that many priests who had been exiled had returned and were secretly moving about the countryside serving masses, marrying couples, baptising babies and officiating at funerals. So in 1709 the crown decided that all registered priests must now take the Oath of Abjuration by 25 March of the following year, which effectively demanded that they renounce their religion:

> *I do solemnly and sincerely profess, testify, and declare,*
> *That I do believe that in the sacrament of the Lord's*
> *Supper there is not any transubstantiation of the elements*
> *of bread and wine into the body and blood of Christ, at*
> *or after the consecration thereof, by any person whatso-*
> *ever; and that the invocation and adoration of the Virgin*
> *Mary, or any other saint, and the sacrifice of the mass, as*
> *they are now used in the church of Rome, are superstitious*
> *and idolatrous …*

The fact that just thirty-three priests in Ireland swore the oath underlines its intolerability. The upshot was that almost every other priest in Ireland was now a criminal.

But the forces of law simply could not cope with the numbers and Ireland, particularly then, presenting such a wild and largely uninhabited landscape, was proving too vast an area in which to effectively enforce the newest penal edict. The cost of significantly increasing the forces of law would be exorbitant, so that same year the monarchy came up with a way to effectively kill two birds with one stone.

> *Anne c.3:*
> *For discovering, so to lead to the apprehension and con-*
> *viction of any popish archbishop, bishop, vicar general,*
> *Jesuit, monk, or other person exercising foreign ecclesiasti-*
> *cal jurisdiction, a reward of 50 pounds, and 20 pounds*
> *for each regular clergyman or non-registered secular*
> *clergyman so discovered, and 10 pounds for each popish*
> *schoolmaster, usher or assistant; said reward to be levied*
> *on the popish inhabitants of the county where found.*

In other words the Crown were not only offering a bounty on the Catholic clergy, but forcing the locals to pay it. The hatred for those who would chose to take up this offer would have no bounds. The peasant, already living a life of bare subsistence, would now have to pay some unscrupulous mercenary to help destroy one of the few comforts to which they clung in life – their faith.

TINKER, TAILOR, SOLDIER, PRIEST HUNTER

Kinsale 31 January 1716To their Excellencies the Lords Justices etc.

The humble Petition of George Hooper of the City of Cork. Sheweth that your Petitioner apprehended one Cornelius Madden, a popish priest and also Daniel Sullivan a popish school master who were tried and convicted at the assizes held for Cork 24 March 1716 and ordered to be transported. The premises considered, may it please your Excellencies to grant the reward.

(Certificate enclosed) that Cornelius Madden was convicted for celebrating mass and exercising his function without being registered

Who were these men, like George Hooper, who were prepared to risk the wrath of the masses and endure their detestation?

An old English children's rhyme provides as good a description of their backgrounds as one might find anywhere:

> *Tinker, Tailor,*
> *Soldier, Sailor,*
> *Rich Man, Poor Man,*
> *Beggar Man, Thief.*

They came from all walks of life, the priest hunters. There was no need to register as an 'official priest hunter' – any disreputable opportunist could simply take up the profession, if he felt up to the task. Some were Irish Catholics, as impoverished as the people among whom they plied their odious trade; others were wealthy beyond the imagination of most. They might be recruited from the ranks of criminals or be former soldiers keen to turn their skills to profit. In some cases they were members of the landed gentry who presumably took up the profession of priest hunting (or 'priest catching' as it was also commonly known) either from some deeply-felt loathing of Catholicism or as a means of reinforcing their ever-more dominant status in Irish society. Many were the official enforcers of the law, sheriffs, magistrates and the like, keen to generously supplement their income from the crown with colossal bonuses. Based on some of the stories concerning these men, a number of them might nowadays be termed psychopathic. Others even came from continental Europe to take up the Crown's generous offer.

And it was generous. Exorbitant even. You can get an idea of how attractive the newly-created profession was by looking at the annual payment of twenty pounds offered to priests who converted. Aware that they would have no other means of monetary support (as their flock would now hold them in ignominy), the Crown made the reward of converting to Protestantism quite generous. In other words a priest could live in reasonable comfort on twenty pounds per annum. Also at the time the annual wage of a skilled tradesman such as a carpenter was just fifteen pounds, so it can be inferred that the vast majority of people who were uneducated and largely unskilled existed on a fraction of this. In that context the possibility of earning twenty pounds (later increased to thirty) for capturing a priest or fifty for a bishop must have seemed to many like the eighteenth-century equivalent of winning the lottery.

And it wasn't as if they were being asked to pursue dangerous criminals or armed and trained soldiers. The men they sought to capture or kill were largely men of peace, one of whose principal aims in life was to preach non-violence. Add to that the fact that many of them were old and infirm and priest-hunting must have seemed like easy money. Yet, as many found out to their cost, some priests weren't quite willing to turn the other cheek and go quietly and besides, they may have been peaceful men of the cloth, but they had a vast army of covert support willing to risk their lives to protect them and seek vengeance should any harm befall them.

Modern culture has made us all familiar with the old posters of America's Wild West that proclaimed 'Wanted – Dead or Alive'. And although the law specifically sought the apprehension only of unregistered priests for transportation or for trial for treason, in reality the forces of law cared little in what condition the victim was delivered to their door. A meeting of the Grand Jury, for example, for Tipperary attempted to have a particular priest certified to be a 'Torie' – a type of armed highway robber, and therefore liable to be justifiably shot on sight:

> *County of Tipperary to wit.*
> *We the Grand Jury at said Assizes in lawful manner*
> *Sworn and charged John Hally of Killerke in the County*
> *of Tipperary, popish priest, who stands indicted that he*
> *contemptuously and unlawfully did endeavour to seduce*
> *and pervert Charles Moore, a professed Protestant of the*
> *Church of Ireland as by Law ... (that Fr Hally be) certi-*
> *fied to be a Torie, robber and rapparee of the Popish reli-*
> *gion, out in Arms and on his keeping and not ameanable*
> *to Law and we pray your Lordships he may be represented*
> *as such.*

In effect the priest hunters were being handed *carte blanche* to use whatever means they liked, and some would take full advantage of the law's blind eye.

WHAT'S IN A NAME?

The British Conservative Party are commonly known as the Tories, but what many of its own members don't realise is that the word 'Tory' derives from the Middle Irish (tenth to twelfth-century) word '*tóraidhe*', which was essentially an outlaw or robber. During the Confederate Wars or the Eleven Years War, which ended in an Irish defeat at the hands of Cromwell, the term was applied to the Irish Confederate soldiers as a term of abuse. Half a century later, the term was adopted as an insult to supporters of the Catholic James II. Eventually the Conservative Party coalesced from the descendants of this group of Jacobite supporters and moderate Whigs, (who would later form the Liberal Party), but the nickname 'Tory' stuck. The origins of the term 'Whig' are uncertain, with two possible sources; it may come from the Scottish term 'Whiggamores' who were opponents of Charles I, or a more disparaging etymology is that it comes from the old English word 'whigg', which meant 'country bumpkin'. From an Irish perspective in the eighteenth and nineteenth century, it would have come as no surprise that outlaws and country bumpkins occupied the opposing sides of the House of Commons.

But in most cases it was simply more practical to take a priest alive, as it would save the hunter the effort of transporting a body over long distances and often through dangerous mountain terrain where avenging peasants might attack him. Yet being captured was often a death sentence in itself for the priest, who at the very least would have to endure months in the filth and squalor of an eighteenth-century prison before being exiled for life.

It is difficult to know how many priest hunters were operating in the period. But given the number of recorded petitions that survived, it is safe to assume that several hundred men were engaged in priest hunting at any given time. These men roamed the countryside usually on horseback in search of their prey, often armed with a flintlock pistol or the British musket known as the 'Brown Bess' among Her Majesty's forces, or more commonly nicknamed in Ireland during the reign of Anne as 'The Queen's Arm' – thus named because no Catholic priest was safe from the long arm of English law. When firearms weren't available to the hunters and on the assumption that they were pursuing unarmed men, any weapon might suffice and swords, knives or even simple clubs were employed. When closing in on a particular priest, the hunter would often recruit others to help him at the cost of a shilling or so each – also a generous reward for a few days' work. These would be mere thugs, often local Irishmen without any means of subsistence or with little conscience. The petition of a priest hunter called Samuel Porter in Cork, made in 1716, although somewhat simpering and coloured with superlatives about his bravery and personal burdens, gives us an insight into how these men operated.

> *To his Grace the Duke of Bolton Lord Lieutenant General etc.*
>
> *The Humble petition of Samuel Porter of Inishannon in the County of Corke. Sheweth That your petitioner for severall years has showed most sincere zeale and affection for his Majestie's service and the Protestant interest by his diligence in apprehending and prosecuting many of the regular and secular popish Clergy. That he performed severall orders and directions from the Justices of the Peace of Corke to the hazard of his life and at great expense with men, horses and arms assisting him. That at the last assizes held for the said county the 6th of August last your petitioner appeared at the perill of his life and brought to justice two popish priests videlicet Charles Carthey and Teige Mahoney for saying mass not registered who obstinately refused to take the oath and were convicted before the Right Hon. the Lord Chief Justice Foster. That your petitioner from his fatigue and rideing in executing said order has laboured under a heavy fitt of sickness to the detriment of his fortune having twelve children and an aged father to maintain. That your Petitioner hopes to bring several priests to justice, they being very numerous and dayly flocking into the kingdom and severall of them by messages and letters have made your petitioner large*

*offers and a yearly sallery and retain for him the good will
of their assemblyes but your petittioner has an abhorrence
to them and does wholly rely on your Grace and Lordships countenance. That popish persons have spirited and
trained up their mobbs in a most violent manner to take
your Petitioner's life.*

S. PORTER. *Received 8 October 1717.*

Elements of Porter's petition are undoubtedly true; some are very likely exaggerations to help progress his claim. Shovelling it on heavily, Porter claims he was fatigued, sick *and* had thirteen mouths to feed, all the while with his life under threat. The latter is the only element of his claim that is likely to be fully accurate as such was the contempt in which these men were held that they were often subject to violent assault, and cases were recorded all over the country of priest hunters being intimidated, burnt out, assaulted, or even killed, some of which are documented later in this book. It's also doubtful he was offered bribes to retain his good will, as the ordinary peasants would not have had the means. It's actually quite likely that Porter's priest-hunting endeavours provided him with a life of some comfort as the same man turns up two years later, this time in Clare where he is petitioning for 'the usual reward' for apprehending a priest named Brady. In addition he sought an extra reward offered by the Grand Jury of County Clare for the crime of high treason, as it seems Fr Brady had returned to Ireland having already been exiled to Europe.

The priest's sentence might well have been execution.

Further evidence of the character of many of these men and of the retribution they might face can be gleaned from a petition made by a priest hunter called Richard Huddy of Ballynoe (an area in east Cork) in 1709. Having seized a priest called William Hennessy, Huddy's house and property were burnt to the ground. Huddy escaped with his life and his plight so enraged the local magistrates that they not only offered a twenty pound reward, but a pardon for life of all crimes, murder excepted, to anyone bringing about the capture and conviction of the incendiaries. Put simply, they were recruiting the lowest criminal elements in Ireland.

But before they could arrest the priests, they first had to find them and much of their information came from informants paid by the crown. These were ordinary people who would hear word of a forthcoming mass or other sacrament through the local grapevine, then betray their fellow Catholics by selling the information to the priest hunter. As hated as informants were, even greater opprobrium was reserved for the occasional priest who chose to sell out his former brothers for profit. Instances of this were rare, particularly as the individual could expect to spend the rest of his life looking over his shoulder.

One such incident was recorded by Primate Hugh McMahon who wrote that he had to fly from his hiding place near Carrickmacross in Monaghan after the local priest hunters had been tipped off by an 'unworthy person whom I had refused a parish'.

Another incidence is recorded in the official documents of the time, which reveal that a John Hennessy, the ex-parish priest of Doneraile in Cork, gave evidence that he'd been in the company of a number of bishops and priests who he named and who had been plotting to raise money for the purpose of restoring James II to the throne and 'put their present majesties and all the royal family to the sword'.

The other source of information on the whereabouts of the priests was eagerly supplied by the Protestant clergy who had their own flock engaged in gathering information as they moved about the community, as can be evidenced from the letter below from a senior Protestant clergyman.

Limerick August 15 1714.

To Joshua Dawson Esq. Sir ... having been employed by the Lords Justices to enquire after the persons mentioned I send you the following account viz. That Daniel Falvey is a Franciscan Fryar formerly belonging to the abby of Irelogh [now Muckross] neer Kilarny in the county of Kerry, is a middle aged man, and lives now with Dennis Mahoney at Drommore in the Barony of Glanerogh in the County of Kerry. That Florence McCarthy formerly guardian of the said abby is a very old man and living now at the five mile bridge within five miles of Kilarny on the road to Macroom and that David Fitz Gerald was formerly a Friar in the abby of Askeaton in the County

of Limerick but he removed out of that county into the
County of Clare but where he lives in that County I
cannot learn.
Your most humble servant, THO. LIMERICK.

Should no information be available to the priest hunter regarding the possible hiding place of a particular priest, his only option was for the wolf to disguise himself as a sheep, blend into the community and wait patiently for word to come of the priest's appearance at the celebration of a sacrament and then to make his move.

With the potential for betrayal and capture awaiting them at every turn, the priests lived a life on the edge of peril and it demanded of them the acquisition of the guile of a fox seeking to outwit a bloodthirsty pack of hounds. From 1709 onwards, those hounds were loosed upon the clergy the length and breadth of the land.

Part Two

MANHUNTING

THE MARTYR OF
INISHOWEN

Much of the historic legacy of the town of Buncrana on the Inishowen peninsula in County Donegal exists thanks to the Vaughan family who were wealthy eighteenth-century landowners in the area. Buncrana Castle, which more resembles a stately house than a castle, was built by a Vaughan in 1718, as was the pretty six-arched Castle Bridge that spans the Crana River. The actual location of the town is largely due to the Vaughans, as it was their introduction of the fledgling linen, cotton and salt-producing industries, which contributed to the continued expansion of the town. But no manmade monument exists to mark one of their most infamous legacies to the locality, merely a rough outcrop of rock jutting west out into Lough Swilly and widely known in the area as Fr Hegarty's Rock. It was at this spot that a Vaughan would carry out one of the most brutal and infamous murders of the penal era. Coincidentally, the rock is almost directly opposite the place called Killygarvan on the western shore of Lough Swilly, where a quarter of a century after the event described here, a similarly-named priest, Fr O'Hegarty, would also meet his end at the hands of a priest hunter.

At the start of the seventeenth century the O'Doherty clan ruled the Inishowen peninsula. After what was known as 'O'Doherty's Rebellion' in 1608, the clan was crushed by crown forces under Sir Arthur Chichester and their lands confiscated and subsequently leased to a Welshman called Sir John Vaughan. Later generations of the Vaughan family served the crown loyally during the turbulent century that followed and were keen supporters and advocates of the policy of Catholic suppression, which was one of the less appealing bequests they made to the infant born around 1650 and given the name George.

George Vaughan rose to the rank of Colonel in the Donegal Regiment of the British Army, (which would later change its name to The Prince of Orange's Own Regiment, leaving no doubts as to where its sympathies lay). Local lore tells us that when George Vaughan returned from his military career he took up residence on the family estate in Buncrana and soon after undertook a strategy of Protestantising the people of the area. His principal means of achieving this was to set up a number of soup kitchens that would offer badly needed sustenance to the poverty-stricken Catholic population, most of whom existed on a precipice of starvation. His apparent benevolence had a catch however – to get your bowl of soup you had to attend Protestant church services. The soup was only dished up on Fridays and a last qualification was that it must be consumed in public. Anyone who partook was granted the derogatory sobriquet 'Friday' before their surname by their Catholic neighbours, as in the 'Friday Dohertys' or the 'Friday Gallaghers' and so on.

Among the more chilling reminders of the family's reign in the area are a couple of stone pillars that are known as Vaughan's Gallows, and evidently keen to maintain the family's fearsome reputation and equally keen to rid the area of the scourge of popery, George set himself up as the local priest hunter.

He knew the road to the eradication of Catholicism would be a long one, particularly if the peasants continued to have their faith ministered to them, and the principal stone in his shoe as he travelled that road was the local priest, Fr Hegarty.

At the General Sessions of the Peace in 1704, along with a number of other priests in the Inishowen area, Fr James Hegarty had officially registered as Parish Priest of Fawn (Fahan). It was recorded that he'd been ordained in 1672 by none less than Oliver Plunkett (now Saint Oliver Plunkett) who was then the Titular Primate of Ireland. He was fifty-five in the year of his registration. The fact that he was registered allowed Fr Hegarty to openly practise his religion within his parish albeit with the usual caveats of not being allowed a curate and so on. Unless he broke the rules of his registration, neither Vaughan nor any of the agents of the law could legally touch him. During his years as parish priest he developed a close bond with his parishioners, which was strengthened by the fact that his family came from the area. His sister, Mary, still lived in the village of Ballynary, a couple of miles to the north of Buncrana. As the sole serving Catholic clergyman he officiated at every key event in the lives of the local peasants, marrying them,christening their newborn children and praying over their graves when they passed away.

Then in 1709, the crown decided to shift the goalposts, passing the edict requiring all registered priests to take the Oath of Abjuration by 25 March of the following year. Required in effect to renounce his most cherished, fundamental beliefs, Fr Hegarty chose instead to go into hiding.

Colonel Vaughan was soon on his trail but months went by and his searching proved fruitless – he could unearth no trace of the priest. Each night as the Colonel retired to the comfort of his bed surrounded by thick walls that kept the chill Donegal winds at bay, Fr Hegarty would emerge from his hiding place and move with stealth about the parish. Christenings, confessions, marriages and even funeral rites were now observed only by candlelight. Masses were few and literally far between, held in the dead of night in remote places, after which the priest would steal away into the darkness before any informer might betray him. So secret was his refuge, in fact, that only one person had been entrusted with its whereabouts – his sister, Mary.

Mary had married a man called Thomas Doherty many years before, her own brother officiating at the ceremony. Her dowry had provided Doherty with a small plot of rough land in Ballynary that barely supplied their needs, but was sufficient to feed them and the two sons she bore. It also provided food enough for Mary to regularly smuggle to her fugitive brother, a task she often undertook in the hours before dawn. Thomas Doherty was not content with his lot. He barely scraped a living off the land and had already succumbed to the temptation of Colonel Vaughan's offer of Friday soup against his wife's wishes. He'd also convinced his grown sons to do the same, so in effect the Friday Dohertys had renounced their religion. Seeing his wife regularly take a supply of their scarce stocks of food to her brother made him deeply resentful.

A year had passed since Fr Hegarty had become an outlaw and as the spring of 1711 approached, Colonel Vaughan decided to up the stakes in his hunt for the elusive priest. He knew through informers that Catholic ceremonies were being conducted, but none could provide advance information of when they would be held so he could lay a trap, and he still had no clue to the priest's hiding place. Fr Hegarty had been appointed Dean of the Parish, a title that made him as valuable a catch as a bishop – he was worth fifty pounds. Yet Vaughan had no interest in the reward; he was extremely wealthy and his vast estate included the most fertile lands in the region. Considering his track record, his motivations were more likely a deep hatred of Catholicism. He decided to offer the reward money along with a sizeable chunk of land as a reward to anyone who would provide information leading to the priest's capture.

Most of the traditional accounts of what subsequently happened are in broad agreement. Vaughan's offer was too tempting for Thomas Doherty to ignore. He lay and watched as his wife rose from their bed in the early hours of a May morning. He let her gather her meagre supply of food and slip out the cottage door and then he quickly rose and set off after her. Her path took her towards the coast and after less than half a mile he could hear the waves of Lough Swilly crashing against the rocks. He watched his wife's dark shape as she descended the gently sloping track towards a large outcrop of rock. She then disappeared into a narrow crevice in the rock face.

Doherty immediately swung about on his heels and took off running towards Buncrana. Arriving exhausted in the town, he roused Vaughan and told the priest hunter the news he'd been waiting to hear. The Colonel hurried to the local garrison and gathered a handful of men to assist him, supplied Doherty with a horse and ordered him to lead them back to the spot.

In the cramped cave the priest gave his sister a parting benediction then urged her to leave as the first hints of daylight were just brightening the sky outside and he was anxious she wouldn't be spotted leaving a sea cave at an early hour and arouse suspicion. She said her goodbyes and set off back up the narrow path, but had barely gone a handful of steps when she saw Vaughan and his men hurrying towards her with swords drawn. To her deeper horror she saw that her husband was pointing the way. She turned and fled back to the cave and cried out a warning to

Fr Hegarty, who emerged from his hiding place to realise he'd been discovered and that he was trapped between the onrushing men and the waters of the lough. He took a last look at his sister's distraught face and decided to take his chances in the sea, and before he could be seized he plunged into the crashing waves.

Vaughan, Doherty and the others gathered on the rock face and watched as the priest battled to stay above the churning waters. Guns were raised but Vaughan ordered his men not to fire. If they killed the priest in the sea his body might never be recovered, and it was needed to provide evidence of their capture.

Fr Hegarty began to realise he had little hope. It was almost two miles to the far side of Lough Swilly and he was a man of over sixty, his body weak from a life of deprivation and hardship. Then, above the roar of the surf he heard Vaughan's voice yelling down to him, offering to spare his life if he swam back and surrendered peacefully. He knew he would face prison and transportation, but given the choice of that or drowning, he opted to return to shore. As he scrambled on to the rocks eager hands clutched at his arms and pulled him up, and he was dragged to the grassy top of the rock and surrounded, his sister Mary's wails a backdrop to the entire drama. Vaughan faced him, ordered him thrown to his knees and with heinous brutality, ordered one of his men to behead the priest, which was done in an instant. Mary's wails now turned to screeches at the horror of what she'd witnessed. She fell to her knees and screamed curses and vengeance on her husband, and beseeched God that she would live to see him dead.

Local legend tells that Fr Hegarty's head bounced eight times as it tumbled back towards the sea leaving eight marks in the rock that are still visible. In all likelihood Vaughan had the head taken back to Buncrana as evidence. He ordered a grave dug and the priest's headless body was buried on the spot where he'd died and where Mary would remain for many hours, her terrible keening carrying far across the waters of Lough Swilly.

In the coming days Mary separated from her husband and sons and went to live with a family called McDonald in Buncrana. It's not known if they were relatives or merely sympathetic to her plight, but it's likely they were financially comfortable as they occupied the only two-storey, slated house in the town. There she spent most of the remainder of her days, lamenting her brother and praying that her husband would not live to enjoy the fruits of his blood betrayal.

George Vaughan was at least true to his word with Doherty. He granted him a large piece of fertile land and paid over the fifty pounds, which would leave the man and his two sons in very comfortable circumstances. The price they would pay was their isolation from almost every other living soul around Buncrana, at least the Catholic souls, and they moved about under the constant gaze of detestation. Vaughan decided to hire them as henchmen; as the Dohertys were despised anyway being a hated 'enforcer' would make little difference to them.

A couple of years after Fr Hegarty's murder, Vaughan was

asked by a friend to help track down a poacher and outlaw by the nickname of 'Stumpy', who had managed to avoid all attempts at capture and lived in remote, mountainous terrain. Vaughan was happy to turn from priest hunter to man hunter and offered the job of tracking down the outlaw to Doherty's two sons, which they eagerly accepted as a substantial reward was being offered.

Little is known about the pursuit of the outlaw, but the story, which is probably apocryphal, goes that they located 'Stumpy' and set off in pursuit of him up a mountainside. They were forced to abandon their horses and chase him on foot, at one point firing their guns and wounding the man in the leg. The outlaw collapsed between two ridges of potatoes and the Doherty brothers believed they'd killed him. But when they came close enough, 'Stumpy' fired two shots and killed both men instantly. The outlaw being the only witness to this event, there is no way of knowing if the brothers truly met their end in this fashion.

Thomas Doherty was now burdened with the task of recovering their bodies. As he followed an undulating track across the hillsides, it is said that his horse, seeing an inviting mountain stream, came to an abrupt halt and lowered its head to drink, throwing its rider whose head struck a rock, breaking his neck. Again, no one witnessed his demise, so either the tale is supposition based on the condition of his body after the fall, or it's a complete fabrication.

Irrespective of the way Doherty and his two sons died, a couple of days later a cart passed beneath the window of Mary's room in the McDonald's house in Buncrana and she witnessed the tragic answer to her prayers. Whether the peasants who detested the Dohertys for their betrayal had lent God a helping hand in bringing about their demise, or by great coincidence, the three men all died on a lonely mountainside within a few hours of each other, is something about which one can only speculate.

Colonel George Vaughan escaped the wrath of Mary Doherty's prayers and lived into his seventies, becoming Deputy Governor of Donegal. His wife's name, coincidentally, was also Mary and she would bear him four children, the second of whom was given his name and who would go one step further than his father, becoming Governor of Donegal. The family would continue to wield their power and influence in and around Buncrana until the following century.

Some time during the 1800s one of Fr Hegarty's successors in the parish of Fahan, Edward Maginn, who would become a well-known advocate and supporter of Daniel O'Connell, returned to the spot where Fr Hegarty was slain. In his company was a Dr Hugh O'Donnell, who was studying at Edinburgh College of Surgeons. The two men dug up a portion of the soil and Dr O'Donnell took it back to Scotland, where subsequent testing indicated that the soil contained evidence of human remains. A fitting grave and headstone was subsequently organised and it lies on the inland side of the popular walking path from Buncrana to the place where he died in 1711, which has ever since been known as Fr Hegarty's Rock. But aside from the well-tended grave a short distance from the rock, the landscape of rocky, heather-covered earth pummelled by the north Atlantic waves betrays little hint of the tangled drama of betrayal, martyrdom, greed and hatred that saw its final tragic act played out at that spot.

Before the days of the priest hunter would end, many more lonely unremarkable places would tell a similar tale.

THE MOST DANGEROUS
MAN IN THE COUNTY

Around the year 1711 rumours were rife of a new Jacobite plot to restore 'The Old Pretender', James Francis Edward Stuart to the throne. Just a few years beforehand, using ships supplied by the French, James had made an attempt to launch an invasion of Scotland and England through the Firth of Forth, but was repelled by an English fleet. Since that abortive 'invasion', the entire Protestant community had been nervously watching the seas for a Jacobite fleet, convinced such a force would simply butcher them in their beds. This was particularly the case in Scotland and in the northern counties of Ireland, where support for The Old Pretender was strongest, as it was widely believed that as a Catholic, James would scrap all the Penal Laws and end the era of suppression. Most Protestants were fearful of the possible violent retribution that might ensue and that they might be disenfranchised as the Catholic community had been.

The forces of the crown therefore regarded the Catholic clergy as the principal agents of Jacobitism and many suspected that cabals of priests were secretly working to raise funds to support a new invasion. In the Ulster counties it became a period of *'Jacobites under the bed'* and every bishop, priest, nun and friar was seen as a potential threat not only to Protestantism, but also to national security. In his book *The Irish Priest in the Penal Times*, the historian and author William P. Burke notes that the authorities expended a great deal of time and effort in finding evidence of Popish-Jacobite plots, and when this was not forthcoming, often resorted to fabrication, such as the letter below, which had reportedly been 'accidentally dropped by a priest in The Four Courts':

> *Dear Brother,*
> *This is to let you know that I received a letter from our*
> *friend the Nuncio from Rome whence I have a full*
> *account of matters abroad. Thank my Jesus, now his most*
> *Christian Majestic hath let our King have 50 thousand*
> *pounds and 30 thousand arms, which will be very soon*
> *remitted to us that we may be able to assist to settle him*
> *upon the Throne of England. I hope it will be done*
> *to that effect that never it shall be in the power of any*
> *damned heretick to give him the least trouble hereafter –*
> *our hope while the world stands and the glory of all the*
> *Roman Catholicks. I hope now we have a fair opportu-*

*nity to begin and give the blow. The Queen is to get her
dose very soon ... I'm told by good hands that the Duke
of Marl will be soon put out of the way which will make
things the better for us. I wish he and all his Party were
damned which in a short time I hope they will be sent to
Eternity ...*

The 'letter' went on in this vein at some length, detailing numbers of men who had committed their support for James and carrying a warning to stand ready and waiting for 'the invasion'. The chances of a priest carrying such a blatantly incriminating document on his person, especially when visiting the headquarters of Irish law, and then being foolish enough to drop it on the floor, were infinitesimal.

A VICIOUS CIRCLE

Such were the numbers of priests returning to Ireland that some of the more fanatical members of the Privy Council's inner circle tried to introduce a bill in 1719 that would put a new form of punishment on the statute books and one they believed would act as a powerful deterrent. They wanted to castrate priests.

*Council Chamber, Dublin Castle, 27th of August 1719.
... After the country hath paid a sum of twenty pounds
to the discoverer of every such offender and been at great
expense convicting them, they are only liable to transporta-*

tion, unless they return after being transported but for so doing are punishable with death. Priests Friars etc. are no sooner transported but new ones come over from France, Spain, or Portugal, so that their number continues as great as ever. The common Irish will never become Protestant or well affected to the crown while they are with Priests, Friars etc. who are the fomenters and disturbers here. So that some more effectual remedy is perfectly necessary. The Commons proposed the marking of every priest who shall be convicted of being an unregistered Priest, Friar, etc. with a large, P. to be made with a red hot Iron on the cheek. The council generally disliked that punishment, and have altered it into that of castration which they are persuaded will be the most effectual remedy that can be found out to clear this nation of the disturbers of the peace and quiet of the kingdom … We are your Excellencies most humble servants.

CHARLES PAULET, Duke of Bolton, ALLEN BROD-ERICK, Lord Middleton, JOHN EVENS, Bishop of Meath, JOHN STERNE, Bishop of Clogher, JAMES BARRY, LORD SANTRY, SIR OLIVER ST. GEORGE, E. WEBSTER, R. TIGHE.

Thankfully, either through a sense of decency or because they believed it would provoke even greater rage among Irish peasants, the recommendation was ignored.

But there were plenty only too keen to believe such dastardly plots were afoot among the priests and soon every document seized was being scrutinised for information about 'the Jacobite conspiracy'. In the northern counties there was also a renewed effort to track down fugitive priests who were believed to be working in factions to ready the Catholic populace for battle. Among the most sought after of these was Fr James Hannah, the Vicar General of County Down. Fr Hannah (variously recorded as 'Hanna', 'Hannat' and 'Hannal') had been registered in 1704 as the parish priest of the tiny village of Kilclief, which rests on the western shore of Strangford Lough. The document recorded that he was ordained in Flanders in 1685 and was at the time forty-eight years old. It's possible that Fr Hannah was one of the few priests who agreed to take the Oath of Abjuration, if only in word and not in spirit, as he continued to carry out his duties to the full after March 1711, although secretly his loyalties were still to Rome – a serious breach of the law.

Henry Maxwell was the local magistrate at the time in County Down and was a keen enforcer of the penal statutes. Although not nominally a priest hunter himself, he frequently recruited men to track down outlaw priests and recorded many of their captures in letters to the Secretary for Ireland, Joshua Dawson. He was a very wealthy and influential man in the area, owned vast tracts of land and would in later years be elected as an MP for three different constituencies (elections in which Catholics had no vote). In the autumn of 1712, Maxwell received orders from Dublin to track down James Hannah with all possible urgency, a task he set about with great purpose:

> Downe October 8, 1712.
>
> Sir, In pursuance to the Order of the Government, Major Morise and I issued our warrant to apprehend one James Hannal whom we look upon to be the most dangerous Priest in this County and if he could not be found, to secure his papers. And that no time might be lost, we sent a party to secure him the very night after the Proclamation came down. He did not lye at his house that night nor has he appeared in this country since, but they brought his papers. Some of these show that he had great authority among them but I send you the copy of one that plainly shows jurisdiction.

Maxwell's letter then documented a long list of priests who Fr Hannah had summoned to a meeting the previous January, thereby proving the priest had been exercising ecclesiastical jurisdiction, a treasonable act, and also adding weight to the 'Jacobite conspiracy' theory.

A hunting party was dispatched to arrest the priest at Kilclief. But Fr Hannah had somehow gotten wind of the approaching men and fled into the open countryside. The area around Kilclief is extremely fertile nowadays, but three hundred years ago the engineering works that kept the water of Strangford Lough at bay had yet to be commenced, and the priest struggled to find a route through a broad marshland for several miles until he came to an area called Ballinarry, about two miles inland. Here he remained for several months, although his precise hiding place is unknown.

But with each passing week the priest hunters were closing in. One in particular was a local man whose name was not recorded in the official documents of the time, although it's possible he was Daniel Mackey, a local publican and who had previously provided Maxwell with information about meetings of priests in his pub. Mackey would have been in the perfect position to pick up any snippets of useful information from gossiping locals and someone's loose lips may have unwittingly betrayed the priest's hiding place.

Eventually Fr Hannah's location was discovered, but the priest managed to elude his pursuers again, now making his way back towards his own parish. He knew he couldn't find sanctuary in the homes of any of his own flock as their dwellings were subject to frequent searches, particularly with an outlawed priest on the loose. With a priest hunter hot on his heels, he fled towards what he hoped would be the sanctuary of a local Protestant farming family called Stockdale, who were sympathetic to his plight. Mr Stockdale quickly directed the priest towards his barn and pulled open a meal-ark, which was a large wooden box used for storing grain. The priest climbed in and waited, listening as the priest hunter acquainted Mr Stockdale with his mission and the farmer hummed and hawed and shook his head, informing the man that no priest had passed the way of their farm. The men left and Fr Hannah breathed a sigh of relief. It's unlikely he remained in the Stockdale household for very long as his capture there would condemn the family to bankruptcy and disgrace among their own community, but he would continue to evade capture for a number of months. Local folklore holds that the Stockdale's barn was blessed for the remainder of his days as not even the severest storm could shift a sliver of its thatch.

As Christmas of 1712 came and went, the hunt for 'the most dangerous man in the county' continued relentlessly and in late January 1713, a local priest hunter finally got his man, although the details of the capture were not recorded. The man's name is curiously absent from all subsequent communications, most likely for his own safety.

Henry Maxwell eagerly reported the news to Dublin on 2 February:

> *Sir,*
> *I formerly gave you an account that I sent to search for*
> *one James Hannal, a priest whom I had reason to believe*
> *exercises Ecclesiasticall jurisdiction in this Diocese and*
> *the most dangerous priest in all this County. I am now*
> *to acquaint you that he is taken and Major Morrise and*
> *I have sent him to the jaile with a Mittimus. I must*
> *tell you that the Priests in this country are very much*

alarmed and disturbed at his being taken and so exasper-
ated at the man that took him that I have been obliged to
give him arms to defend his house from their insults. The
sub sheriff has been with me since the Priest's confinement
and told me that he had clapped a new arrest upon him
for marrying a couple of our church clandestinely, which
crime I leave to the Government whether it be bailable. I
waite your directions.

Sir, Your very humble servant, H. Maxwell.

A year passed before Fr Hannah was brought to trial and while no proof of a conspiracy to dethrone Queen Anne could be established, a crime that would have merited execution, there was ample evidence that the priest had been in breach of multiple penal statutes. In particular, the crime of marrying two Protestants, which would have required their conversion, was viewed as particularly grave. He was sentenced to transportation and committed to Downpatrick Gaol while arrangements could be made. At the time Downpatrick Gaol was in a horrendous condition. The overcrowding was so serious that male and female prisoners were crammed together in the same cells, a thing unheard of at the time. The cells were filthy and disease was rampant, as when a prisoner fell ill he or she would most likely be left in the cell as whatever limited medical facilities existed were constantly crammed. Besides the ordinary prisoner, even the insane were housed there. A visitor described the smell in the prison as 'intolerably offensive'.

For whatever reason Fr Hannah was abandoned into this squalor for almost a year and a half. At one point the gaoler recorded the presence of the priest in his institution and his eagerness to have the cleric moved is clear, however his letter suggests also that sufficient funds were not available to pay a ship's captain for transportation. (The annual cost of transporting prisoners from the jurisdiction at the time was about one hundred pounds.)

> *Down Patrick 2 Nov. 1714.*
> *Sir, There is no one in the Gaol of the County of Down under sentence of Transportation but one James Hannal a popish priest. He has layn in Gaole about fowerteen months and has been about halfe of that time under the sentence of Transportation. George Lambert Esq., one of the Justices of the Peace and I have used our endeavours to have him put off and have had him severall times att Portaferry but could gett noe shipp that would receive him. We shall do our utmost to gett him transported as soon as possible we can.*
> *Your most humble servant, Robert Jones.*

Fr Hannah was finally put aboard a ship at Portaferry at the narrow entrance to Strangford Lough some months later, but neither his story, nor that of the priest hunter who captured him, ended there. The ship had barely left the harbour when a storm blew up and drove the vessel northwards along the beautifully-rugged Antrim coast. The vessel was dashed against the rocks and wrecked, but it seems that most managed to reach the safety of the shore, as Fr Hannah certainly did and as a prisoner he wouldn't have been a priority when it came to saving lives. It seems however that the captain, perhaps because of his politica or religious sympathies or maybe because he determined for himself that God's hand was evident in the priest's fate, decided to release his prisoner. Over the coming weeks the priest somehow made his way back south towards his home parish. He found a new hiding place in the townland of Castleskreen at a place called Black Bush Well, and took up precisely where he'd left off, as though his arrest, imprisonment and brief adventure on the high seas were nothing more than a troublesome fly to be swatted and forgotten about.

The two years he'd been absent had not been kind to the priest hunter, having to live every day since he'd captured Fr Hannah with one eye looking over his shoulder. In his communications with Dublin Castle, Henry Maxwell had alluded to the fact that he'd had to supply arms to him to defend his home from the rage of the local Catholic peasantry. Such was the ill-feeling that the man decided it would be wise to use his ill-gotten gains to fund a long trip abroad, probably in the hope that the event would have been forgotten about by the time he got back. But the Catholic peasants, it seemed, had long memories.

The priest hunter returned some years later and was shocked

to discover that Fr Hannah was back in business, secretly serving masses and carrying out the other sacraments. It's safe to assume he decided against a second betrayal, such was the animosity he experienced on a daily basis, as Fr Hannah continued to serve the community for more than a decade after he'd returned. Such was the admiration of his work that Rome appointed him the Archdeacon of County Down. He lived to the age of sixty-eight and was buried in Down Cathedral graveyard. The inscription on his tombstone read:

> *In this tomb lies the body of Reverend James Hannah*
> *who left this world on the twentieth day of December*
> *1723.*
> *First and foremost a Christian.*

The man who had almost been responsible for putting the priest in an early grave was not so lucky when he shuffled off his mortal coil. Having lived the remainder of his days as a pariah within the community, when he died the local peasantry pursued him with their hatred even beyond the grave and took it upon themselves to erase all trace of his earthly existence. After the man's funeral, they destroyed his headstone then disinterred his body and dumped it at a crossroads. He was re-buried, but the locals once again dug up the corpse and threw it in a ditch where it was located by the man's relatives, who buried it for a third time. But so driven were the locals by the wild justice of revenge that they continued to unearth the decomposing remains and leave it exposed as a warning to any who might follow the man's trade. Eventually his relatives had to transport whatever was left of him to an island on Strangford Lough.

The priest hunter's reward very often came at an exorbitant price.

THE LONGFORD FOX

Many priests became, through necessity, quite adept at evading the priest hunters and as we've seen, some even escaped their clutches after their initial capture. But pride of place in this regard must go to Fr Bryan McHugh from County Longford who repeatedly confounded the authorities and the mercenary priest hunters for almost a decade by means of fox-like cunning.

The village of Newtowncashel nestles on the north eastern shore of Lough Ree in Longford and affords its inhabitants a fine view of much of the thirty kilometre-long expanse of water and its multitude of islands, many of which, even during the age of the Penal Laws, were of ancient religious significance. Around the lough's shores can also be seen a number of mass rocks and holy wells where Fr McHugh, his forebears and successors undoubtedly presided over forbidden services under cold, moonlit skies.

HE STOOPS TO CONQUER ...

The following letter makes reference to some of the illegal Catholic gatherings in the Longford/Roscommon area, the writer bemoaning the lack of enforcement of the penal laws banning such activities. What is interesting on another account, is that the writer was the uncle of the poet, Oliver Goldsmith, who had been raised in Longford and whose father was a local Anglican curate:

Elphin 22 Aug. 1704.

My Lord, We have a well in the neighbourhood of Elphin commonly called St Mary's Well, to which vast numbers out of severall distant places lately came and they are to meet there again sometime in September next. This is taken no notice of here, which occasions this complaint to your Lordship. We live among a people who are very apt upon the least encouragement to grow insolent; they ought therefore to be under the habitual awe of government and not suffered to trample upon so late an Act purposely provided against their superstitious and riotous meetings. Edward Goldsmith.

Luckily his nephew grew up with a more tolerant and enlightened view of the world.

In 1704, Fr McHugh (also referred to as 'Hughes') was officially registered as the parish priest of Cashel, County Longford and while the authorities may have suspected that he was performing clerical duties that breached the strict statutes that governed the lives of registered priests, they had failed to catch him in the act and no information had been forthcoming from informers. Then after four years without any apparent blots on his copybook, Fr McHugh was suddenly charged with what was then regarded as an especially heinous offence – he'd married one Edmund Geraghty and one Elizabeth Byrne who were Catholic and Protestant respectively.

Particularly during the first half of the eighteenth century, most Protestants viewed mixed marriages and those who conducted them with contempt and they held little sympathy for the guilty member of their brethren. In the minds of many Protestants, marrying a Catholic was tantamount to treason and brought shame and humiliation to the family. If one imagines America's Deep South one hundred years ago and the outrage a white girl marrying a black man might provoke, the situation in Ireland at the time was not markedly different between Protestant and Catholic in terms of relative social status and basic rights. A Catholic priest, as the facilitator of the crime, should, they believed, be subject to the full rigours of the law. The case of Fr Timothy Ryan from Limerick illustrates the feelings mixed marriages evoked. In 1722 he officiated at such a ceremony and when word of the marriage reached the authorities, they quickly had him hunted down and committed to Limerick Gaol where he remained for several months until his trial. He was subsequently found guilty of 'marrying a Protestant man and a Catholic woman contrary to an act of Parliament' and to the horror and shock of his Catholic flock, condemned to death and hanged at Gallows Green, which is now the area known as Garryowen.

Fr McHugh would have been well aware of the seriousness of the accusation, but in his case, there are indications that the entire charge was trumped up. On a very superficial level, the names of the bride and groom – Byrne and Geraghty – are more associated with the Catholic community. A subsequent deposition taken from the pair also supports the priest's innocence:

> *Co. Longford.*
> *Information of Edmund Gyreaght and Elizabeth, his wife, taken before John Wilson and Thomas Kennedy, Justices of the Peace for said County. Who being sworn on the Holy Evangelists say that they are of the popish religion and were married by Mr Bryan Hughes on the 12th of August 1708 and further depose that they did profess the popish religion at the time of their Marriage etc.*

Fr McHugh appealed to the Lord Lieutenant, the Duke of Ormond, stating that he'd been brought to trial before he'd had time to prepare and swearing that he'd been assured the couple were both Catholics. The fragile nature of the prosecution evidence probably saved him from the death penalty, yet Fr McHugh was sentenced to transportation and committed to the infamous Newgate Prison in Dublin. Because of the seriousness of the charge he knew he would in all likelihood languish in Newgate for years before his transportation would be effected.

Like the previously-mentioned Downpatrick Gaol, Newgate Prison, which originally stood near Christ Church Cathedral, was in a horrendous condition. A contemporary Parliamentary report by a Mr Froude describes its condition:

> *A den of infamy ... in a room 12 feet square and 8 feet high, there were frequently fourteen people and occasionally twenty ... wretched objects were lying naked on the ground, some dying, some dead of cold and hunger. Some had been four days without food of any kind. The stench among the naked, starving felons was so intolerable that the Committee fled after a stay of half a minute.*

The historian William P. Burke suggested that while the official line was that the authorities simply wanted to rid the country of priests through transportation, they were aware that hundreds of priests managed to return and therefore many were often simply left in prison until they died, evidence of which can be seen in the records of the religious orders. The petition below from two Catholic priests pleads for their sentence of transportation to be carried out; while it is evident that transportation was something to be dreaded, for most, awaiting it in the squalor of prison was infinitely worse:

17 December 1722.

*The humble petition of Thomas Blunt, George Martin
and James Dugan, Prisoners in Newgate. Humbly
sheweth that your petitioners having been convicted
some years ago of being Regulars [priests] have been
since detained close prisoners whereby they are not only
impaired in their health but also reduced to the lowest
ebb of indigence and want. May it therefore please etc …
that we may be transported as soon as there is an opportunity.*

Fr McHugh surely saw a similar fate ahead for himself and decided his only choice was to escape. His means of achieving this is not recorded, but there were several possible routes to freedom. The official malfeasance he no doubt witnessed in the prison may have worked in his favour. The keeper of Newgate Prison, Ashenhurst Isaack, was a deeply corrupt man who exchanged money for favours, including allowing prisoners to flee into the night. (His successor was known to have earned over a thousand pounds through extortion – an impossibly large sum of money at the time.) Previous to Fr McHugh's conviction, a man called Lecky had contrived to escape by dressing in his wife's clothing, and it was not uncommon for priests of the era to dress as women to evade capture. Also when a Catholic inmate died, a priest might be permitted to perform the burial rite beyond the prison walls. By one of many possible stratagems, Fr McHugh passed beyond the walls of the prison and immediately set about returning to his diocese in Longford so he could resume ministering to his flock as soon as humanly possible, as he had sworn to do. It may seem odd that he chose to return to the 'lion's den', but in the context of the time it is perfectly understandable. As long as he was absent, his flock were without official means of expressing their faith and without his holy guidance, and therefore, in the priest's mind and in the minds of his parishioners, in great danger of eternal condemnation to hell. While these notions may seem extreme to us nowadays, at the time people truly believed that such a fate was infinitely worse than anything the English forces could inflict upon them.

But the wily priest was not content to live in his parish as a fugitive. He'd had the audacity to forge an order for his release from prison, signed by no less a dignitary than Joshua Dawson, future Secretary for Ireland, then Clerk of the Privy Council. Upon his return he went directly to the offices of the local magistrates and waved his 'release paper' in their faces. He then returned to his position as the officially-registered priest of the parish, much to the delight of his flock.

His freedom to wander about his parish unmolested was shortlived, however, as within months the priest's discharge papers were discovered to be forged. A hunting party was dispatched to track him down, but the elusive priest managed to evade immediate capture. But it was now post-1709 and placing a bounty on the clergy's head had entered the statute books. A

Grand Jury branded him a 'tory and rapparee' and offered the official reward for his capture. Two priest hunters called Timothy Kinnett and Thomas Cursen were soon on his trail, but failed to locate him for several months. Their inability to track him down is understandable considering the loyalty and support the priest evidently enjoyed in the area and the fact that Lough Ree offers a multitude of island hideaways, indeed many of the islands had served just that purpose during the previous centuries. At length however, Fr McHugh was apprehended by Cursen and Kinnett, and although the precise circumstances of his capture are not known, he had remained at large for over two years. Yet again he was marched off to Newgate in Dublin to await transportation.

On 11 July 1712, the Lord Justices issued a proclamation detailing the priest's troublesome history and offering another reward of twenty pounds – incredibly Fr McHugh had effected his second escape from what was then Dublin's largest prison. His loyalty – and brazenness – is evidenced in the fact that once again Fr McHugh returned to Longford and resumed his illegal activities.

The priest hunters were again on his trail, but once more demonstrating his talent for evading capture, a further two years would pass before any trace of the slippery priest could be found. An official document from 1714 records the fact that Fr McHugh had been identified as having taken over from a deceased priest in the parish of Shrule, just six miles to the east of his home village.

Yet it would be January of 1716 before the priest hunters Kinnett and Cursen finally tracked him down at a place called Mosstown. His ability to stay at large for so long a time might be explained by the fact that the area features a long underground passage connecting two castles, which during the previous decades had been used by the locals for the purpose of hiding from attacking Cromwellian forces. According to the testimony of the two priest hunters, Fr McHugh was taken 'at great hazard to their lives', which is probably true; given the loyalty and courage the cleric had demonstrated in continually escaping and returning to serve his home county, the local peasantry would have been enraged at his seizure, the third of his career.

They brought Fr McHugh before the local Justice of the Peace, Robert Newcomen, who granted them a certificate confirming the capture, which they needed to claim their reward. The priest was committed to Longford Gaol, where he remained, likely under tight security, for several months before being brought to Dublin for transportation. The capture was officially recorded thus:

> *The King against Bryan McHugh.*
> *Whereas Bryan McHugh the defendant was convict*
> *att a generall Assize &c. held at Longford celebrating a*
> *marriage between a Protestant and a Papist contrary to*
> *the statute and thereby incurred the pains, penalties and*
> *forfeitures of a Popish Regular, and was sent to Dublin in*
> *order to be transported beyond Sea pursuant to said Act*

> *but the said McHugh made his escape and returned again*
> *to the County of Longford, but by the directions of the*
> *then Lords Justices was again apprehended in ye County*
> *of Longford and again made his escape and a reward of*
> *Twenty Pounds was offered to any person or persons who*
> *should apprehend the said Bryan McHugh in order that*
> *he might be brought to justice. Now Timothy Kinnett*
> *& Thomas Carsen this day make oath that they were*
> *the two persons who by virtue of the said Proclamation*
> *apprehended the said Bryan McHugh att Mostown in the*
> *Barony of Moydow & Parish of Kilcommock & conveyed*
> *him to the Goale of Longford where he was left in safe*
> *custody, and was thence as these examinants hear brought*
> *up to Dublin by order of His Majesties Writt of Habeas*
> *Corpus.*
> *July 1716.   W. Caulfield.*

Collecting their twenty pounds wasn't quite the formality the pair expected, as the authorities seemed to be in two minds about the confirmation that these men were the actual captors. Letters were batted back and forth for months between Dublin and Longford, eventually requiring the personal intervention of the Robert Newcomen, the Justice of the Peace, who wrote to the Lord Justices assuring them that the men had indeed captured the priest and that they 'doubly deserved' their reward as it was 'with great hazard and difficulty that they took this man and are often insulted by their Popish neighbours'. The reward was ultimately granted, but as many a priest hunter was learning, it seems Messrs Kinnet and Carsen weren't to enjoy much peace and quiet in the Longford area for many years to come.

What the above claim for a reward didn't record, or what the local authorities in Longford hadn't yet learned, was that weeks previously, and quite unbelievably, Fr Mc Hugh had effected yet another escape from Newgate, and this time the gaoler actually offered a further ten pounds' reward for his apprehension. The account of this also provides us with a colourful description of the priest:

> *Just after 9 a clock at night one Bryan McHugh alias Hues a convicted Popish priest made his escape out of Newgat-gaole. A middle-sized man, full shoulders, a thin pale face, down looking with a cast in his eyes, swarthy complexion, wears a scald brown wigg, long nose, wears a dark frize coat and vest: whoever secures the said priest so that he may be brought to justice, shall have ten pounds paid him or them, by John Saunderson Gaoler.*

After that nothing more is recorded of the wily Fr McHugh, although the above report was issued in November, and it is safe to assume that the priest was still at large some months after his latest flight from imprisonment. And given his cunning, he may well have evaded capture for the rest of his days.

In the ancient graveyard of Shrule, where he served for a time while on the run, a handful of weatherworn, mostly illegible, memorials are still visible, devoted to a number of Catholic priests from the penal era. Perhaps, knowing his proficiency at escaping the long arm of the law, and his enduring determination to return to and serve his beloved flock, one of those faded stones marks the final resting place of the Fr Bryan McHugh, the Longford fox.

BETWEEN THE DEVIL AND
THE DEEP BLUE SEA

onsidering that priests who had already been transported faced a possible death sentence if they set foot
in Ireland again, it is astonishing just how many were prepared to
run the risk. Beside those devoted souls, the numbers of priests
entering Ireland who had not previously been convicted was
considerable. These consisted principally of men who had been
secretly smuggled abroad as children or young men to be educated in the priesthood in France, Spain or Portugal and were
now assigned duties in a parish that was filled with hostile forces
waiting to pounce should they be discovered. While these men
didn't risk the death penalty on their initial capture, if it could
be determined that their parents or benefactors had provided the
means of their education in the priesthood abroad, their spon-
sors would forfeit all their possessions for life, lose all inheritance
rights and be barred from all offices of the state. Anyone found

harbouring or helping such a person also faced enormous fines and imprisonment.

Yet the Catholic clergy came in their thousands during the penal times. They were driven by a level of faith that is difficult for us to comprehend in this day and age. They believed that the laws that governed their destinies were ordained by a much higher power than the British crown. And of course there would likely also have been a large element of patriotism, as Catholicism had already become inextricably linked to Ireland's destiny as a nation, and their lack of freedom to practise their faith was reflected in the oppression under which their flock existed on a daily basis. Perhaps also, for some of the younger men, there was an element of adventure involved, as though they were soldiers being sent into enemy territory to rescue their fellow countrymen, if not from the yoke of English domination, then at least from eternal damnation.

The authorities were urged to use 'their utmost diligence in apprehending all such regular or other popish priests who shall come into this kingdom' and if they were found to be negligent in this duty, the consequences were considerable:

> … *every such justice and other officer shall for every such neglect forfeit one hundred pounds, one moiety to the King, the other to the informer or person that shall sue for the same, and be disabled from serving as a justice of the peace during his life.*

Senior Protestant clergymen, among others, were not remiss in pointing out the failures, as they saw them, of the authorities in curtailing the influx of priests. In 1715, the Archbishop of Dublin wrote to Secretary Sunderland:

> *For want of a due execution of the laws many priests are come in from foreign parts and there are in the country Popish bishops concealed that ordain many. Little inquiry of late has been made into these matters.*

The Protestant Bishop of Derry, in a similar vein, was outraged in 1723 at the continuing arrival of, and nerve of, the Catholic clergy in his county:

> *The present insolence of our Popish clergy is unspeakable. Our law makes it death for any of them [returned priests] to officiate; and yet I am abundantly assured that very lately in my own diocese four or five masses were openly said by as many different priests ...*

A report from early in the century gives a sense of the perseverance and courage of some priests, and of the penalties they risked. In 1700, Fr Daniel McDonnell from Mayo attempted to smuggle himself back into Ireland through Galway port. The unfortunate priest was captured before he'd even set foot on dry land and thrown into prison while he awaited transportation. A reluctance on the part of the ships' captains, probably because they feared Catholic retribution, and the apparent indifference of the authorities, meant that fourteen months would pass before he was put back onto a ship and returned to Spain.

> *County of the Town of Galwey had presented that the*
> *Judges of Assize should apply to their Excellencies that*
> *care might be taken for the transportation of the said*
> *Daniel McDonnell. Their Excellencies were pleased to*
> *answer that they had endeavoured to get Transportation*
> *for convicted Regulars but that the Masters of Ships to*
> *whom application had been made showd an adversness*
> *to take them on Board. I being satisfied with this answer*
> *and assurance of the Lords Justices I did conceive any*
> *further application in this matter was unnecessary.*
> *6 September Anno 13 (of the King's reign)*
> *Munster Circuit. Com. Civit.*

The following year the priest was back in Ireland, this time under the alias Patrick Hubbane. But his freedom among his flock was short lived and he was arrested and thrown into prison again. The authorities were in no hurry to transport him again it seemed and he languished in prison for years, his health deteriorating. His devotion to his faith brought him to a miserable end as related in The Irish Ecclesiastical Record:

> *A.D. 1707, Daniel Mac Donnell, of the convent of*
> *Urlare, County Mayo, having returned from the con-*
> *tinent, was discovered on board the ship, which lay at*

anchor, as a religious, and immediately flung into prison, where he was detained fourteen months in irons; at length he was obliged to reembark for France. Again venturing to Galway, he was arrested a second time, thrust into prison, and kept there over six years. He at length, broken down by suffering, resigned his soul to his Creator.

With countless others like Daniel McDonnell willing to risk venturing into Ireland, and encouraged by panicked sheriffs and magistrates, the priest hunters soon realised the rich pickings that were to be had around Ireland's coasts, although seizing these illegal clerical immigrants was not without its dangers, both from their sympathisers and the crews of the ships that carried on the illicit trade.

In September 1709, an informer reported that he'd seen one Patrick Grady of Crookhaven in West Cork row out to sea to meet a passing ship. Having disappeared on board for a considerable time, Grady reappeared with what were described as 'eminent men' who the informer believed to be 'friars and clergy out of France' and proceeded to row the men towards Schull. Once ashore a second man called Mahon took charge of the new arrivals and escorted them to his house where he fed and sheltered the clergy for several days before conducting them to Cork city. Both men were armed for the duration of the operation and were clearly alert for the intervention of any lawman or priest hunter and prepared to use their weapons to defend themselves.

The fate of Grady, Mahon and the others is unrecorded, though it is likely that even if the clerics managed to get safely to Cork and disappear, as their facilitators were now known to the law and had illegally borne arms, they would quickly be arrested and imprisoned upon their return.

The conveyance of priests into Ireland on cargo ships and fishing boats was equally risky for a vessel's captain, who would at the very least face a fine of twenty pounds and imprisonment at the will of the law and seizure of his craft. Yet there were many willing to carry their human cargo. Some did it purely for the profit, passage usually being paid for by the priest's seminary abroad, others because they were Catholic sympathisers. An incident in Dungarvan in June 1713 illustrates the inherent dangers involved. A priest hunter called Pierce Sherlock, with the sanction of the port surveyor and in the company of a handful of 'officers', boarded a recently-arrived ship and hidden in the hold discovered an elderly man who confessed to being a priest called Cornelius Reynolds who had been absent from his homeland for over thirty years, but was returning not to preach his creed, but to spend the remainder of his days with his elderly sister. Earning little sympathy, the priest was hauled ashore and packed off to Waterford Gaol to await trial. The authorities then sent out a larger force with the intention of seizing the vessel and arresting the captain, but to their shock found themselves facing twenty-five armed crewmen ready to do battle. As they drew near shots were fired into the boat. They hit nobody but, in the confusion, the ship's Captain Butler weighed anchor and fled the harbour.

Though priest-hunting was a dangerous profession, the rewards were too good for the relentless hunters to be discouraged. Cork and Kerry, with their jagged coastlines and countless remote inlets proved popular disembarkation points for priests. But their return to Ireland was often brief, their feet not even touching dry land before some mercenary would stick a musket in their face. Below are a few samples of their endeavours to prevent the influx of clerics.

From Kinsale, a priest hunter called George Pepper writes:

> *Yesterday I took a Jesuit in his habitt whom I understood said some seditious words. The priests taken on board our privateers are suffered to go aboute and preach everywhere which I feare will be of ill consequence.*

Robert Hill, a priest hunter in Cork, netted himself a considerable catch when he managed to seize no less than four priests on a cargo ship:

> *To Joshua Dawson, Dublin Castle.*
> *Four Irish priests are brought to Gaol this day havinge left Nantz twenty dayes past and came in the Mary of Galloway to Baltimore which was loaden with salt and Indigo. R. Hill, Port of Corke.*

Besides Cork and Kerry, almost every county with a western

shoreline brought its haul of Catholic clergy. Records such as those below also point to the use of soldiers, ex-soldiers or country gentlemen as priest hunters, and to the huge financial burden placed on the head of the ordinary Catholic peasants who had to foot the bill for these men's reward.

> *5 April 1716.*
> *We find that Lieut. George Green of the Abbey of Limerick did take John Butler, a popish priest, for celebrating mass, we therefore present that twenty pounds sterling be raised on the popish inhabitants of [name of parish obliterated] and paid to the said George Green as a reward.*

> *11 April 1717.*
> *We present £20 to be raised on the popish inhabitants of the County to Captain John Odell for his good service in taking Teig Sullivan, a popish non-juring priest. We present £10 to be raised on the popish inhabitants of the County to Capt. John Odell for his service in taking Thomas FitzGerald, a popish schoolmaster.*

A priest hunter called Hodges reported in 1712 on his pursuit and capture of one Donagh Sweeny, who had been smuggled into Ireland having been educated in Sorbonne in France. Hinting that Sweeny was in fact a bishop due to the reverence paid to him by other Catholic clergymen, he also recounts a tale of a young man who had never been abroad yet had been ordained in

Ireland, implying that his captive had conducted the ordination. Hodges recounts that his search for the young curate had forced him to try to flee the country during which escape attempt the unfortunate curate had drowned.

Towards the middle of the eighteenth century, the rewards for the priest hunters and the subsequent burden on the peasants had grown considerably as it had fallen within the remit of the local authorities to increase the rewards by special proclamation if they thought the outlaw priest of particular influence or importance. In 1746 one Thomas Price petitioned for a reward of one hundred and one pounds – a vast sum of money – for the capture of a James Corbally. By now it seems some priest hunters had taken to the high seas to intercept approaching ships and search them for smuggled clergy:

> *The humble petition of Thomas Price to their Excellencies*
> *the Lords Justices etc. Sheweth That one James Corbally*
> *a Reputed priest was taken Prisoner by the Ambuscade*
> *privateer and brought into the harbour of Corke ... he*
> *prays etc. for the sum of £101.*

One obviously slippery priest called Flan Brody had previously been captured in 1711 at Sixmilebridge in Clare. Brody subsequently remained at large for the next four years, no doubt due in part to the fact that he also went by the name James Brown and also by the name Dennis Culligan and probably a myriad of other aliases. The priest was eventually caught in Limerick in 1715, committed to Limerick Gaol, where he languished for some time before being put aboard a ship for transportation. Incredibly the deft Fr Brody somehow managed to escape the ship, possibly while it was still docked. When the authorities learned that he was at large again, they clearly decided they'd had enough.

> *We the Grand Jurors at the general Sessions of the Peace held this 8 day of October 1717 for the said County do find and present the said Flan Brody alias Brown alias Culligan to be a Tory, Robber and Rapparee out and upon his keeping and guilty of High Treason against his Majesty's Crown and Dignity and we pronounce that we will secure and pay unto any person or persons who after this day shall seize and secure the said Brody, alias Brown alias Culligan within the said County so as he may be brought to Condign punishment the sum of twenty pounds sterling.*

Officially branding Brody as a 'Tory, Robber and Rapparee' effectively meant he was fair game for any self-styled priest hunter with a musket or a sword. It's not known whether the priestly pimpernel was ever caught or killed, but given his fondness for aliases (besides those officially recorded above he was also known to go under by the name of 'Bruodin') and combined with his obvious escapist skills, it's quite possible he survived.

Undeterred by the dangers of imprisonment, pursuit and death, the seas around Ireland continued to wash ashore countless Catholic clergy during the penal era and despite the attentions of the hunters and the officials of the law, most actually found their way to their designated parishes all over the country and settled into a life of secrecy, deprivation and self-sacrifice.

But all too often they were called upon to make the ultimate sacrifice.

MAKING A KILLING

The track from Milford in Donegal thundered to the sound of men on horseback guided by the first cold rays of light from the sun that rose on the second day of March 1734. At their head rode a man with visions of gold sparkling in his eyes, by name of Buchanan, local magistrate and priest hunter. His men, or 'yeomen', as they were recorded, were equally keen to share in the promise of rich spoils that lay just ten miles to the east on the shores of Lough Swilly. The yeomen were employees recruited from the surrounding estates of wealthy Protestant landowners, and would have eagerly answered the call. Another official communication from the time describes Buchanan's men simply as 'Protestants'.

Buchanan's destination was the parish of Killygarvan on Lough Swilly's western shore and the rare prize he and his band sought was the capture of none less than the Bishop of Raphoe, Dr James Gallagher, at that time worth all of one hundred pounds if taken.

It seems sadly appropriate that Lough Swilly, from the Irish

'*Loch Súilí*', means lake of the eyes, as from the moment Bishop Gallagher revealed his identity to his flock a greedy gaze fell upon him and would soon after report his presence in the area. Besides tending to the people's spiritual needs, he'd come to Killygarvan disguised as a vagrant as part of his duties of administration, which continued secretly despite the persecution. Until recently a Rev. Thomas Caulfield had ministered the parish and was apparently liked by the authorities who referred to him as a 'quiet, inoffensive priest'. The fact that Bishop Gallagher dismissed Caulfield from his position and replaced him with an elderly priest called Fr Peter O'Hegarty suggests there was something amiss about the man's relationship with their Protestant rulers. But it wasn't long before word reached the local magistrates that a bishop was in the area and a determined effort was set in motion to root him out.

On Sunday 1 March, the bishop decided to hold a clandestine confirmation ceremony for the local children and unavoidably, word had to be spread about the community of the coming event. Among the flock was a paid informer, who glimpsed Bishop Gallagher's face when his beggarman's disguise was necessarily discarded. With the ceremony complete, the bishop decided to take refuge that night with Fr O'Hegarty. Accompanied by some locals they set off for the parish priest's dwelling, a tiny hut near the shore of Lough Swilly, a wild place carpeted by sally trees and cut through by a myriad of streams. As they rested in the cabin that afternoon, a local was seen approaching, but he was a trusted friend of Fr O'Hegarty and he was admitted. The man had been asked to deliver a note from a wealthy Protestant landowner named Potter, inviting him to dine at his home that evening. As a good number of Protestants abhorred the repression of Catholics, such invitations weren't unheard of, and it was possible that Potter might have wished to meet such a prominent Catholic. Dr Gallagher considered the offer for a few moments, but his years of evading capture had made him cautious and he immediately suspected that Potter's invitation might be part of a ruse to lure him into the open. He asked the messenger for his opinion of Potter and if he thought he should accept, to which he received the reply:

> *'Más maith leat a bheith beo, ná téigh.'* – 'If you want to continue living, don't go'.

Dr Gallagher is reported to have spent a restless night, perhaps disturbed by the invitation and the messenger's warning, wary that Potter and associates wouldn't leave it at that. Several times he rose and determined to leave, but was dissuaded by the others, as he didn't know the region sufficiently well to travel alone by night.

He was right to be nervous, as it seemed the delivery of the message was merely a means of discovering his whereabouts and it was probable the messenger had been followed. During the night, word had been sent to Buchanan in Milford, who quickly set about assembling a group of men to seize the bishop. By dawn the following day, Buchanan and his yeomen had the priest's refuge almost in their sights.

Finally giving up on sleep, Dr Gallagher eventually rose before dawn, donned his beggar's garb and furnished with a meagre supply of food, said his thanks to his elderly host, mounted his horse and set off alone along the bridle path to Rathmullan in the dim early light.

No sooner was he out of sight of the cabin, than Buchanan and his men thundered up and encircled the dwelling. Drawing his weapon, Buchanan yelled 'Out with the Popish bishop! Out with the felon!' but his only reply was the frail, trembling voice of Fr O'Hegarty, who – no doubt fearing blood would be shed – emerged and informed the priest hunter that the bishop was no longer there. The riches he'd imagined having slipped through his fingers, Buchanan had the cabin and surrounding area searched, but no trace of the bishop was found. He decided to settle for the lesser prize – the twenty pounds reward for a priest, whom he could prosecute for taking part in the Confirmation ceremony, but also for hiding the bishop – a wanted criminal.

Buchanan ordered Fr O'Hegarty's hands bound and as his helpless followers watched, the aged clergyman was led off on foot on the tortuous journey across the wild landscape towards Milford. Enraged, the locals secretly took flight and managed to get ahead of the party, spreading the word as they went that the hated priest hunter had seized their pastor. By the time they reached the tiny hamlet of Glenalla, nestling in the shadow of Cnockaffrin Hill, which appropriately means 'Hill of the Mass', rising a thousand feet above them, a large crowd of Catholic peasants had assembled. As Buchanan and his troop entered Glenalla, they launched a bombardment of stones at Fr O'Hegarty's captors.

Buchanan reacted swiftly; he was the only armed member of the party and knew that they might soon be overwhelmed. With his yeomen desperately trying to deflect a rain of stones with their arms, he turned towards the helpless priest and aimed his weapon. A moment later a shot rang out and the old priest lay dead by the roadside, a musket ball in his head. The bombardment abated, the attackers stunned by the brutal murder, and in the lull Buchanan threatened them with a similar fate. Some accounts of the incident say that Buchanan ordered his men to place the priest's body on a horse so they would have the proof necessary to claim the reward and afterwards threw the body into the tiny Lough Columbkille just to the east of Milford. Other versions say that, terrified they would be torn to pieces, they simply fled the scene at a gallop and left the priest's body at the roadside.

Two days later the Protestant Bishop of Kilmore, Josiah Hart, recorded the event although his account omits the murder and seems to imply that the priest was rescued. The letters appears to be more an attempt to foster unease by implying that the Catholic community was on the point of rebellion.

To George Doddington, the Secretary, 4th March, 1734:

The Bishop of Raphoe acquainted the Duke of Dorset
[Lord Lieutenant] this morning in the great room that
the Popish Bishop having removed a quiet inoffensive
priest and put a turbulent fellow in his place, Dr Rogers
had issued a warrant for apprehending him. As they were
carrying him to the County Gaol, guarded by severall
Protestants, some of them gentlemen, a great body of
papists attacked them, wounded severall and arrested
[seized] the priest. Letters from my own diocese are full of
apprehensions that some mischief is brewing. In the more
settled parts of the country ecclesiastics had to lie perdu.
[Remain out of sight]

Unaware of the bloody fate that had befallen his priest, Bishop Gallagher continued his flight for many weeks, and finally found safe refuge on a small island in Lough Erne, eighty miles to the south. He remained there for a year during which time he wrote a renowned volume of sixteen sermons, many of which are still referenced by the Catholic Church today.

He then moved south by stealth, always in fear of being captured or slain, and came to settle in the Bog of Allen in the midlands, his home for much of the considerable remainder of his days consisting of a small concealed hut of mud walls and straw thatch, which despite its isolation and obvious discomforts, at times served as a tiny seminary where he trained and ordained priests. It wasn't his only refuge however, as he continued to travel the country administering the affairs of the church and ordaining priests. Despite the constant threat of capture, Dr Gallagher also managed to publish his *Sixteen Irish Sermons* in Dublin and his duties even required him to travel to Paris in 1741. He returned undetected the same year and a few years later was back in Donegal and was once again keenly, but unsuccessfully, sought by the authorities:

> *Londonderry April 29 1744.*
> *Sir According to his Grace the Lord Lieutenant's direc-*
> *tions I have made all the Enquiries I possibly could and*
> *find that there is a Popish Bishop of the name of Gal-*
> *lagher in the County of Donegal and likewise that there is*
> *a Friary neare Ballyshannon but how many friars I cant*
> *give an exact account. This is all the information I gott*
> *from the severall Constables of the severall Baronyes and*
> *if I heare of any more I shall return them as directed.*
> *CHARLES MCMANUS, Sheriff of Donegall*

Although he had many more narrow escapes from the clutches of the priest hunters, they never caught him and despite the privations of his life, he remained at large and active until his death in 1751 at the age of seventy.

Fr O'Hegarty's murder was by no means an isolated act, although the killing of priests was the exception rather than the rule. That said, in the climate of the age there was little to prevent a man like Buchanan from killing a priest in cold blood if he chose to do so. There was no fear of a trial for murder or even any loss of position. And although many prominent Protestants were openly opposed to the repression of Catholicism and the activities of the priest hunters, largely they were powerless to intervene, because to the authorities in Dublin and London, the death of the likes of Fr O'Hegarty's meant just one less old priest to corrupt the populace.

The locals are said to have recovered the priest's remains (either from the lake or the roadside) and buried him the following day in the graveyard next to the tiny church in Killygarvan. He remained a figure of reverence and martyrdom to the people for generations and a memorial plaque today marks the place where he died.

Part Three

SURVIVAL &
RESISTANCE

EVADING THE HUNTERS

Ennis 13 May 1712.

Sir, Donogh O'Brien, Brigadier General and Mr Thomas Hickman joyne their diligence with myne, but I believe it would be easier at this tyme to ketch soe manye wolfes or foxes than those priests. And it is a great affliction to me that I am found at this tyme to make any Excuss.

Yours, W. BUTLER.

The Protestant churchyard at Shanrahan in Tipperary may have been a place of eternal rest for many locals who had passed away, but around the mid-eighteenth century, beneath the gravestones, concealed in the ancient vault, another soul lay at rest, though it was anything but eternal. Fr Nicholas Sheehy, PP of Clogheen was wanted for treason and was pursued with great enthusiasm by the priest hunters of the day. As the search intensified the priest knew he would require someplace he could hide by day that his pursuers would be unlikely to search. Fortunately he was much liked in the broad neighbourhood not only by his own flock, but also by many Protestants. Among them was a man named Griffiths, a farmer whose land adjoined the local churchyard. Between them they concocted a plan to conceal the priest during daylight hours in the vault under the graveyard, beneath the bones of those long gone and the feet of mourners laying loved ones to rest. To stay alive Fr Sheehy had to spend months on end with only the dead for company. Then as soon as night fell, he would clamber, benumbed, from his living tomb and creep to Griffith's house where the farmer warmed him by a fire and fed him, before he would go out into the night to tend to his flock. Although he would eventually surrender himself to the authorities, the priest hunters never once thought to search for a Catholic priest in, of all places, a graveyard.

Such were the stratagems required of the clergy as they went about their business in the dangerous world of eighteenth-century Ireland. It is recorded that the Reverend Coyle, Parish Priest of Kells, spent most of his adult life dressed as either a peasant or a beggar and living a transient existence, sleeping in haylofts and garrets and the houses of the poor. The Bishop of Kilmore, who was a good musician, travelled his diocese disguised as a Highland bagpiper. Fr John Barnewall, Parish Priest of Ardbraccan in Meath would frequently go one better. He often eluded the local priest hunters by moving about dressed as a woman, a dark shawl concealing his face. Fr Barnewall also came up with another novel – if extremely uncomfortable – hiding place. He had a local peasant turf-cutter construct a large rick of turf that was actually hollow inside. His pursuers likely rode past the rick a hundred times, never giving it a second glance from the myriad of other such turf piles on the bog, little aware that a small fortune in the shape of a prone priest, shivering with the damp and cold, was lying under his nose.

Others resided in holes dug into the bogs, in caves or in hovels of mud erected on remote hillsides. A letter from Reverend Forstall, Bishop of Kildare and Leighlin, relates how friends had given him shelter, but such was their terror of being caught harbouring a Catholic clergyman that he decided to leave them and seek shelter in the wilds.

> *… on this account [of his friends' terror] I have constructed for myself a hut or thatched hovel, in a marshy wood; there I took up my abode, but was attacked by agonizing pains that brought me almost to the point of death. Sick though I was, I have abandoned the place, for I could no longer endure my sufferings there.*

Fr Phelim Conlon resided in a similarly wild, though evidently more agreeable, abode near a small rise called Cornee or 'the round hill', situated just to the north west of Mohill in Leitrim. The priest travelled the area disguised as a piper and returned from his ministrations to his 'home' in the Cornee bog that surrounded the hill. Here he and a colleague had excavated a large hole deep down into the turf, which they'd then covered in a thatch of heather on a level with the surrounding landscape. One could approach to within a few yards of their hiding place without noticing anything untoward. It served Fr Conlon well, as he survived as Parish Priest of Mohill for twenty-seven years, before he is said to have died there alone.

So-called 'priest holes' offered a slightly more comfortable existence. Although more commonly found in the large stately homes of sympathetic Protestants in England, Ireland had its share. Priest holes were tiny rooms often ingeniously concealed behind a panel or a wall or beneath the floorboards of a large house. One such was discovered in 1996 during renovations at Barberstown Castle near Straffan in County Kildare, having successfully remained undetected for two and a half centuries. Some small cottages were also said to have cruder, but none the less appreciated, priestly accommodations, usually consisting of literally a hole dug straight into the earth beneath one of the building's rooms, and then covered over with boards which were themselves covered in hard-packed earth. Some are said to have featured a small tunnel leading to a concealed entrance in a nearby field, which allowed easier access and offered a means of escape in the event of an emergency.

A man alone trying to evade the hunters for years on end had a difficult enough feat to accomplish, but trying to remain unseen while administering the sacraments, particularly mass, which by its nature would attract a large gathering of people, would present an even greater and more perilous challenge. Most people in Ireland are familiar with the Mass Rock, the secret altar on which the ceremony was conducted. Many of these can be seen nowadays simply sitting by the roadside – there is a well-known mass rock in Ballymacspeake in Derry that sits in a local's front garden. But in penal times roads were few and far between and even these now highly-visible examples would in those days have been far removed from civilization; for anyone who has done any hill walking in Ireland, it's also possible to see some of the locations as they were in the days of the priest hunters, as one will occasionally come across these usually flat-topped boulders often inscribed with a crude cross in the most remote, bleakest places, hours' walk from even the nearest track.

Attending mass was a dangerous, uncomfortable and usually exhausting business for all concerned, yet given the thousands of known mass rocks in the country, even these considerations did little to deter the priests' flock. Besides the remoteness of the location, the quality of the land on which the rocks were chosen, usually bog or mountainous, infertile terrain, meant that it was little visited by the landowners. Densely-wooded landscapes were also favoured as they discouraged priest hunters, who usually travelled on horseback.

Writing to the Protestant Archbishop of Dublin in 1714, a magistrate called Kennington bemoaned the difficulty he had apprehending priests in the wild Kerry landscape:

We do live in a remote part of the county twenty miles
from the sea coast ... so that by this means and that of
being a mountainous country the new herd of Popish
priests have shelter there with impunity.

Often a number of mass rocks were located relatively close to each other so that the site of the mass could be moved at short notice. And one particularly clever artifice employed by the priests was to choose a rock close to a stream. The congregation would then walk to the rock through the stream, leaving no trail for their pursuers to follow.

Once the congregation had gathered, usually in the dead of night or just before dawn, lookouts were then positioned at multiple points around the area to warn of anyone's approach. Only when all necessary precautions had been taken would the priest make his appearance, emerging from the body of the peasantry clad as they were and donning the priestly vestments, which would have been kept in secret by a different nominated man or woman since the previous celebration.

Even then, only a select few trusted individuals would know the identity of the priest and further precautions were often necessary to conceal his identity in case a priest hunter disguised as a peasant had infiltrated the congregation. Usually the priest would wear a veil over his face or if the mass rock was sufficiently large, he would remain concealed behind it and only his voice would be heard. At some point during the service, gifts of food or whatever miniscule amounts of money could be afforded were made to the priest to allow him to survive and the moment the mass was complete the priest would divest himself of his vestments and disappear into the darkness or surreptitiously mingle back into the crowd. Even those to whom his garments were entrusted would be forbidden from making any inquiries as to where he was next headed or where he was living. It was a case of the less one knew, the less one could be forced to reveal.

Whispers, rather than chanted responses were the order of the day at most clandestine masses, as the collective voices of a large group might be carried a great distance across the open countryside. The 'speakeasy' nature of these gatherings is hinted at in a letter from a hunted priest, one Dominick Deane, in which he arranges a mass in subtle terms.

> *July 27 1710.*
> *I shall see you on the 22 of the next, as this enclosure*
> *requires. You summon all yours to meet where you shall*
> *think most convenient which I believe may be at the*
> *place where we met last, and be it timely in the morning,*
> *without horses or servants or any sorte of noise which is*
> *all now.*
> *From your Brother,*
> *Dominick Deane.*

In some cases mass was celebrated in a peasant's hut. This was particularly risky for all as the penalty for anyone who permitted a mass to be said on his property was thirty pounds fine and a year's imprisonment. News of the impending and usually rare celebration of mass would travel a locale by word of mouth and no strangers were informed. On arrival at the hut, the small flock would see only an improvised curtain from behind which the priest's voice carried the words of the rite. Besides protecting the priest's identity, this allowed the worshippers to truthfully swear they had no knowledge of the celebrant. For the same reason, when a new priest was being illegally ordained, several clergyman present would simultaneously lay hands on the new priest so that he could truthfully say he didn't know the name of the man who ordained him, ordination being an extremely serious offence.

In their attempts to locate and identify priests, the authorities eventually took to searching sacks of letters intercepted on incoming ships. Anything that looked like it was from Italy, Spain, Portugal or France – all countries known to provide sanctuary to clergy – was opened and read in the hope that it would provide clues to various priests' locations and names. The letter below was written in 1751, and although implementation of the Penal Laws had been relaxed by then, the writer yet urges caution in correspondence:

To Mr James Madden at Milick near Eyrecourt in the
Co. of Gallway Ireland per London.
Dear Laurence. Last post I was agreeably surprised by
some lines from you in Mr Rourke's letter, a favour I

*had so long before expected. If you have written before
to our College it was certainly an error I had forgot to
apprise you of as it is probable maney letters to me were
intercepted. You will for the future be more cautious and
follow the directions in Mr Rourke's letter. I wish ear-
nestly to know the state of your affairs.
Salamanca, October 1751.
WILLIAM NUGENT.*

Making a report to Rome a few decades earlier in 1714 on
the state of affairs in Ulster, Dr Hugh McMahon, Archbishop of
Armagh, commented on the dangers the priest hunter presented
and the care that must be taken when writing letters:

> *The people watch for the heretics [the priest hunters]
> who we fear the most, and do not let them come near the
> priest, but they sometimes succeed ... In no mission in
> Christendom is correspondence with Rome so difficult as
> in Ireland.*

Dr McMahon thereafter began to employ ciphers to avoid
detection, and would use the address of a non-clergyman and
a *nom de plume*. Aware that a large percentage of their pursuers were uneducated, sometimes even illiterate, the priests wrote
much of their correspondence in Latin and signed off with the
phrase *'e loco refugii nostri'*, meaning 'from the place of refuge'.

The normal practice when a priest received a letter that might implicate him or anyone else in illegal Catholic practices was to immediately destroy the evidence. Unfortunately in the case of the Parish Priest of Ballinrobe, Father Patrick Duffy, he failed to destroy a collection of letters he'd been receiving from two priests called Dominick Deane and Miles Stanton. Their correspondence to him was likely written under the light of a stub of candle in some godforsaken hovel and then carried about secreted in a boot or the lining of clothing. The many letters give us an insight into the world of fear in which the priests lived:

> *Reverend Sir,*
> *… I am very sorry I cannot encouradge you (to visit*
> *me), for my present circumstance is such as you know,*
> *and cannot well admit visits. Wherefore it will be more*
> *expedient and discreet to send communications by paper*
> *than take the paynes of all this way, and hazard perhaps*
> *great evils.*
> *Your owne, Dominick Deane.*

> *Reverend Sir,*
> *There is an Information made against us in Dublin;*
> *upon the Information, orders were sent to the country*
> *to bring us to question. Yett all will signify but little. Si*
> *Deus pro nobis quis contra nos? (If God be for us, who*
> *can be against us?) We must all keepe close these three*
> *weeks to come.*

Your owne, Dominick Deane.

Reverend Sir,
… I shall be glad to hear from you if anything occurs at
present. We will keep very close till the Assizes be over and
till we know further of the designes of Mr Birmingham.
[A local priest hunter]
Your owne, Dominick Deane.

And in this one the unfortunate Deane hopes for a pair of shoes:

Reverend Sir,
… Pray at your leasure order a paire of shewes made for
me as if for your selfe, and be it somewhat bigger then
your own shewe, the heel not very high and well nailed.
Your owne, Dominick Deane.

We are also given a clear insight into the levels of secrecy that the priests were required to observe to evade capture:

Reverend Sir,
The times are bad and we have reason to observe caution.
You take great care of yourself lest you be surprised as
we are informed is intended. You must keep no sort of a
station or meeting, but from village to village serve your
people at unseasonable hours. I dare not goe further your
side. I believe you may better serve or distribute the sacred

129

> *liquor [the holy oils] in some house there at the Neale*
> *than where we thought to meete this day. Which is the*
> *most discreet method you can take to serve the soule of our*
> *friend [a recently deceased Protestant sympathiser who*
> *had converted to Catholicism] and you are not to keep*
> *them long to make a show.*
> *I rest Sir your owne, Dominick Deane.*

Unfortunately, the Fr Duffy to whom these letters were addressed had committed the cardinal sin of retaining all the papers he received. When he was captured by a priest hunter called Robert Millar all his documents were seized and among the papers found was a papal absolution for several priests, Duffy included, for having taken the Oath of Abjuration, which in itself provided the evidence the authorities needed to prove Duffy and the others guilty of a treasonable act. This would lead to the arrest of several other priests and the incident highlighted how a single, simple lapse could bring so many priests to ruin. His papers also revealed that Deane and Stanton were in fact aliases for Fr Dominick Lynch and Fr Francis Burke. While Fr Duffy was found guilty, imprisoned and transported, Lynch and Burke remained at large for the rest of their days, thanks largely to the continuing secrecy that was evident in their letters.

In another piece of correspondence, the aforementioned Dr Hugh McMahon also makes reference to another secret – and somewhat strange – practice designed to evade detection. This was the holding of a kind of 'imagined mass' with the priest *in absentia*. He tells us that it was not unusual to see peasants with their hands joined in prayer, each quietly mouthing the prayers of the mass. In some distant spot a priest had begun the rite, observed from a distance by a follower who would signal that the ceremony had commenced. This signal would be relayed over an area so that the community could participate. McMahon wrote.

> *Not uncommonly one would come across men and women with their hands joined in prayer having got the signal that mass was begun and thus they united themselves in spirit with those who afar off were praying on bended knees although they could not see the priest. It often happened to myself when saying mass by night that not a soul was present except the man of the house and his wife not even the children, for they could not be trusted with the secret. There is a penalty of £30 and a year's imprisonment on any who permitted mass to be said in his house or anywhere on his premises.*

This strange, scattered congregation would be denied sight of their beloved priest, but more importantly, he would also remain invisible to the priest hunter.

By means of disguises and codes, secret hiding and meeting places, by covering their trails and constantly watching their backs and by trusting only a close circle of friends, many priests, using means that would do a modern-day spy proud, continued to remain free and alive and bring the faith to the people. Yet all their secrecy and cunning was often not sufficient to remain at large unaided, and they gladly accepted assistance from those the authorities would least suspect – the Protestant community.

PROTESTANT RESISTANCE

The attempts to suppress or eradicate Catholicism in Ireland were not based purely on some form of maniacal bigotry, certainly not in the sense that it would be understood today. While it is undoubtedly true that bigotry was the motivation for a substantial number of Protestants, the anti-Catholicism was as much to do with politics as religion and also driven by a very real fear. Tales of events like The Massacre of St Bartholomew's Day in 1572 when as many as thirty thousand Huguenots were butchered by Catholic mobs in Paris or of more recent vintage and much closer to home, when the Catholic rebellion of 1641 resulted in the deaths of up to twelve thousand Protestant planters in Ulster, were passed on through the generations and held up as vivid reminders of the threat of 'popery'.

Catholic and Protestant alike would ultimately revile the priest hunters, but for most of the first half of the eighteenth century they plied their trade with impunity. The Irish House of Commons had voted in 1709 that the profession provided 'an honourable service, deserving of the nation's gratitude.' Ironically the 'nation' as defined by the then parliament, excluded all Catholics and Presbyterians, who comprised over ninety per cent of the population.

Yet not every Protestant believed the Catholics who lived among them were constantly planning to butcher them in their beds. As the eighteenth century progressed more and more ordinary Protestants came to see the repressive Penal Laws as unjust and cruel and on many levels, downright impractical. The laws fostered an air of resentment, unease and suspicion, and also interfered with everyday commerce. Catholic workers, for example, might not try too hard to impress a Protestant employer and the more extremist papists were already engaged in a long-running campaign of maiming livestock, burning barns, poisoning drinking water and so on.

But many liberal-minded Protestant men and women considered the Penal Laws immoral and offensive. Ultimately the abhorrence these men felt regarding the treatment of Ireland would move them to form the Society of United Irishmen in the late 1700s, to campaign for Parliamentary reform. The words of perhaps the most famous of those, Theobald Wolfe Tone, spoken from the dock on the occasion of his court-martial, give us a sense of the feeling of these men towards their downtrodden compatriots:

I have laboured to abolish the infernal spirit of religious

*persecution by uniting the Catholics and Dissenters. To
the former, I owe more than ever can be repaid. The
service I was so fortunate as to render them they rewarded
munificently but they did more: when the public cry was
raised against me, when the friends of my youth swarmed
off and left me alone, the Catholics did not desert me.
They had the virtue even to sacrifice their own interests to
a rigid principle of honour. They refused, though strongly
urged, to disgrace a man who, whatever his conduct
towards the Government might have been, had faithfully
and conscientiously discharged his duty towards them and
in so doing, though it was in my own case, I will say they
showed an instance of public virtue of which I know not
whether there exists another example.*

Yet helping their Catholic neighbours could be a risky business
for the average Protestant, and often quite dangerous. Should a
Protestant be discovered harbouring a Catholic priest, for example, he could count on being cold-shouldered at the very least
by many of his own community or even those within his own
family. He could also incur the loss of his property, fines or face
imprisonment, especially if he was a man who held public office.
The crown had officially stated that 'all magistrates who neglected
to execute these laws, were betrayers of the liberties of the kingdom.' Yet many Protestants, of all classes, were prepared to run
the risk of penury, shame and imprisonment in an effort to help

their Catholic neighbours. One example from 1711 shows how a number of Protestant Dissenters were willing to face prosecution rather than assist the forces of law in a 'priest-hunt':

> 25th October
>
> *Walter Dawson, Esq. one of her majesty's justices of the peace for the county of Armagh, having lately in pursuance of the proclamation issued by the Lords Justices and Council, for apprehending regulars of the Popish clergy, given a warrant for apprehending one MacGuire the titular dean of Armagh, the constable employed in that service commanded several persons to go and assist him in taking the said dean, among whom were some Dissenters, who absolutely refused to assist the said constable, for which refusal they are to be prosecuted at the next assizes to be held for the said county.*

Besides helping priests to avoid detection, innumerable Protestants also helped their Catholic neighbours to retain their lands and possessions, which would have been forfeit under the Penal Laws. The so-called 'discoverer' was in effect the white-collar version of the priest hunter, but the rewards could be vastly greater and the danger almost minimal. These men spent their time travelling the country and trawling through legal documents relating to land and property ownership in search of any anomalies or evidence that a Catholic who still retained some property or wealth was infringing the law, which could mean the confiscation of all he possessed, a portion of which would be granted to the discoverer. Mathew Palin was one such, a former lieutenant in King William's army. Palin took a legal action against the Fitzgerald family in Westmeath as a result of which all their lands were forfeit to the crown, Palin being rewarded with a quarter of the property.

In another case a Catholic called Farrell who lived in Longford, had decided to convert to Protestantism in order to purchase some lands. A number of years later a discoverer called Tomlinson uncovered a tiny technicality in the man's documentation. Conversion to Protestantism required the person to 'take the sacrament' within six months of his declaration of conformity to the religion. Tomlinson discovered that Farrell had only converted officially after six months and *three days*. The court ruled in his favour and Farrell lost all his property and was also ordered to pay costs, reducing him to complete penury.

As a means of helping Catholics to escape such injustices, many Protestants secretly took the title deeds of a Catholic friend and held it in their name, yet returned all the profits from the land to the true owner. Because the Penal Laws were in force for over a century it was often necessary for the title deeds, not to mention the sense of justice, to be passed down through the generations. The Bryans of Jenkinstown in Kilkenny for example, had been a prominent and wealthy Catholic family whose land would have been lost to the crown had it not been for the Protestant Marquises of Ormonde, whose family held the Bryans' title deeds in their own name and passed them down, father to son for over a hundred years until the day when the Penal Laws were finally revoked, at which point the Bryans' estates were returned to their rightful owners.

At the other end of the scale, an impoverished Protestant blacksmith in Tipperary was the official 'owner' of a large estate that had been the property of a Catholic family for whom he'd previously provided little more than horseshoes. Legally the possessor of enough farmland to make him a very wealthy man, the blacksmith simply allowed the Catholic family to continue running the estate; all documentation recorded that monies from rents and so on were being paid to the Protestant blacksmith yet the man refused to take a penny for his trouble and simply continued in his former role as the family's blacksmith for the remainder of his days.

Concealing or altering documents was one thing, trying to shield a Catholic priest or bishop from the agents of the law was far more dangerous. Yet in many cases, Protestant courage formed the last line of defence between the priest and the hunter.

A PROTESTANT SPY
AT COURT

The Catholic church at Ardbraccan in County Meath had already been watching over the faithful for over seven hundred years when Fr John Barnewall was appointed to the parish in the late seventeenth century. The original tower, now a thousand years old, still stands watch today. But the winds of change would soon banish the priest from within its stone walls to the open hillsides, woodlands and riversides of the area just to the west of Navan.

Ardbraccan is actually something of a misnomer – it means 'high point or hill of St Braccan' – as the general area boasts little in the way of high hills. Mostly it is flat and fertile, the landscape only occasionally interrupted by a small rise or hillock. If was from this place that Fr Barnewall proceeded to Navan in 1704 when required to register himself by law as the practising popish priest of the parishes of Ardbraccan and the surrounding lands.

He was then aged forty-seven, having been ordained in 1680 in Kildare, yet he would continue as priest to the community for many decades to come, despite a price being put on his head when he refused to take the Oath of Abjuration five years later, and was forced to flee into the night. The reason for his continued service was in part due to his own physical strength, to the loyalty of his flock and in no small measure to the help he received from Protestant families in the neighbourhood.

Fr Barnewall seems to have been hunted with a particular vigour, possibly because he hailed from a well-known family of Catholic nobles who had raised forces to oppose Cromwell's armies in the previous century and whose lands had subsequently been confiscated. For years he survived on the goodwill of his flock, taking shelter in their outhouses and haylofts, eating the food they supplied to him in ditches or in hedgerows. He celebrated countless masses in forest glades and by the banks of the Boyne and the Blackwater, the location changed each on each occasion, the meeting place whispered from ear to ear about the parish at only the last moment to avoid detection.

His most ardent pursuer was a man called Sir Richard Barker (or Baker), who resided on the banks of the Blackwater River and who had developed a fearsome reputation as a priest-catcher over the years. Little is recorded about Barker's background, but his title would seem to suggest he was a man of means and probably occupied some position of authority, such as local magistrate. It's unlikely his motivations for pursuing priests with such vigour were monetary, and more than likely were political or borne of religious intolerance. His *modus operandi* was not uncommon; to pay a collection of informers to keep their ears open about the region for any hint of a priest's appearance.

His Protestant peers around Navan and Kells weren't exactly supportive of his efforts and it is said that the family of Sir Thomas Taylor, who would later serve as MP for Kells, often sheltered fleeing priests in the grounds of their very sizeable estate of almost eight thousand acres. Another, Robert Waller, was of even greater assistance to Fr Barnewall, and seems to have enjoyed considerable popularity among the native peasants for his efforts.

Despite Barker's repeated attempts to locate Fr Barnewall, such was the secrecy and stealth with which the priest's activities were organised and his hiding places conceived that years passed without any solid information manifesting itself. Eventually Barker resorted to the oldest trick in the priest hunter's manual – feigning an oncoming bereavement in a Catholic family; the last rites being the one sacrament that could not be deferred, the priest was obliged always to take his chances. Barker assembled a collection of underlings in a house at a place called Martry, almost equidistant from Kells and Navan, and sent word that a man in a nearby cottage was near to death. Hours would pass before the priest would hear the message and then make his way to the area, during which time the discussion of their plan was overheard by their Catholic servant girl, who soon after quietly stole from the house into the night and ran along the track until she met the approaching priest, warning him that he was walking into a trap.

The priest escaped on that occasion, but it wouldn't be long before Barker and his minions were on his trail again; as they soon began to suspect that one of their own was working to thwart their efforts.

Robert Waller was a prominent Protestant magistrate in the county and a wealthy landowner. As it transpired, the principal reason Fr Barnewall had been able to avoid detection so successfully for years was that he was regularly supplied with information on the authorities' intentions, including those of Richard Barker. The priest and Waller had a friendship that stretched back many years. They were about the same age and Waller was a considerate landlord and a popular figure with the Catholic peasantry.

But it seems Waller's attempts to help Fr Barnewall may have eventually become a little too obvious as Barker's next ploy was to again despatch a messenger into the community who spread the word that Richard Waller needed to meet with the priest on a matter of urgency. This time Barker positioned men about the Allenstown demesne, crouching in hedges and behind trees and haystacks, invisible against the dark cloak of the night. Some hours later the priest arrived and no sooner had he hurried through the gates when the shout went up and several dark figures rushed out to surround him. With a multitude of weapons levelled at him, he had little option but to surrender and was hauled off to Trim Gaol before Waller had any notion of what was happening beyond his walls.

When word reached the priest's friend the following day he was enraged, but knew that Barker was well within his rights. He seems to have had little fear of being prosecuted for abetting a fugitive, perhaps because the priest had been taken outside the walls of his home or perhaps because his influence and reputation among his fellow Protestants was such that he knew they would not support any prosecution of him. Waller determined to use that influence to good effect and spent the next weeks driving his carriage along the tracks and boreens that cut through the mostly flat fields and dense towering woodlands that defined the Meath landscape of the age, visiting each of his fellow Grand Jury members and encouraging them to find the priest innocent of his crime, perhaps urging them to consider the ill-feeling that the arrest would cause among the peasantry, which was not only bad for business, but could also make life dangerous.

At the next Assizes the priest's case was heard and Waller had done his work well, as Fr Barnewall was found not guilty and released, and although no record of the trial survives, it appears that despite the 'not guilty' verdict he was barred from ministering to his flock in any form. Such a ban would be of little consequence to the priest who had grown used to the privations of a life lived in frosty by-ways and moonlight forest clearings.

Robert Waller was reported to have come to his aid on another couple of occasions some years later when a relative of the priest decided to ease his burden somewhat by making him a gift of a fine horse. Unfortunately another of the Penal Laws forbade a Catholic to own a horse with a value greater than five pounds and furthermore empowered any Protestant who offered that sum to be entitled to seize the horse. Riding through the townland of Greetiagh, just to the north of his parish, Fr Barnewall was halted in his tracks at a crossroads by one of the band of priest hunters who had been involved in the earlier attempts to capture him. Seeing an opportunity to make up for lost earnings, the man immediately demanded that the priest sell him the horse for five pounds, a fraction of its value. Fuming, but with little choice the priest dismounted and handed the reins to the man. But as he pushed his feet into the stirrups and prepared to gallop away he suddenly felt the clergyman's hand on his arm. In a moment of inspiration the priest demanded his saddle and bridle back – they weren't covered by the legal statute. The man responded with a few profanities as the priest informed him he would be a thief in the eyes of the law if he took the saddle. When that made no impression, Fr Barnewall, who was a tall, broad-shouldered individual, struck the man a tremendous blow on the side of the head with his whip handle, then seized him by leg and arm and hauled him from the horse, pitching him head first into the Meath dirt. He then duly remounted and trotted away. The enraged man immediately hurried to the nearest authorities, only to be referred to the presiding magistrate of the day, who just happened to be Robert Waller. Hearing the man's tale, Waller berated him for his behaviour and informed him he was lucky not to be on a charge of attempted robbery, and duly sent him packing.

Another minor incident is recorded involving Robert Waller and Fr Barnewall. On his way to perform one of the sacraments in a cottage near Waller's Allenstown home, Fr Barnewall encountered his friend on the roadside talking to a notorious priest hunter named Pilot. The man was actually inquiring of the magistrate if he had any information about Fr Barnewall's whereabouts, clearly unaware of the friendship that existed between the pair. The priest was disguised as a pauper, garbed in a coat of coarse frieze and sporting a tattered peasant's hat, his vestments concealed in an old satchel across his shoulder, and Pilot failed to recognise him, but was immediately suspicious nonetheless.

Feigning innocence, he greeted the pair with a cheery 'Good morning', at which point Pilot demanded his name. Offering some fictitious name, he asked the same of the priest hunter. Informed it was 'Pilot' he apparently couldn't resist the reply: 'Your name, sir, [sounding like 'Pilate'], 'bodes no good to a Christian.'

An apparently irked Pilot immediately blocked the priest's path, at which point Waller interposed and pulled the priest hunter aside saying 'Let him pass, let him pass, he is a mere beggar.'

As the years began to take their toll on Fr Barnewall, Waller actually provided him with a secret sanctuary within his own estate. This was a time that the authorities were particularly active in seeking out wayward priests and Waller agreed a means of operating with the priest and a number of the local peasants. When someone required the priest's services a man or woman would be despatched to find Waller and would then loiter suspiciously in open view of the magistrate and whatever company he might be keeping. When Waller would approach and ask what their business was, the peasant would apologise and explain that he was in search of a particular individual, using an alias for Fr Barnewall. Waller would innocently tell him to 'be off', and at the first opportunity get word to the priest that he was needed in such and such a place.

Besides disguising himself as a beggar or a peasant labourer, Fr Barnewall also frequently dressed as a woman when he needed to move about during the daylight hours and as has been recorded in earlier pages, even lived for a time in a specially-constructed, hollow rick of turf. By these means and with the priceless help of Richard Waller he continued to minister to his flock until he was an octogenarian. Unfortunately, his principal protector's death in 1731, left him more vulnerable. Although the magistrate's two sons Robert and William continued to assist the priest during the following years, the relentlessness of the priest hunters finally paid off. Sometime after 1737, the aged priest was caught in the act of celebrating mass while garbed as a beggar, surrounded and bound, then taken to Navan Bridewell (see panel) where the twenty pounds reward for his capture was finally claimed. On this occasion, not even the influence of the Waller family could save the priest from prison and trial.

BRIDEWELL – THE IRISH CONNECTION

Ireland's two largest cities both still have Garda stations bearing the unusual name 'Bridewell' – at Chancery Lane in Dublin and on Cornmarket Street in Cork. Although there is an Irish link to the name, to find its origins one has to look beyond Ireland's shores and as far back as the reign of King Henry VIII. In the early sixteenth century, a palace was built for the king on the banks of the Fleet River in London. Among the important meetings held here was that in 1528 of a senior papal delegation convened to discuss the monarch's desired divorce from Catherine of Aragon. The building was located close to a holy well known as 'St Brigid's Well', or more commonly called 'Bride's Well', named for one of Ireland's patron saints, Brigid of Kildare. Henry VIII's dwelling adopted the name and became known as 'Bridewell Palace'. Some years later, the monarchy donated the building to the City of London for use as housing for homeless children and prostitutes, but within a few years it had been turned into a prison. Soon other prisons in England, Ireland and even the United States (Chicago Bridewell) began adopting the term as a generic word for a prison. Eventually almost every prison in Ireland was known as a 'Bridewell', such as Navan Bridewell referred to in this chapter. The original building in London was demolished in the nineteenth century and use of the term was discontinued in Britain, but the name lives on in Dublin and Cork, with its etymology involving the curious mix of an English monarch's palace and an Irish patron saint.

Two weeks later he was transferred to Dublin, probably to Newgate Prison, and there the official record of his existence ended. Among the locals, various tales were told of how he met his end, some undoubtedly exaggerated to support their view of Fr Barnewall as an official martyr to the faith, but even the most restrained of these – that he lived out his days in the squalor of a crammed prison cell – present a brutal picture of the old man's last months of life. A man called William Forde Esq, who was the Town Clerk of the Corporation of Dublin and a native of Meath, claimed he knew for a fact that Fr Barnewall had been executed in Dublin. Another account, the most commonly believed among the local population, is that the priest was put aboard a ship for transportation that stopped in an English port for supplies. While he was on the deck a crewman pointed him out as a Catholic traitor to a mob on the dock, who then dragged the priest from the ship and hanged him on the spot. Although possible, it seems unlikely that a prisoner would be allowed on deck and a ship's captain would almost certainly have intervened if a mob invaded his craft, particularly as he may have forfeited his transportation fee if the prisoner was lost.

Robert Waller's family continued to reside in the area and his second son, William would in future years build the impressive five-bay, four-storey Allenstown House, which would stand for almost two hundred years before being demolished in 1938. The family's efforts to help Fr Barnewall and other priests were deeply appreciated in the Navan-Kells area and the Waller family would continue to enjoy deep popularity among the peasantry for generations after. A hint of this can be gleaned from the fact that, more than a century after Fr Barnewall's death, it was reported that the peasants exhibited 'very extraordinary joy' when a young male Waller descendant won a horse race held at Ratholdren near Navan in May of 1865.

But the Waller family's religious tolerance was by no means unique and without the help of countless other Protestants during these dark years, many more Catholic priests, bishops, schoolteachers and ordinary peasants would have fallen under the shadow of the priest hunter.

SANCTUARY BY
THE BOYNE

Meath was not a good place to be during the penal era, having gained notoriety as the birthplace of Oliver Plunkett, who had been hanged, drawn and quartered in 1681 at Tyburn in London. The circumstances of his trial, which was little more than a kangaroo court, and his dignified acceptance of his fate (when the sentence was pronounced after the prolonged process of conviction, he said '*Deo Gratias*' – 'Thanks be to God') had long since conferred martyr status on him. His place of birth at Loughcrew became a place of pilgrimage and the ancient passage tomb on the nearby Sliabh na Caillí became an important meeting place for priests and their followers throughout the era. A mass rock can still be seen on the top of Sliabh na Caillí.

For obvious reasons, the county attracted a large assortment of priest hunters who saw the opportunity for rich pickings; an example of one such is given below. The unfortunate victim in this case was one James Plunkett; although he was only distantly related to Oliver, his name would have pricked the ears of the mercenaries. It is interesting to note that the hunter in this case, Charles Woodward, was formerly a lawman who had decided to devote his energies to his new, more profitable career:

> *To their Excellencies the Lords Justices etc.*
> *The humble petition of Charles Woodward late (ex) High Sheriff of Meath.*
> *Sheweth That your petitioner apprehended one James Plunkett a Popish priest for saying Mass out of the parish for which he was registered, contrary to the Statute. That at the Assizes held for the County of Meath 9 July 1716 the said James Plunkett was tryed and convicted for saying Mass in the parish of Kilsker in the said County being only registered Priest for the parish of Killeagh and thereupon ordered by the Court to be transported pursuant to the Statute at your Petitioner's prosecution as by Certificate enclosed. That your Petitioner was at great trouble and expense in prosecuting the said James Plunkett and prays the Reward mentioned.*

Fr Plunkett had avoided detection up to that point thanks largely to the numerous sanctuaries that were provided by a number of influential Protestants around Meath, one of whom was Peter Ludlow of Ardsallagh Castle, which sat on the banks of the Boyne, and was just a few miles distant from the area served by the priest. Ludlow was widely known among the Catholic clergy as a man who regularly provided sanctuary and sustenance and utterly detested the priest hunters, which is extraordinary considering that he was also the High Sheriff of County Louth.

In 1715, the year previous to Plunkett's arrest, Ludlow had successfully stood for Parliament for the Borough of Dunleer, the records of which indicate that of the ninety-one people who voted for him, one was married to a Catholic and three had not taken the Oath of Abjuration, which gives us some hint as to his leanings.

Ardsallagh Castle (which means 'the height of the sallows or willows') stood on the south western bank of the Boyne, a couple of miles from Navan, and just to the west was the tiny hamlet of Oldtown, where, posing as a peasant farm worker, there secretly resided in a farmhouse a priest called Fr Clarke who had been befriended by Peter Ludlow. Most people in the area at the time were familiar with the case of Fr John McGoona, who in an earlier time had tried to escape a priest hunter by swimming the Boyne, but unfortunately died of hypothermia in the attempt. With this in mind Ludlow had provided Fr Clarke with a boat specifically for the purpose of crossing the river safely and making it to the sanctuary of the castle. On numerous occasions, when word of the presence of priest hunters in the area reached his ears, Fr Clarke availed of the escape route and lay low in Ardsallagh until the storm abated, whereupon he would return to the farmer's cottage and resume his illicit duties.

On one occasion, however, three priest hunters from Navan managed to learn that a priest, disguising himself as a farm hand, was hiding in a cottage in Oldtown; they surrounded the farmer's home before he had time to flee, trapping him inside and alone. But Fr Clarke, like many other priests of the time, was not the surrendering type; in fact he was reputedly a tall, broad-shouldered man whose daily exertions ministering to his flock had given him a particularly athletic build. The men had naively come unarmed, no doubt believing that three of them could easily handle one priest. As they yelled for him to give himself up, Fr Clarke seized the farmer's blackthorn stick and hid it in the folds of his coat, then walked out to face his would-be captors. The three rushed him at once, but the priest surprised them with his sudden violence, connecting the heavy blackthorn with backs and arms and heads with such ferocity that within a minute the three had retreated to the road. As they departed, cursing and bruised, they shouted warnings back to Fr Clarke that they would return and this time in the company of armed lawmen.

He had no doubt they would be true to their word and quickly made for the boat that Ludlow had supplied. When he reached Ardsallagh he explained what had happened, much to Peter Ludlow's amusement. If the men wanted the authorities in this district to come to their aid, he explained, they would need the sanction of the local acting magistrate, who happened to be Peter

Ludlow himself.

As the three men had to take a circuitous route across the medieval Kilcairn Bridge to the north they didn't arrive at Ardsallagh for some hours, by which time Fr Clarke was resting comfortably within the castle. Ludlow emerged and asked their business and the three recounted the attack by the priest, showing him their wounds as evidence and requesting an order from the magistrate for the recruitment of armed men to hunt the priest down. Ludlow listened patiently then expressed incredulity that a single priest could overpower three men. Their passionate insistence that they were telling the truth was met with a nod, after which Ludlow told them to wait at the front door. Inside, he had a servant fetch him a horsewhip, and then returned to face the failed priest hunters, startling them with his outrage that they had allowed themselves to be thrashed by a single papist priest. He then began to wield the whip wildly, adding scars upon their scars as he chased them down the avenue, his curses following in their wake.

It wasn't recorded what transpired when he returned to Ardsallagh, but it's not difficult to imagine the Catholic priest and Protestant magistrate spending the evening laughing themselves hoarse over brandies.

What ultimately became of Fr Clarke is not known, but no record of his ever having been captured exists. The Ludlows continued their efforts to help their Catholic neighbours through the generations and this, along with their general philanthropy towards the poor of the community, earned them a lasting place in the people's memory.

THE 'HAUNTED' ROOM

The lengths to which another Protestant gentleman would go to help a Catholic priest would almost put those of Richard Waller and Peter Ludlow in the shade. Texts from the era don't refer to this man by name although they do inform us that he resided in the Manor House at Ratoath in Meath, so he was most likely a Mr Corballis, whose family had a long history in the area and whose name still adorns various businesses and streets and even the local Ratoath shopping centre. It's possible – likely even – that Corballis, as a prominent local gentleman and magistrate would have known Richard Waller in some capacity as they were almost neighbours and undoubtedly crossed paths in their official capacities.

The priest who benefitted from Mr Corballis' benevolence was also of a renowned bloodline – Dr Michael Plunkett was a first cousin of none other than Saint Oliver Plunkett who had been martyred in 1681. Born in 1652, Michael was tutored by his renowned cousin and was employed as his secretary for a number of years. After his ordination he went to Rome to expand his studies and while there received several letters from Oliver Plunkett that had been written from his condemned cell in London's Newgate Prison. He returned to Meath sometime in the 1680s with royal approval (during the reign of the more liberal Charles II) as 'Dr Michael Plunkett, one of the Masters of our Chancery of Ireland, to the Rectory of Dunboyne'. When Dr Patrick Tyrrell was executed in 1692 at the hands of Williamite supporters, Plunkett was appointed in his place as Vicar General Apostolic of Meath, a post he would occupy for over twenty years. Required to register in 1704 he was recorded as 'Popish priest of the parishes of Ratoath and Rathbeggan, aged fifty-two, living at Ratoath.' It seems the authorities at the time were unaware of his more elevated position, which would have made him subject to immediate arrest. During these years he served his flock from a tiny, mud-walled, thatched chapel in Ratoath, which was apparently screened from public view by other buildings. His pathetic 'chapel' would eventually be closed up and like most of his fellow clergymen, the caves and woodlands of the county would eventually serve as his church. Besides his own parishioners, he also earned the respect and friendship of many of the Protestant gentry in the area. Many of these men connived to help him carry out his ecclesiastical duties, which allowed the priest to evade arrest for decades.

But not long after his registration, he was discovered to be more than a mere parish priest. An official report from a few years later provided a comprehensive list of senior Catholic cler-gymen and their subordinates, which included his name and title – Doctor Plunkett, Vicar General of Meath. The same report lists his coadjutors, which interestingly gives us another insight into the methods employed by the priest hunters, who it seems would go so far as to imitate priests as a means of infiltrating their ranks:

> … *Fr Grady, supposed [suspected] by the Romans (Catho-lics in general) to be a spye, he lately clameing the Reward of £20 for two priests …*

What is certain is that by 1709, Dr Plunkett was wanted by the authorities. As a Vicar General, and bearing such a distin-guished name among the faithful, he would have brought in a handsome reward.

The man most in pursuit of those riches was a priest hunter called Thompson, who resided somewhere on the road between Ratoath and Navan. Sometime around 1715, Thompson is reported to have tracked down the priest and with a band of minions, pursued him some miles southwards across the Dublin border towards Luttrellstown. With Thompson almost upon him, Fr Plunkett fled into estate of the Luttrell family and sought shelter in their barn, where he hid behind a col-lection of harnesses. One of the priest hunter's minions appar-ently arrived and searched the barn but, miraculously, didn't find the priest. His escape was by a hair's breadth and he knew he wouldn't always be so fortunate. Luckily for him, help was at hand from a longtime friend.

Corballis decided to create a more permanent refuge for the hunted priest and one where the priest hunters would never think – or dare – to search. He had an upstairs room in Ratoath Manor House permanently locked and on some pretext forbade all but one of his servants to enter it. This one trusted servant was given the task of secretly stocking the room with food, water, clean clothes and bed coverings. He was also instructed to conceal a ladder in a ditch at the rear of the building. Like Richard Waller, Mr Corballis was a magistrate and often had access to inside information on the movements and intentions of Thompson and his band and whenever he learned of a plan to mount a search, he had word sent to Dr Plunkett to make for the Manor House with all possible speed. The servant would watch for his approach and then quickly retrieve the ladder and place it against the side of the house, allowing the priest to clamber up into the locked room, where he would remain until the storm abated.

The authorities at the time were particularly active in trying to apprehend Catholic priests in Meath; its proximity to the watching eyes of Dublin Castle demanded the rigorous pursuit of outlaw clerics and arrests were frequent right across the county, including that of Fr James Plunkett, possibly a relation of Michael, who was captured in 1716 by an ex-sheriff turned priest hunter called Woodward.

Concerned at the continued pressure for arrests from Dublin, and also in consideration of Dr Plunkett's advancing years –

he was now in his mid-sixties – Corballis decided to make the arrangement with the room a permanent one. Fr Plunkett was surely delighted when Corballis informed him, used as he normally was to sleeping in barns or even ditches. From that point, having spent each night moving stealthily about the extensive parish performing mass, officiating at funerals, weddings, baptisms and so on, all under the constant fear of capture, the priest would return exhausted to the manor house before dawn and use the ladder to climb to the open window of the room, where he would spend the day resting. Each morning the servant would quietly remove the ladder and replace it in the ditch and as soon as night fell would prop it against the window again and give a signal to the priest that it was safe to descend. The fact that a man in his sixties would continue to live such an exhausting and perilous life in terms of exposure to ill health and possible capture, gives us a sense of the depth of belief in the hereafter that people of the time held. For example, an unbaptised infant who died would be sent to limbo, where the child would spend eternity deprived of the beatific vision, or not at one with God. And with such a high infant mortality at the time, parents desperately needed their baby baptised at the first possible moment after birth to save them from such a fate. The concern about their fate in the afterlife could be even worse for adults. Due to the privations under which they lived, the average life expectancy (when deaths of infants aged a year or less are included) was thirty-five years. So in essence nobody wanted to be walking around for very long with a mortal sin blackening their soul, which would see them condemned to the eternal flames of hell. Their priest was their only possible salvation from this fate. Which goes some way to explaining why the aged Fr Plunkett was willing to climb down ladders in the middle of a freezing winter's night and set off across the bleak countryside to minister to his flock.

The servants in the manor house reputedly came to believe that the reason the room was kept permanently locked was that it was haunted, and the creaking floorboards they heard as Dr Plunkett moved about reinforced their superstitious belief, which undoubtedly wasn't discouraged by Corballis.

The 'ghost' secretly lived in the manor house for years on end, but his lifestyle increasingly took its toll and ultimately Corballis' servant was forced to carry the priest 'piggy-back' style up and down the ladder, although his forays about the parish were becoming less and less as the years passed, venturing out only in emergencies. In his final days he became a permanent resident and had to be almost nursed on a daily basis, and it seems almost prophetic that the very building where he lay is nowadays Ratoath Manor Nursing Home.

Thanks to Corballis, neither Thompson nor any other priest hunter ever caught the cleric and he continued to dwell in his lonely, secret chamber until he died in 1727, at the age of seventy-five. He was buried in the old cemetery at Killegland, a couple of miles to the east of Ratoath and on the two hundred and fiftieth anniversary of his death in 1977 local residents reset his weatherworn, centuries-old tombstone. Between the words '*Momento mori*' (loosely meaning 'Remember you must die' or 'Remember your mortality') is a carving of a skull and crossbones, which was a common Catholic symbol of death in the eighteenth century. It also served as a warning that danger is close at hand, which is particularly fitting considering the perils that Dr Michael Plunkett had endured for most of his adult life.

DIFFERENT SIDES
OF THE COIN

Two closely related branches of the Croasdaile family illustrate clearly the differing opinions of certain members of the Protestant ascendancy to the hunting down of Catholic clerics. Referred to in texts as 'the priest hunter, Richard Croasdaile', this man resided in Loughrea in Galway and was another of the gentrified class of hunter, his family owing vast estates in Leitrim, Galway, Mayo and Clare, so presumably his motivations were not monetary, and he appears to have been widely disliked among the local populace. A couple of records of his activities survived:

> *To John Lyons Esq. H.M. Castle of Dublin.*
> *Loughrea 24 Feby. 1743.*
> *Sir I received my Lord Chief Justices warrants against*
> *two popish priests, which shall be strictly obeyed by me to*
> *the utmost of my power. As the papists who live here has*

[have] the earliest Intelligence for the priests being taken
upp in Dublin, they all fled here from their convents and
fryerys but as the two priests I am to pursue live remote
and in the country I hope in some short time to give you a
better account of them.
Richard Croasdaile.

He seems to have been busy in the following year as he compiled a list of almost thirty outlaw priests:

To John Lyons Esq. H.M. Castle of Dublin.
Loughrea 30 March 1744.
Sir Yours of the 3rd should have been answered some
time but I could not inform myself of half the number
of Popish clergy in this County. At the other side (of the
page) you have the most perfect list I could make.
Richard Croasdaile.

In stark contrast to Richard, his relation Henry Croasdaile in Laois not only abhorred the treatment of the Catholic clergy, but actively helped them. He also treated priest hunters with contempt.

In the mid-eighteenth century, the Protestant curate of the parish of Rosenallis in Laois, the Reverend Thomas Hackett, compiled a report for the authorities on the 'state of popery' in his area. He seems to have harboured some fears of being murdered in his bed by aggrieved Catholics, as included in his report is the following:

> *The parish containeth the whole Barony of Tinnahinch,*
> *yet there is not one Justice of the Peace in the whole*
> *Barony. Quere. [Query] Whether a militia quarterly*
> *array'd would not be a natural security to the Protestant*
> *inhabitants, and a check on their Popish neighbours from*
> *entertaining any levelling schemes subversive to the peace*
> *of his Majesty's faithful subjects.*
> *Thomas Hacket of Nutgrove, near Mt. Mellick, Co.*
> *Laois.*

The absence of Justices of the Peace in the area can be explained by the fact that several years before, Richard Pigott of Capard and Henry Croasdaile of Rynnthe, two Protestant Justices, had been removed from their positions, Pigott for harbouring a priest in his home, Croasdaile for refusing to participate in a priest hunt. This had been a costly exercise for both men, as besides the loss of revenue they incurred by being stripped of their office, the law imposed steep financial penalties on uncooperative members of the legal fraternity: fifty pounds for not apprehending an unregistered priest; one hundred pounds for knowingly permitting a priest to enter Ireland from abroad; one hundred pounds for conniving at the presence of a bishop or regular clergyman in the country.

Both men were obviously wealthy and could bear such losses, or at least were prepared to in the defence of Catholic clergy. But

Henry Croasdaile was prepared to go much further than merely concealing a priest. His loathing of those engaged in priest hunting is evident in the account given by one of the breed (name unknown) in a hearing before the Lord Justices of Maryborough:

> When I approached this Justice (Croasdaile) and asked
> for a privy interview, on learning my business, spoke to
> me in a loud menacing voice and with oaths declared
> that he had foxes and wolves and deer to hunt and that
> he would in no wise hunt men. Then he used my body
> very shamefully.

A young Catholic called Daniel Meehan, who was employed on Henry Croasdaile's estate, recounted the incidents that led to the two Justices' fall from grace. The above-mentioned priest hunter was in the Rosenallis area in search of an outlaw cleric and his inquiries led him first to the Piggott estate at Capard. Armed with information doubtless supplied by a local informant, he accused Richard Piggott of hiding a priest and worse, permitting masses to be held on the grounds. Piggott vehemently denied such a charge. (There was actually a chapel on the estate that was regularly used for Catholic masses.) His actions were all the more admirable considering that just a couple of generations beforehand, his grandfather had fought in Cromwell's armies and the lands on which he stood had been confiscated from Irish gentry and granted to his family. But somewhere down the generations the Piggott family had some form of 'road to Damascus' conversion to tolerance, and Richard Piggott gave the priest hunter short shrift and sent him packing.

The man's next stop was Rynn and the estate of Henry Croasdaile, where he sought to recruit the Justice into a hunt for the clergyman. Croasdaile calmly beckoned the young Daniel Meehan and told him to saddle two horses, one for the Justice and one for himself, and to bring his hounds around to the front of the house, clearly giving the priest hunter the notion that he was preparing to join the search. While waiting for Meehan to return, Croasdaile casually engaged the man in small talk for several minutes. Seeing the lad trot up on a horse with a second in tow, a pack of excited, barking hounds clustered about the horses' legs, his demeanour changed utterly and he quickly mounted his beast, stared down at the priest hunter and said:

> Sir, I have hunted the deer. I have hunted the hare and
> the fox. I have hunted the wolf. But you sir, are the first
> man I will have hunted. Get back on your horse, because
> I will give you a sporting chance before my hounds start
> to chase.

The startled, terrified man quickly did as commanded and leapt on to his mount, galloping away down the avenue without another word. Croasdaile then turned to the young Meehan and told him that they would 'drive that vile wretch from the neighbourhood'. Clearly relishing the experience, he yelled 'Tallyhoe!' and took off after the priest hunter with a pack of yapping dogs in his wake. Meehan followed at a gallop and up ahead he saw the panic-stricken priest hunter tumble from his horse, but with one foot caught in his stirrup so that the animal dragged him the last few yards along the avenue and through the gate. The undoubtedly bemused Meehan rode ahead of Croasdaile and secured the runaway horse, then freed the battered, bruised and trembling priest hunter's foot from the stirrup. Croasdaile arrived moments later and the pack of yelping dogs surrounded the terrified man, but were trained not to attack without command. The priest hunter pleaded for mercy as Croasdaile's horse danced slowly around, towering over the terrified man. The Justice then warned the man never to show his face in Rosenallis or to come near the estate again or he would not get off so lightly. He told Meehan to help the man to remount, and the now-ragged figure of the priest hunter took off along the road.

While he never did come near the place again, he wasn't going to forget the matter and immediately reported it to the authorities, as a result of which Henry Croasdaile was deprived of the office of Justice of the Peace, which given his anything but peaceful treatment of priest hunter, seemed quite appropriate.

JUDICIAL MURDER
IN CLONMEL

The single most infamous atrocity of the penal era in the eighteenth century was surely that concerning Fr Nicholas Sheehy in Tipperary in 1766. Although the case only indirectly relates to the subject of this book, that of priest hunters, it merits inclusion because it served to underline the deep religious and political divisions and motivations that defined the age. It also starkly demonstrated the marked contrast between different strands of Protestantism, whereas on one side some were willing to come to a Catholic priest's aid, while others sought his destruction and their own enrichment through any and all corrupt means possible.

The event was all the more disturbing as it came at a time when the implementation of the penal laws had been relaxed. This had come about through various circumstances such as the death of The Old Pretender, James Francis Edward Stuart, removing the threat of a Catholic monarch with a genuine bloodline. Another factor was the ending of the Seven Years' War, which among other things saw Britain sign a treaty with Catholic France. Prominent Catholics had also managed to persuade the more liberal Protestants in Britain that their faith presented no threat to the British monarchy. Lastly the Age of Enlightenment was dawning, which saw intellectuals across Europe begin to challenge traditional ideas about religion and faith.

Certainly the persecution of priests had almost ceased and Catholic ceremonies were being openly practised without harassment from the authorities. While it was still impossible for a Catholic to aspire to high office, many had improved their lot through skill and hard work and a blind eye was turned to certain levels of property ownership that were technically illegal. But the gulf between the ascendancy and the ordinary peasant was still vast and many of the wealthier class sought to maintain the status quo.

Nicholas Sheehy was born in Fethard to the north of Clonmel in 1728 but raised in Newcastle, some twenty miles to the south near the county border with Waterford. His siblings were a brother William and a sister, Catherine, who in adulthood would marry a Richard Burke. It is a reflection of the increasingly liberal times that Burke was a Protestant and a cousin of the renowned philosopher and statesman, Edmund Burke. As a young man, Nicholas was sent abroad to be educated in France, a fact that would later be used against him. He decided to enter the priesthood and continued his studies at Louvain in Belgium and at Salamanca and Santiago de Compostela. He was ordained in 1750 at the age of twenty-two. In the letter below, composed just a few days before his ordination, he writes to a younger friend who has embarked on a journey abroad to commence his own priestly education, wishing him good fortune in his studies. He also refers to his own current ill health giving us a personal insight into the medical practices at the time, and expresses worry about his own mother's health.

> Dear Paul,
>
> This day we received Deaconship from the Bishop of Tuam at his house and are to be priested next Sunday come seaven night. Please to pray we may receive it worthyly and you may be sure I will not forget you at the altar but will daily beseach the Almighty to give you grace to persevere in your holy undertakens to the last with satisfaction and health to undergoe your Noviceship. The latter [i.e. health] we wanted here since your departure so much that at the same time Mr Roche, Paddy Luis and I have been confined to our beds at the same time. Paddy's disease is dubious. Some judge it to be an ague, and others say it is the ptisick [chest infection], he goes off to morrow with his father for Madrid, for the physitians ordered him to change climate … the Doctor though he tended me for three weeks he knew not my sicknes,

> *varying daily in his sayings and prescriptions so that he*
> *pestered me with bleeding, purging, phisicking [purging*
> *the bowels with a laxative] and his glisters [enemas], tho'*
> *I believe they were of no service ... My mother is in a bad*
> *state of health whom I recommend to your prayers who I*
> *dread will (soon) depart this life ... hoping you will have*
> *me with yours as soon as possible dear Sir.*
> *Yours for ever to command.*
> *Nicholas Sheehy*

During the ensuing decade, the maturing Fr Sheehy began to minister to his flock around Clogheen, which lies ten miles to the south west of Cahir, and in which parish he would eventually be appointed Parish Priest. He soon experienced first hand the privations endured by the common peasant on a daily basis. Although the practice of their religion was no longer repressed as in the past, he began to witness the terrible poverty that the Penal Laws had wrought and how they had forced many Catholics to the brink of starvation. He became extremely vocal about the repressive statutes and in a prelude to the land wars that would follow a century later, his sermons and letters were soon filled with condemnations of the evictions of tenants by wealthy landlords and the elimination of common pasture through the building of enclosures, which meant the peasant farmer would now have to rent grazing land where it had formerly been free to use. He also publicly condemned the practice of tithes being levied on Catholics. These represented ten per cent of a person's earnings to be paid directly to the Protestant Church; they usually went directly into the coffers of the local vicars and ministers, in their case the Rector of Clogheen, John Hewitson and the Reverends Foulkes and Sutton, who employed a man called Dobbyn as 'tithe proctor' or the collector of tithes. What inflamed the Catholics even more was that Dobbyn had decided to make a little more for himself on the side, and levied an extra tax that he named 'Marriage Money', requiring all couples married by a Catholic priest to pay five shillings.

In response to these injustices, an agrarian resistance group known as the Whiteboys started a small riot near Clogheen in 1762, during which a wall that enclosed a plot of formerly common land was knocked down. The local Protestant ascendancy were becoming increasingly concerned at what they saw as Fr Sheehy's stirring of the hornet's nest, and immediately seized on the riot as a means of ridding themselves of the troublesome priest. Several of them made sworn statements that Sheehy and several other people who were respected in the Catholic community had incited the riot and were therefore guilty of conspiracy against the state.

A true bill was found against Edward Meehan, Nicholas Sheehan [Sheehy], Nicholas Lee, John Magan, John Butler, and Edmund Burke charging them with compassing rebellion at Clogheen on the 7th of March and

the 6th of October, second year of the King, (1762) and
unlawfully assembling in white shirts, in arms, when they
did traitorously prepare, ordain, and levy war against the
King.

The accused were brought for trial in 1763, the principal witnesses against them being a man called John Bridge and a woman called Moll Dunlea. Bridge had formerly been a Whiteboy himself and had turned informer after he had been tortured while in prison and forced to give evidence against Sheehy and others at the behest of the Protestant Rector, John Hewitson, the principal landowner in the area, Sir Thomas Maude (whose father was responsible for the building of their magnificent country manor, Dundrum House) and another major landlord, William Bagwell.

Bridge was apparently dim-witted to such an extent that he was described as 'a driveling, begging idiot'. Moll Dunlea was regarded locally as 'an abandoned character', which was a euphemism for a prostitute. Some years earlier Fr Sheehy had excommunicated her and the widely-held belief was that she had been bribed to testify.

Local history recounts that after a short trial, the jury, who were Protestant to a man and some of whom liked and respected the priest, found the accused not guilty. No detailed record of the trial survives, but it seems the judge, Richard Acton, must have expressed strong doubts about the credibility of the witnesses, as afterwards he became a pariah within the wealthier Protestant circles in the locality and was the subject of such abuse he was ultimately forced to quit his position and move to England.

Despite walking out of the Clonmel courtroom a free man, Nicholas Sheehy's troubles were only beginning.

Within months of the first trial, the main prosecution witness, John Bridge, disappeared and this was used as a pretext to once again arrest the priest. Accusations were made that Sheehy and others had conspired to murder the informer, after which they had disposed of the body. A reward of fifty pounds was offered for evidence leading to the priest and his fellow 'conspirators' conviction. As in the days thought consigned to history, Fr Sheehy was forced to go on the run and there was a brief resurgence of the profession of priest-hunting.

Such was his popularity, not only as a priest, but as a campaigner against social injustice, he had plenty of help from the community, Catholic and Protestant alike. Constantly on the move, hiding in farmer's lofts or in the wilds of the Galtee Mountains, the priest was sheltered by several Protestants, including a man called Griffith, a tenant farmer, who helped to conceal the priest in the churchyard vault that adjoined his land. It was here that Fr Sheehy remained for months on end, emerging at night to secretly conduct his religious duties.

Following representations made by the influential elite in Tipperary, the Dublin authorities were prevailed upon to raise the stakes in the hunt for the priest. A year after his flight, in 1765, they issued a proclamation for his arrest for inciting treason and rebellion, and one that included an almost unheard of reward.

> *By the Lords Justices & Council of Ireland*
> *A Proclamation.*
> *Whereas Nicholas Sheehy, Popish Priest in the County of*
> *Tipperary, stands indicted at an Assizes held for the said*
> *County for High Treason and Rebellion. And whereas the*
> *said Nicholas Sheehy has since absconded, and We have*
> *received information upon Oath, that he is concealed in*
> *some part of this Kingdom, and has since been concerned*
> *in several Treasonable practices to raise a rebellion in*
> *this Kingdom. We the Lords Justices and Council, do*
> *therefore hereby publish and declare, That if any Person*
> *or Persons, do, within the space of Six Calendar Months*
> *from the date of this Our Proclamation, apprehend the*
> *said Nicholas Sheehy, and lodge him in any one of His*
> *Majesty's Goals, such Person or Persons shall receive as a*
> *Reward The Sum of Three Hundred Pounds Sterling. And*
> *we do hereby strictly charge and command all Justices*
> *of the Peace, Mayors, Sheriffs, Bailiffs, and all other*
> *His Majesty's Officers, civil and military, and also all*
> *other His Majesty's loving subjects, that they do use their*
> *utmost endeavour to have the said Nicholas Sheehy appre-*
> *hended. Given at the Council-Chamber in Dublin*
> *13th day of February 1765*

The huge reward brought every would-be priest hunter from

the woodwork and made it almost impossible for Fr Sheehy to venture out. Every face he saw, Catholic or otherwise, was now subject to the temptation of the riches offered and the country-side was daily crawling with men searching for him. It was surely only a matter of time before he would be discovered. Left with little alternative, he wrote to the Under Secretary for Ireland, Thomas Waite, and offered to surrender on condition that his trial was held in Dublin. Waite agreed and a few days later Sheehy left his underground tomb and surrendered to the authorities.

He was fortunate that the arresting magistrate was a sym-pathetic Protestant called Cornelius O'Callaghan, who wasn't prepared to risk the priest's life by entrusting his transport to Dublin to his Clonmel colleagues. He ordered that a troop be brought from another part of the county who had no knowledge or malicious intent towards the priest. O'Callaghan went further; he offered Sheehy a hundred guineas and urged him to flee the country, but his offer was declined as it would have been seen as the action of a guilty man.

Fr Sheehy was conducted to Dublin in early 1766 and his arrival was recorded in the *Dublin Gazette*:

> *About 8 o'clock on Wednesday night, Nicholas Sheehy,*
> *a popish priest, charged with being concerned in several*
> *treasonable practices to raise a rebellion in this kingdom,*
> *for the apprehending of whom Government offered a*
> *reward of £300, was brought to town guarded by a party*

of light horse and lodged by the Provost in the Lower
Castle Yard.

The trial on 10 February was again brief; the jurors were once more wholly unconvinced by the witnesses and the judge ordered his release. But the priest had barely set foot out into the streets of Dublin when he was once again arrested, this time for conspiring to murder John Bridge, whose body had never been found. As he was led away his supporters spotted one of the local landlords, William Bagwell, who had travelled to Dublin to witness the priest's trial and re-arrest. It was reported that a shout went up from the enraged crowd:

A groan for Maude, Hewitson and Bagwell, the priest-
hunting bloodthirsty magistrates of Clonmel!

Bagwell was forced to run for his carriage and with the crowd in close pursuit, flee at a gallop from the street.

Fr Sheehy was brought back to Clonmel in chains and imprisoned while awaiting trial. Several others were simultaneously arrested as part of the so-called conspiracy to murder Bridge. These were Ned Meehan of Grange, near Clogheen, Edmund 'Buck' Burke, who was Fr Sheehy's cousin, James Buxton of Killroe, James Farrell of Rehill and one Pierce Byrne. The latter three were to be tried separately for the murder.

In the weeks and months before the trial, Fr Sheehy and his supporters had tried to win some support from two prominent

Catholic clergymen, principally Dr Pierce Creagh, the archbishop of the diocese and Fr William Egan, the Parish Priest of Clonmel, who was said to be very influential among both Catholics and Protestants. But it seems both men lacked the courage that thousands of their predecessors had displayed during the preceding century. The bishop had previously condemned the actions of the Whiteboys and was worried that supporting Sheehy might be interpreted wrongly as a subtle condoning of the attacks on landlords. He sat on the fence throughout the entire episode. William Egan refused point-blank to speak out in favour of his fellow cleric, fearing that the relaxation of the Penal Laws of recent years might end. Despite pleas, particularly from Sheehy's sister Catherine, the door to his house remained stubbornly shut.

In the days leading up to the trial, Clonmel was effectively put under martial law. A contemporary account records the atmosphere:

> *Every avenue was guarded with Drogheda's light horse,*
> *and to get in or out was attended with difficulty and*
> *danger … On the day of the trial a party of horse sur-*
> *rounded the court, admitting and excluding whom they*
> *thought proper; while others of them with a certain*
> *Baronet (Sir Thomas Maude) at their head, scampered*
> *the streets in a formidable manner; forcing into inns and*
> *private lodgings in the town; challenging and questioning*

all new comers; menacing his friends and encouraging his
enemies.

The trial, the third of Fr Sheehy's life, was hurriedly convened
on 12 March 1766. The men's accusers were leaving nothing to
chance on this occasion and the jury was loaded with supporters of the wealthy land-owners and Protestant clergy, who feared
Sheehy's influence might force a change in the tithe laws. The
man responsible for jury selection was Sir Thomas Maude himself
and among those he chose were Osmonde Tothall, a prominent
landowner and direct descendant of a Cromwellian settler, Jonathan Willington of the stately Castle Willington, whose family
owned almost three thousand acres of land in the area, and John
Bagwell, brother of William who was another of Sheehy's main
adversaries. Sheehy and Meehan were unable to secure the services of an attorney in Tipperary, but finally managed to recruit a
sympathetic Protestant lawyer called Sparrow, from Dublin.

The first charge put to Sheehy was that he was involved in a
plot to facilitate an invasion of Ireland by the French, leading
ultimately to the usurpation of King George III. The only evidence produced to support this was documents proving he had
been educated in France. Their apparent motive for murdering
Bridges was that he knew of their conspiracy and after he had
testified against them concerning the riot, they had killed him to
prevent his revealing their complicity in the invasion plot.

Reverent Hewitson, who was also a magistrate and one of

Sheehy's and Meehan's accusers, then introduced three witnesses to the murder of Bridge. The first was a man called Toohey, a horse thief who had to be conducted from his prison cell to testify and arrived dressed in 'a coat of superfine blue cloth and waistcoat and breeches of black silk', gifted to him to present an appearance of credibility. He swore that he had been present as one of a party of Whiteboys when Sheehy threatened Bridge with death if he testified about the French invasion plot. When Bridge refused to comply, Pierce Byrne struck him on the head with a rock and Meehan did likewise with a billhook, which was the fatal blow. Toohey then said that Sheehy swore all present to silence and to be 'true to the King of France'. (Despite the charge of horse-theft against Toohey, which could carry the death penalty, he was subsequently set free without trial.)

The next witness was a young tinker boy called Lonergan who was said to be quite dim-witted, and who testified that he met the party on the way to dump the body and that the priest had given him three half-crowns to keep quiet.

The third witness was Moll Dunlea, the 'abandoned character' who had previously testified in the earlier trials and was given no credence by those juries. Dunlea had been put in 'protective custody' in the Clonmel barracks where she had been showered with new clothes and food and drink from the town's finest tavern 'The Spread Eagle'. (While there she is said to have been on intimate terms with a soldier called Brady, but after the trial took up with Toohey.) Dunlea swore on oath that on the night of the murder, she was present in her mother's house along with one Michael Kearney, and the priest had arrived and asked Kearney to accompany him. She had followed and witnessed Sheehy and Kearney rejoin the other Whiteboys as they buried the body at a place called Ballysheehan, two miles from the place where the alleged murder had taken place.

Sparrow, in defence, suggested to Dunlea that it was strange to have carried a body so far, requiring great effort and exposing themselves to possible witnesses and capture, but Dunlea could offer no explanation. He then called her mother, Ann Hullan, who swore that Moll slept in the same bed with her that night and never left the house and that Kearney had not been present.

The trial descended into complete farce when Sparrow called Fr Sheehy's main witness in his defence, Nicholas Keating, a respected local Catholic. Keating swore that Fr Sheehy had spent the entire evening of the alleged crime in his house in Tubba-ret, some eight miles away. At this point Hewitson stood up and claimed that Keating was a wanted man and had been implicated in the murders of a sergeant and corporal during the rescue of nine Whiteboys in Kilkenny. The judge immediately ordered Keating's arrest and he was spirited from the courtroom and taken to Kilkenny Gaol. Keating was later tried and cleared of the crime.

The jury found Fr Sheehy and Ned Meehan guilty and the courtroom exploded into a crescendo of screeches and sobbing. The following morning the judge asked if they had any reason to offer as to why a sentence of death should not be passed. Meehan remained silent, but the priest gave a composed response:

> My good lord, I am aware that your question is a mere form, and anything I could say would have no effect; still, as the opportunity is afforded me, I must say that I am entirely innocent of the heinous crime of which I have been convicted. Not only am I innocent thereof, but, to the best of my belief, no such murder has been committed. I am almost fully persuaded that this very John Bridge is still living, for we have the clearest evidence that, some days subsequent to the date of the supposed murder, the man was seen alive and in good health, and took leave of his friends, to go either to Cork or Kinsale, to embark for some foreign country. Knowing, or at least believing, this to be the case, I protest against the entire proceedings, as regards Meehan and myself, and will protest until the latest moment against the shameful injustice, the gross perjury, the deadly malice, of which we are the victims. In conclusion, I must declare that, notwithstanding all this, I bear these unhappy men who persecute me even to death, not the slightest ill-will: I leave them in the hands of a just God, knowing that He will deal with them according to their deserts. That is all I have to say. I leave God to distinguish between the innocent and the guilty.

The judge then passed sentence:

> *You shall be hanged, drawn and quartered, on Saturday*
> *next, the 15th inst; and may God have mercy on your*
> *soul, and grant you a sight of the enormity of your crimes.*

The priest calmly thanked the judge for his good wishes and expressed his confidence that God knew of his complete innocence and that, doubtless, all men must ultimately answer for their crimes. Less forgiving was his attorney, Sparrow, who rose and cried out to the judge, 'If there is any justice in heaven, you will die roaring.'

The trial was recorded in the press of the day:

> *Cork Chronicle, March 13, 1766.*
> *Yesterday, March 14, Nicholas Sheehy Popish Priest of*
> *Shanrahan, County Tipperary was capitally convicted at*
> *the assizes at Clonmel and received sentence of death to be*
> *hanged and quartered for the murder of John Bridge, a*
> *person who was to have been an evidence against him for*
> *his trial for Rebellion and Treason at the Court of Kings*
> *Bench, Dublin, but was murdered after the issuing of*
> *the Lords Justices proclamation apprehending Sheehy, in*
> *order to facilitate his escape from Justice.*

Two days later, Fr Sheehy and Ned Meehan were led through a wailing sea of local Catholics to the place opposite St Peter and Paul's Church in Clonmel. There they were hanged, taken down before they were dead, cut open and their entrails torn out. Their limbs were then cut off, followed by their heads, which were mounted on spikes in front of Clonmel Courthouse. Fr Sheehy's head was left there for ten years as a ghoulish warning to others.

Catherine Sheehy pressed her hand against the ground stained with her brother's blood, walked to the home of Fr Egan, the Parish Priest, and imprinted a bloody handprint on the cleric's door in a grim denunciation of his Judas-like behaviour in not standing by Fr Sheehy's side. The priest was vilified in the town for years after.

Two months later the same judgment was passed on the other 'conspirators' and they were similarly executed.

As previously alluded to, Edmund Burke, Privy Council, was a cousin to Richard Burke, husband of Fr Sheehy's sister Catherine. Burke was a Protestant (with a Catholic mother) and a renowned philosopher, political theorist and prominent parliamentarian in England. He is nowadays regarded as the founding father of conservative liberalism and Winston Churchill would write of him as 'a foremost apostle of liberty'. In the months subsequent to Fr Sheehy's execution, he came to learn of the nature of the sham trial and raged against the injustice. His anger at what he termed 'judicial murder' is evident in letters he wrote to an associate in Tipperary:

We are all in a Blaze here with your plots, assassinations, massacres, Rebellions, moonlight armies, French Officers, and French money. Are you not ashamed? You who told me, that if they could get no discovery from Sheehy, they would cool and leave off their detestable plot mongering? You think well of Ireland; but I think rightly of it; and know, that their unmeaning Senseless malice is insatiable; cedemus patria! [Save us from the state!] I am told that these miserable wretches whom they have hanged, died with one Voice declaring their innocence: but truly for my part, I want no man dying, or risen from the dead, to tell me, that lies are lies, and nonsense is nonsense. I wish your absurdity was less mischievous. And less bloody. Are there not a thousand other ways in which fools may make themselves important? I assure you, I look on these things with horror; and cannot talk of such proceedings as the effects of an innocent credulity. If there be an army paid, and armed, and disciplined, and sworn to foreign powers in your country, cannot Government know it by some better means than the Evidence of whores and Horse Stealers. It is late; and I am vexed and ashamed, that the Government we live in, should not know those who endanger it, or who disturb it by false alarms; to punish the one with knowledge and vigour; or to silence the other with firmness. Adieu.

Fr Sheehy's sister, Catherine, arranged to have the pieces of his headless body transported to the graveyard at Shanrahan, where his remains were buried before a crowd of thousands. In the years after, she repeatedly went to the courthouse and begged to have his head taken from the spike, to no avail. Finally, a decade after her brother's murder the authorities relented and the head was interred with the rest of his body.

Local folklore held that Sir Thomas Maude descended into madness and died screaming that Sheehy's spirit was dragging him down to Hell, and that several other jurors met with gruesome deaths through sickness or through revenge at the hands of the peasants. Moll Dunlea was said to have fallen drunk into a cellar in Cork a few years after and cracked her skull open, killing her instantly, although a different version of her demise tells that she was found dead in a Kilkenny ditch, possibly the victim of retribution. The executioner, a man called Darby Brahan was stoned to death by a crowd in Kilkenny for having carried out the deed. ·

Two years after the executions, it was reported that John Bridge was located in Newfoundland and was completely unaware that a trial had been held for his 'murder'.

Because of Clogheen's associations with Fr Sheehy and its symbolic importance in the struggle against religious intolerance, Daniel O'Connell chose it to address a crowd of fifty thousand people on 28 September 1828. One year later Catholic Emancipation would finally end the centuries of religious repression.

Shanrahan Cemetery, just over a mile to the west of the village of Clogheen is today a picturesque, peaceful spot, the gravestones nestling under the shade of trees and watched over by the ancient church tower, with a small river rolling placidly by just a few yards away. Fr Nicholas Sheehy's headstone can still be seen there and has no shortage of visitors, as he is still widely held to be a martyr for his faith. The graveyard once served him as a place to hide from the brutality of the time, and ever since has served as the place where he finally found an eternal refuge.

THE FOUR CORNERS
OF IRELAND

It is difficult to gauge the general extent of sympathy within the Protestant community for the plight of their Catholic neighbours, but undoubtedly it was more prevalent than one might glean from broad histories of the time. From counties in every province spring tales of Protestants or Presbyterians secretly resisting the will of the crown and concealing or saving priests from the clutches of the bounty hunters.

Although the authorities in Clare, for example, were usually vigorous in their attempts to control and arrest priests, even among their own numbers there seemed to be some who appeared to be dragging their feet. When the High Sheriff of Clare, William Butler, was instructed from Dublin to issue warrants for the arrest of *all* priests, he procrastinated to such an extent that he was soon having his wrist slapped:

> *… his Excellency and their Lordships are extreamely*

surprised to find there are so many popish priests in your
County and no account from you of your having seized
and committed any of them to Gaole ... I am again to
repeat to you their former commands in causing all popish
priests, whether they have taken the Oath of Abjuration
or not or whether they are registered or not to be immedi-
ately seized and committed to Gaole. His Excellency and
their Lordships do highly resent your neglect and disregard
of their orders. So as to compensate your omission, you
will exert yourself with more than ordinary diligence and
zeal in seizing and comitting the priests, and in returning
an account with a Certificate of the Gaoler of the County
of the number and names of the priests committed.
Dawson, Dublin Castle, 4th March 1711

Even then it seems that Butler was hesitant, replying a week later, '... the numbers of papists are so great that the priests are hed from us.' And two months later Butler's (unenthusiastic) efforts had met with little success. In fact he seems to openly demonstrate a degree of compassion for priests who had been captured:

Ennis 13 May 1712.
Sir I came hither to attend the special sessions when I
hoped to have some popish priests brought in but mett
with no more than two that I sent as by the inclosed
Certificate ... one more seized and brought to me latelye

*to a Countye Courte who fell into fitts of the ague which
I was informed credibblye attend him for a considerable
tyme paste and therefore I did not commit him being in
manifest danger of losing his life. And it is my greatest
trouble that I should leye under the censure of his Excellency and the Lords of the Counsell for not succeedinge
in theire committment or that their Lordshipps should
thinke that I would in the leaste either neglect or disobeye
their orders.*

Yours W. Butler.

One of those doing the seizing in Clare was a priest hunter called Harrison, who, in the company of several minions, managed to track down one Fr Cunnan in the tiny village of Cloonmore, just a few miles south of Ennis. What's likely to have put them on the priest's trail was the pre-dawn celebration of a mass in an open field, word of which always presented a danger as it could easily fall on an informer's ears. Harrison and his band arrived with such stealth that there was no time to hide or to disguise the priest, who – still clad in his vestments – took off across the boggy field in a panicked flight, the hunters in pursuit on foot. He made directly for the nearby lands of Charles Phillips, a Protestant magistrate who had befriended him. Some minutes later, breathless and exhausted, he located Philips in a field and with no time to find a hiding place, the magistrate told him to quickly remove his outer vestment. He immediately donned the garment himself, told the priest to make for his house and hide there and without further ado, took off into the countryside. Thompson arrived moments later and in the early morning light, saw the priestly figure fleeing across the fields and hedges. He and his band continued their chase, giving Fr Cunnan ample time to escape.

It wasn't long, however, before the hunters caught up with the magistrate and seized him. Not knowing what Fr Cunnan looked like, they naturally assumed they had their priest and duly hauled him off to Ennis to claim their reward. Arriving too late to bring their prisoner before the local magistrate, they locked up Phillips in their house and spent the night carousing, reportedly buying drinks all round on the promise of the wealth that would soon be coming their way. The following day they hauled their 'priest' before the magistrate, who happened to be the Reverend Adam Caulfield, a close friend of Phillips. Upon seeing his fellow magistrate brought before him accused of being an outlaw priest, Caulfield is said to have exploded with laughter, much to Harrison's chagrin. The magistrate explained his actions by saying that he 'wished to see how these fellows were able to run'. After the laughter had died away in the courtroom, the case was immediately dismissed and Harrison and his crew went away penniless, and now burdened with the debt of their premature celebrations. Charles Phillips was said afterwards to be 'the most popular man in the county'.

Another close pursuit and escape thanks to the efforts this

time of a number of non-Catholics is that of Dr John McColgan of Donegal. His identity and location in a cottage in Muff are said to have been revealed by a fellow priest who had incurred the wrath of his superiors, possibly for denying his faith to save himself from persecution. Forced to flee north into the mountainous area around Slieve Snaght, the bishop was given refuge for several days in the remote cottage of a Presbyterian farmer called James Davis. But as a prominent bishop with a price on his head, which at that time was one hundred pounds, he was being widely hunted by every mercenary in the county. The situation being too dangerous, Davis conducted Dr McColgan to the shore of Trawbreaga Bay, which is the most northerly bay in Ireland, and gave him a small boat in which the bishop rowed a couple of miles across the bay to a place called Glasha, north of Carndonagh. Here Dr McColgan was grateful to accept the help of another Presbyterian farmer called Joseph Campbell. The assistance of men of this faith was probably due to the fact that members of their own religion had not escaped the wrath of the Penal Laws – they were barred from holding any public office, their marriages were not recognised by the state and they had to pay tithes to the clergy of the Protestant Church of Ireland. The bishop remained concealed in Campbell's farmhouse for some time, the farmer going about his business as though nothing untoward had occurred, all the while keeping one eye on his plough and another on the horizon for the approach of armed strangers.

And eventually they reared their heads, moving through the area searching cottages with impunity. Luckily, one of Campbell's neighbours warned him of their approach and without hesitation, he unyoked the two horses from the plough, hurried to the cottage and told the bishop to mount one of the animals. Familiar with the paths and tracks of the area, he then led the bishop at a gallop all of twelve miles to the west and the tiny village of Leenan on the north western shores of Lough Swilly. The local fishermen, realising they had a bishop in their midst, quickly abandoned their work and once again Dr McColgan, who was almost sixty, found himself fleeing across the sea to safety in Fanad. The priest hunters apparently located his hiding place on Campbell's farm and reported, somewhat colourfully, that they 'found the nest, indeed, but the bird was gone'. Joseph Campbell's fate is not recorded, but he is likely to have suffered greatly for concealing and aiding the flight of a bishop, most likely with the loss of his property. After hiding in Fanad until the hunt abated, Dr McColgan made his way to Omagh in County Tyrone, where he managed to remain undetected for the remainder of his days. He died in 1765 and at his own request was buried in Culdaff graveyard, back in his beloved Inishowen.

On the other side of Ireland in County Down, Fr Edmund McGraddy, who was a contemporary and close colleague of Fr Hannah (see 'The most dangerous man in the county'), was also to benefit from the help of several non-Catholics. A Mr Craig, a Protestant who was ironically a descendant of the Clerk of the

Peace for County Down, actually facilitated Fr McGraddy celebrating mass on his farm while he stood on a nearby hillside watching for the approach of priest hunters. Local lore held that Mr Craig and his family enjoyed good fortune and health for the rest of their days, which was naturally interpreted as some form of divine 'thank you'. But Craig wasn't alone in attracting God's good grace. Tracked down eventually, Fr McGraddy was fleeing for his life on foot from a 'posse' consisting of an officer of the law called Hutton and a collection of local volunteers, recruited on the basis of a possible reward. The priest came to a river into which he plunged and swam to the far bank (again according to local lore he 'leapt the Glass River') just as the band of hunters arrived on the other side. Unbeknown to the rest of the men, their leader, Hutton, was actually a close friend of Fr McGraddy and had been obliged to demonstrate his enthusiasm for 'priest-catching' for the benefit of his superiors. The river, however, presented Hutton with an excuse to abandon the chase, deeming the current too dangerous to tackle. One of his band was not to be so easily discouraged and judged the danger worth the possibility of reward. The man hadn't counted on Fr McGraddy's ire. While he may have feared the band of men, Hutton's action had now left the priest with just a solitary pursuer, and Fr McGraddy wasn't the type of man, priest or not, who would be willing to turn the other cheek and go quietly. He found himself a solid branch and remained out of sight as the would-be priest hunter struggled against the river's current. When the man clambered breathless and worn out from his exertions, Fr McGraddy laid into him with the branch with such ferocity that the man reputedly bore visible scars of the beating for the rest of his days. Besides ensuring Fr McGraddy's escape, the Hutton family was said to have helped numerous other priests to evade the authorities and in keeping with the fervent religious beliefs of the time, local tradition assigned the Huttons' prosperity as God's reward for their behaviour.

Besides the Huttons and Mr Craig, the area seems to have been well stocked with sympathetic Protestants, as a Mrs Cleeland is said to have once directed another fleeing priest to her bed to escape the priest hunters! Arriving on her doorstep bathed in sweat from his flight, he told the woman that a band of men were close behind and begged her help. The good lady whisked the priest inside to her bedroom, directing the priest to climb under the blankets. When the priest hunters arrived she claimed she had seen no Catholic friar and the only one present was her husband, who was sick in bed with a terrible ague. She brought them inside and showed them the 'feverish' priest, who was still sweating terribly from his exertions, and fearful her 'husband's' sickness might be catching, they quickly made their exit.

It is in dark times such as those of the penal era that genuinely benevolent, tolerant and farsighted individuals are revealed to the world. Prepared to put their own personal and financial safety at risk, those Protestants who recognised the injustices of the age and stood against them in their own small way, whether they were poor or wealthy, could all be rightly called noble men and women.

The flip side of the coin revealed those who sought only to profit from the oppression, be they Catholic or Protestant. But many of the priest hunters would discover there was a heavy price to pay for the blood money they earned.

Part Four

RETRIBUTION

MURDER IN THE
NAME OF GOD

To understand the feelings that the capture, imprisonment or killing of priests roused in people's hearts is difficult to convey in the context of the modern world, particularly given the scandals that have been associated with the priesthood in recent decades. Yet even the reverence with which the Catholic Church was held in Ireland in the first half of the twentieth century pales into insignificance compared to the devotion of Catholics in the eighteenth century.

The people of the time, it must be remembered, had little in the way of quality of life; every waking hour was expended in the struggle to put food on the table. Their homes were cramped, squalid, cold and damp. They had little or no means of fighting disease and many simply endured years of pain or discomfort with a stoic acceptance that it was part of their lot. They married young and their offspring had only a slim chance of surviving past childhood. The average life expectancy in the eighteenth century was about forty years. Life was brief by today's standards and incredibly gruelling. Given this context, it is not difficult to understand the fervour of people's religious beliefs. God offered meaning to their pitiful existence. They could accept the life of misery they had been handed because an eternal life of happiness awaited them in the next world.

The priest was seen not merely as a representative of the church who steered them on the right path. He was their conduit to God. He officiated at all of the rituals necessary to reach heaven; he baptised them and erased original sin; he gave them communion, which granted them a tangible connection to God; he was their confessor, their means of cleansing themselves of their misdeeds; he wed them and sanctified their union; he prayed over their dead and eased the path of their spirit through the gates of heaven. Even in the devoutly Catholic days of, for example, 1950s Ireland, the loss or death of a priest, while tragic, wasn't calamitous. There would always be another to replace him. But during the penal era, the loss of a priest was as a knife through the heart of the community. It might be years before the man could be replaced, during which time all of the aforementioned necessities of Catholic faith would have to be done without.

When a priest was captured or killed, beyond the human dimension of the loss of a beloved friend, people experienced a terrible fear that their chances of eternal life were greatly diminished. So it's not surprising that their feelings towards the ruling classes, the informers and the priest hunters swayed between a passive malevolence to an active quest for vengeance. While the notion of doing violence railed against their priests' very teachings, many felt powerless to ignore the rage in their hearts. And although some priests did themselves fight back, none were prepared to take another human life, or do serious violence to the priest hunters, whereas some among their congregation were ready and willing to do just that.

An anonymous letter sent from Limerick by a priest hunter, identified only as W.D., in many ways sums up the people's devotion and the possible consequences of seizing a priest. W.D. had come to believe that a conspiracy was afoot to raise money from the Catholic masses to finance an invasion by a foreign prince and that the priests' method of achieving this was to 'oblige penitents to give a certain sum' to hear confession, in effect to charge to charge for absolution. A long list of priests is supplied who were allegedly engaged in this practice. It is highly doubtful a single penny was handed over in this manner as it would have brought extreme sanction down on the priests' heads, but W.D. may have chosen to interpret people's offerings for the priest's subsistence as some sort of fee. The financing of invasions by bishops and priests was also a common theme used by those wishing to stir up anti-Catholic feeling. The reason W.D. remains anonymous is evident:

Limerick January 30 1744.

To his Grace William Duke of Devonshire.
… they stirr up their penitents and give them such hearts
that they are willing to doe anything rather than disobl-
idge their pastors. And my Lord unless you prevent this
business the whole kingdom is in danger. All these Gentle-
men both priests and friars now being in the kingdom of
Ireland ought to sweare allegiance publickly to the King,
and if this be not done his Majesty's person is in danger. I
cannot at present discover [reveal] my name lest I should
be murthered but send out a protection for the person
who writes this and then you will know more. The Eter-
nal God preserve your Lordship and that both peace and
plenty may attend his Majesty's subjects.
Yours for ever W. D.

No action is recorded as having been taken to suppress this 'conspiracy' and it's likely the authorities regarded W.D.'s story as a flight of his imagination. But he was certainly correct on a couple of points: that the Catholic peasant would do anything rather than disoblige their pastor and that given the opportunity, there was indeed every possibility that the devoted faithful might well 'murther' him.

Attestation of that fact can be seen in an event that occurred near Kells sometime in the early part of the eighteenth century that seems darkly humorous from a present-day perspective. The Fr Myles O'Reilly who was recorded as being thirty-nine years of age and resident in Sheepstown in the year of registration, had been illegally serving mass in the ruin of an old chapel near the village of Kilskyre. As he was a registered priest the celebration of mass was permitted within his own parish, so either he was acting outside his permitted area or he had offended the sensibilities of the law in some other way. For whatever reason he had become the target of a number of priest hunters in the area. Two men in particular, whose names are recorded only as 'P' and 'G', had been scouting the parishes with pricked ears in search of a clue to the priest's whereabouts. While visiting the old graveyard at Kilskyre chapel, a local happened to spot the pair skulking about, observing the chapel and its environs. He quickly relayed this information to a couple of the men in the parish. At dawn the following Sunday Fr Reilly commenced serving mass in the old chapel, unaware that two of his faithful congregation had designs other than goodwill to all men.

Although the area around Kilskyre is today mostly flat and fertile farmland, then it was covered in dense woodland, and through the trees a lookout spotted the approach of 'P' and 'G', now bearing firearms and clearly intent on defending themselves against any interference from the peasantry.

The lookout took off for the chapel and whispered his news to the two men inside, who quietly sneaked from the chapel and collected the clubs they'd secreted nearby. They then took up hiding places either side of the track along which 'P' and 'G' approached. As the priest hunters passed the pair leapt out and felled them instantly and as described by Dean Anthony Cogan in his history of the Meath diocese, they 'knocked out their brains'. What happened to the bodies of the priest hunters wasn't recorded, but it's likely they were dumped somewhere in the woods and found at a later date. The devoted men's work complete, the pair then dutifully returned to the chapel to catch the end of the mass. Not surprisingly, Fr Reilly's persecution abated greatly after that and he was largely left alone, which was probably a mystery to him, but something he likely attributed to 'God moving in mysterious ways.'

PEASANTS TO THE RESCUE

While the peasantry were clearly willing to take life in the defence of their clergy, they were also willing to risk their own as can be seen in the case in March 1754 of a priest in Tipperary who had been arrested for some violation of the Marriage Acts. The incident also demonstrates the widespread fervour that could be roused in the multitudes when a priest was under threat. Orders were sent from Limerick to Tipperary for an armed force to proceed to Cashel and to seize the priest and return him to the city for trial, a journey of some forty miles. They were also to conduct what appears to be the chief witness safely to the city, who is identified only as a 'young Lady'.

Having arrested the priest the force of twenty yeomen proceeded along the road under the vengeful gaze of the locals who followed the small train of carriages and mounted horsemen until camp was made at nightfall. Word had spread meanwhile about the priest's arrest with astonishing speed and at dawn the following morning the arresting sheriff Jonathan Lovett found himself surrounded by a mob of a hundred men and women in front and the same number behind their party. As they proceeded, the mob continued to grow in number and confidence; the constant clamour of insults and curses accompanied them at every step; the young female witness or informer was subject to a barrage of threats and foul language. Becoming increasingly nervous, Lovett sent a number of his men to gather as many local Protestant men as they could from about the area, which they successfully did. These were assigned the task of conducting the woman to Limerick and a path was forced through the mob, allowing the group escorting the woman's carriage to escape along the road. But the captive priest remained the principal focus of the baying crowd.

By the time Lovett and his small force of yeomen crossed the county border, the number of peasants had grown to five hundred. Their demands for the priest's release bringing no satisfaction, they finally began to hurl stones. At that point Lovett ordered his men to fire into the crowd and one peasant fell dead and several others were wounded. But the rain of missiles was so great by now that the yeomen found themselves unable to reload their single-shot muskets. The sheriff described 'vast multitudes running down every hill to the place they heard the fire' and he and other witnesses estimated the numbers surround them now in the thousands. As the stricken party tried to make some small headway along the track they were suddenly beset on either side by a swarm of men who had been concealed in thick furze bushes that line the track. As these made to release the priest, stones continued to bombard the yeomen, seriously injuring the sub-sheriff and two yeomen and leaving each and every one of them bruised and battered. Helpless to prevent the rescue now, they watched as the priest was spirited away into the crowd and as the cheers for his liberation rang around the hillsides, Lovett and his band fled towards the safety of Limerick.

Lovett was castigated later for failing to bring sufficient numbers to guard the priest and ordered to investigate the incident with all due haste and to try to recover the clergyman. It appears he was unsuccessful on both counts, as can be seen from his letter to his superiors:

> *Kingswell, 6 April 1754*
> *You mentioned that it is necessary for me to send up*
> *proper Informations of the rescue but if you was here you*
> *would see it was not in my power to gett any at present,*
> *for the Priests have such an influence on the people that*
> *time must be the only thing that gives me hopes of getting*
> *such as will be of service.*
> *Yours, Jonathan Lovett.*

Lovett subsequently survived an attack by two men with pistols and his family were the subject of constant threats. The Protestant vicar of Tipperary even rallied to the sheriff's side in an attempt to convey the scale of the attack and placate the authorities.

> *On his arrival at Tipperary with twenty soldiers no*
> *attempt at rescue was apprehended till they came near*
> *Limerick, but as some insolence was used in examin-*
> *ing the coach that travelled the road from Tipperary*
> *and many threats were uttered against the young Lady*
> *that was to prosecute, he and his friends apprehended it*
> *reasonable to send the priest by the military force and all*
> *the neighbouring Gentlemen were summoned to convey*
> *the Lady that was to prosecute. Had they all attended*
> *[meaning the entire Limerick garrison] I feare it would*
> *be fruitless for I heare there were thousands, and many of*
> *them armed.*
> *Yours, Rev. Armstrong, Vicar of Tipperary.*

There is no record of the priest ever having been recaptured and such was the intimidation directed at Lovett and his family, that they were eventually forced to abandon their home in the village of Kingswell and move into the relative safety of Tipperary town. Recounting Lovett's fate some months later, Joseph Damer of Shronell, a neighbouring magistrate added:

> *The Common Papists are insolent and provide themselves*
> *with arms. We hope the Lord Chief Justice in his charge*
> *to the Grand Jury will let the county know their duty and*
> *raise the spirits of the now insulted poor Protestants ...*

The Tipperary/Limerick rescue by outraged peasants wasn't the first or the last time 'insulted poor Protestants' would experience the common man's wrath, or that a priest would be wrested from the very clutches of the priest hunters. Forty years before the above incident, several priests were rescued in a strikingly similar fashion from a hunter called Power in Loughrea in Galway. His party were surrounded by three hundred or so locals and managed to free most of the priests, but the arrival of a large force of mounted dragoons scattered the peasants before the last of them, Fr Ambrose Madden, could be freed. In fact capturing priests in the general Connaught region was a dangerous occupation around that time. Following an outbreak of agrarian revenge attacks across the province, Dublin Castle had decided that the Catholic clergy were the prime conspirators behind the trouble:

Dublin Castle 4 Mar. 1712.
My Lord, His Excellency and Council have reason to
believe so much mischief could not be carried on without
the connivance and knowledge if not the concurrence
of the priests, so their Excellencies gave directions to the
Justices of the Peace in the Counties of Gallway, Mayo,
Roscommon and Clare to commit all the priests of the
popish religion in their respective counties to Gaole.
Jos. DAWSON.

RIGHT UP HIS STREET

Joshua Dawson, whose name appears so frequently on communications regarding the capture of priests and who actively encouraged the suppression of Irish Catholicism, was immortalised for his efforts by having one of central Dublin's most famous streets named after him, although he shares the honour with his ancestor, Harry Dawson, who is credited with having laid out the original street along with Grafton Street. Joshua Dawson was the Chief Secretary for Ireland, which although subservient to the position of Lord Lieutenant, in practice was the most powerful political position in the country. The Dawsons owned large estates in Londonderry and Joshua also gave his name to the town of Castledawson in that county. His most recognisable contribution to Dublin, however, is undoubtedly the Mansion House, home of the Lord Mayor. Dawson was also a property developer and in between issuing orders for the hunting down of priests, he financed the erection of the iconic structure in 1710. Five years later Dublin Corporation purchased it to use as the Lord Mayor's official residence. Joshua Dawson also served as MP for Wicklow from 1713-14. He died in 1725, aged sixty-five. There is an irony in the fact that one of Dublin's most loved thoroughfares is named after a man, who in his day, was utterly despised by the vast majority of Ireland's population.

The decision to arrest even registered priests naturally caused even greater outrage. Most of the priests in the province disappeared before they could be captured and in Roscommon there was a particularly vigorous effort to round them up, which culminated in a bold attempt to rescue a Fr James Kilkenny from the very clutches of a priest hunter.

In October 1715, having evaded the law for four years, Fr Kilkenny was finally tracked down by a number of priest hunters. But the priest's flock wasn't going to relinquish their pastor without a fight and a collection of locals gathered, including a number of women, and intercepted the priest hunter's party as they conducted the cleric toward Roscommon Gaol. They forced the men to release their prisoner and then beat them senseless and disappeared into the night.

But their daring was to come at a price. The authorities in the county were so affronted that they issued a proclamation for the priest's arrest with a reward of one hundred pounds, five times the normal bounty. What's more, the priest hunters had managed to identify four of their attackers: Patrick Bakin, Mary Bakin, Una McManus and Margaret Tristan. A further reward of twenty pounds was offered for each of their captures. The large sums on offer certainly stimulated the imaginations of Roscommon's priest hunters and within days they were arriving from all over the county. The beating of their fellow hunters during the rescue seems to have aroused a large measure of caution among them and they clearly decided that on the old maxim of safety in numbers as a few weeks later no less than six men – Christopher Marshall, Samuel Belshier, Edward Jones, Thomas Griffiths, Martin Wilcox and John Clifford – set out to seize the unfortunate Bakins. Having learned of the Bakins' location, they rode the ten miles south of Roscommon town to the tiny backwater of Carroward then waited until nightfall before surrounding the cottage and yelling for the Bakins to surrender. Roused from their bed, Patrick and Mary Bakin had no time to effect an escape or to summon help and were left with no alternative to surrender. The details of their trial have been lost, but it is known that after a period in prison, Mary was found guilty and fined twenty pounds, which sum was vastly beyond the means of an ordinary peasant, so unless the community managed to scrape together the money, she would have been given a long prison sentence or been condemned to transportation to a penal colony. Patrick Bakin's sentence is unknown, but given that he was a man, one can only imagine that it would have been greater than Mary's.

As they languished in prison, they may have taken some comfort in the fact that Fr James Kilkenny was never recaptured. But their faith and loyalty had cost them dearly.

BEASTLY VENGEANCE

The venting of anger by the peasantry was not limited to the hunters, the informers and the magistrates; an episode from Carlow in the middle of the century demonstrates that cruelty was not the sole preserve of the priest-catcher.

In March 1744, a priest hunter called Philip Bernard recorded in a letter that he had gone in search of one Fr James Taffe, parish priest of Carlow town, but that the cleric had managed to escape; despite an extensive search he could find no trace of the man and believed he had left the county. In reality Fr Taffe had simply gone underground and continued to fulfill his duties for all of seven years before a chance encounter on a road with another hunter called George Brereton, who recognised him and seized him on the spot.

It was soon evident that the priest had made friends among the Protestant community during his time at large, as many of the more influential ones were indignant at the arrest. The previous decade had seen a relaxation of the penal laws during which time many more Catholics had forged links or even friendships with the Protestant community. Unfortunately 1744 saw a widespread and often violent campaign mounted as a result of a rumoured Jacobite invasion by Charles Edward Stewart (Bonnie Prince Charlie), son of James, 'The Old Pretender'. This campaign outraged Catholics and many Protestants, and their influence might have led to Fr Taffe's release had the peasants not reacted to the arrest as they did. No sooner had word of the priest's incarceration in the county gaol spread, than a large mob assembled in the town. Brereton was spotted in the street on a carriage driven by two horses and the crowd immediately gave chase, pelting him with sticks, stones and mud. His escape route cut off, the priest hunter abandoned the carriage and sought temporary sanctuary in the house of a friend, in the hope that the military would soon arrive and disperse the crowd. But before they did, the peasants decided to vent their anger on the man's unfortunate animals. A knife flashed and the horses' blood spilled on to the Carlow street as the mob maimed them brutally, among other things, cutting off their ears. Brereton surely listened to the terrible wails of his beasts and contemplated his fate should they manage to capture him.

Their brutality did not serve their priest well, for despite the high regard in which he was held by many Protestants, such was the anger at the mob's action that Fr Taffe was sentenced to twelve months in prison after which he was to be transported. Some months later, with his health declining, a Mr Dorset made the following plea on the priest's behalf:

> ... *the said John Taafe submitted to the said Indictment*
> *and was thereupon ordered by the Court to remaine in*
> *Gaol for the space of twelve months and to be afterwards*
> *transported as we should think fit. Upon some favourable*
> *circumstances submitted to us in his behalf we think it*
> *fit to extend his Majesty's mercy unto him as to the said*
> *Confinement.*
> Dorset

Dublin Castle wasn't feeling particularly merciful however, its ire at the Carlow disturbances not having fully receded, but it did consent to allow the priest to be transported as soon as a ship became available without having to complete his full prison sentence. He was never heard of in Ireland again.

Unfortunately the maiming of animals wasn't only committed during the spontaneous venting of a mob's rage, but was often part of a planned strategy of retribution against the ruling class. Most of the magistrates, the justices and the sheriffs were 'gentlemen farmers' – they oversaw the running of large estates, but rarely got their hands dirty. This was usually their primary source of wealth and frequently when a priest was taken the more militant among the peasants would strike back at the business interests of those deemed responsible. The principal method of doing this was the practice of 'houghing' cattle, sheep and horses – cutting the Achilles tendon in the hind limb – which besides being agonising for the animal rendered them fit only for slaughter. At other times the animals would simply have their throats cut in the dead of night. Barns and stables were set ablaze and the animals within condemned to a horrific death. Less cruel, but equally costly to the landowners, was the wrecking of enclosures, the burning of crops or the dumping of an animal's carcass in a well. This cruelty was by no means unique to Ireland as across Britain and Europe animal maiming was seen a relatively easy means of striking out at a landowner who was judged to have mistreated his tenants.

Outbreaks of these agrarian attacks usually followed a clampdown by the authorities on the activities of the priests. Many believed that the Catholic clergy was behind the attacks and actively encouraged the practice, but in general priests abhorred this cruelty perpetuated on their behalf.

A sense of the outrage stirred by these attacks and of where the blame was apportioned can be gleaned from the letters below, the first from a prominent Protestant clergyman in Galway in response to the sinister activities of a character called Eaver, who was the leader of a band of agrarian guerillas.

> *Tuam March 3 1712-3.*
> *… I do assure your Grace as many of the priests as I*
> *discoursed of Eaver and houghers to know how they*
> *stood affected or disaffected to the practice of houghing. I*
> *could never observe by their speech or behaviour that they*

disliked or disapproved the practice. I could never hear that any one among them made as much as an exhortation against it but on the contrary if we may judge of the inclination of all by the conduct of some, your Grace with all reason will judge that they are deeply concerned in promoting this wicked design.

Yours, George Foster

In the following letter from Roscommon the writer, Gilbert Ormsby, a Justice of the Peace, has clearly worked himself into a blind fury over a recent 'houghing' of a neighbour's cattle and in effect assigns all his earthly troubles to priestly influence among the peasants and pines for the days of Cromwell's butchery of the clergy:

Tobervady 12 Mar 1711-2.

… I hope the Government will take notice of it [the continuing attacks] and rather that I find these barbarities dispose the papist to renounce his scurvy religion for I reckon that all our unhappiness and misfortunes proceed from the Priests to whom the greater men communicate their designs and they stirr up the common people to execute them. Nor do I believe we shall ever be safe or quiet till a wolf's head and a priest's be at the same rate. Such a time I remember and then there was not a quieter populace in the world.

Yours, Gilbert Ormsby

KEEPING THE IRISH WOLF FROM THE DOOR

Besides the men who spent their time in the pursuit of priests, from the mid-seventeenth century another band of bounty hunters, mostly Englishmen, were at work in Ireland. Their prey was not human, but the wolf. Up until the eighteenth century Ireland had always had a substantial population of wolves, and indeed, the animal enjoys a prominent role in Irish mythology. Cormac Mac Airt, the high king of Ireland, for example, was said to have been raised by wolves and had learned to communicate with them. Ancient ringforts were built partly to protect against attacks by wolves. In the years before the Cromwellian invasion, it is estimated that the wolf population may still have been as high as one thousand, and due to the massive loss of human life and the depopulation of the landscape because of the Cromwellian wars, their numbers were on the increase. The counties of Galway, Mayo, Sligo and Leitrim, with large unpopulated areas, boasted the highest wolf population.

The English Government considered the threat the wolves posed to humans to be so great that they imposed a ban on the export of Irish wolfhounds, which were used to hunt wolves. In 1652 they went further, introducing a bounty for the killing of a wolf; six pounds for a female; five for a male; two pounds for a sub-adult; ten shillings for a cub. As the English authorities didn't want bands of armed Irishmen roaming the land, the offer was mainly directed at their own countrymen and in 1656 alone almost four thousand pounds was paid out in wolf bounty. Having survived in Ireland for twenty thousand years, the animal finally lost its battle for survival when the last wolf was hunted down and killed by a sheep farmer called John Watson from Ballydarton in Carlow in 1768.

As the bounty on a priest was almost four times that of a wolf (see panel), one can only assume that the bloodthirsty Mr Ormsby meant that he wished to literally see priests' heads delivered to his doorstep.

But while the agrarian unrest may have been largely in response to the repression and arrest of priests, they were mostly the work of small groups of peasants acting independently. A petition to Dublin Castle by twenty-four priests who had been imprisoned in Clare County Gaol in response to a recent spate of attacks, pleads their innocence and repugnance:

> *Tuam March 3 1712-3. GEO. FOSTER.*
> *To their Excellencies the Lords Justices.*
> *… your petitioners are informed that the reason for which they are soe imprisoned is on account of the late houghing and killing of cattle and sheep in this County*

221

> *which is a practice they utterly abhor and detest and*
> *which they have endeavoured and will endeavour to*
> *prevent all they possibly can …*

But the vicious circle of priests being hunted down followed by revenge attacks followed by more repression would continue nonetheless for as long as the Penal Laws endured. And while the Protestant community largely enjoyed wealth and prosperity thanks to their benefactors who had conquered Ireland in previous generations, many lived their lives looking over their shoulders or lying awake at night listening for unfamiliar voices and sounds outside their walls or fretting each time they ventured out on the highway.

The threat of violence always hung heavily in the air.

AN INTIMIDATING PROSPECT

There seems little doubt that one of the reasons the rewards for capturing priests and bishops were set so high was to compensate for the stigma, fear and intimidation the hunter would have to endure, probably for years to come. This was especially the case if the man lived in the immediate area or even within the county – the rural grapevine was constantly alive with tales of the deeds and identities of priest catchers and informers. The documentation that has survived the era is littered with references to threats to person and property of these men:

> *Offaly 1714*
> *We desire you will be pleased to acquaint his Grace and*
> *their Lordships that the late insolent behaviour of the*
> *Papists of the County, as we apprehended, is chiefly owing*
> *to their priests not being brought to justice who have of*

late publickly exercised their functions. And severall of the Justices of the Peace who were active in summoning persons to give evidence against them and taking examinations have been threatened for their behaviour towards them.

Dublin 1720
That the Irish papists did severall times endeavour to destroy your Petitioner by secret practices and open violence so that your Petitioner is in perfect fear of his life …

Carlow 1739
There was a priest taken last week by Mr Wolseley for marrying a Papist to a Protestant and accordingly was ordered by him to be carryed to Carlow Jail but was mett by the way by near 500 people and rescued from Mr Wolseley's servants and the Constable … [the papists] have already attempted to murder a Justice of the Peace and a trooper who gave examinations against them and threatened Mr Wolseley, Mr Preston the Parson of the Parish and several other gentlemen. I write this at the desire of Mr Wolseley, Mrs Burton and severall others to beg your Lordship will lay them before the Government that we may have an order for the troops.

As late as 1760, by which time the worst of the repression

had passed, a priest hunter in Cork called Robert Powell was shot and seriously injured after he'd captured a Fr David Welsh for secretly marrying a Protestant and Catholic. Interestingly, the avenging party of five people included the Protestant groom, a female maidservant and two others also called Welsh, possibly relations of the priest:

> Whereas David Welsh of Mitchelstown a popish priest
> was indicted at the last Assizes of Limerick for solemniz-
> ing a clandestine marriage on the 4th day of June last
> between John Webb of Cooliveghy, yeoman, and Margaret
> Powell, spinster, and whereas the said John Webb and
> Patrick Cahure of Cooliveghy, Charles Welsh of Tulla,
> mariner, and Mary Jones of Durragh a servant maid
> all in the said County Limerick together with a person
> commonly called by the name of Captain Welsh were also
> indicted at the said Assizes for way laying with intent to
> murder Roger Powell, gentleman, on the 16th day of last
> June, the said John Webb and Charles Welsh having each
> of them discharged a gun at said Mr Powell wounding
> him in the face and body.

The petition goes on to relate that all the accused parties had since fled the county and requests that they be proclaimed out-laws. But despite the seriousness of the charges, the authorities demurred, possibly because of the changing climate or because of the general ill feeling that by then existed towards the profession of priest hunting. In other words, they had little sympathy for Powell.

Most ordinary folk, of course, would not be willing to go so far as to kill one of these men, either because of moral and religious reasons or because they feared ending up on the wrong side of the law – or the end of a rope. But if they were not prepared to take a priest hunter's life they were keen to ensure that his life was lived in fear. Men were stigmatised, threatened, their families abused, their property destroyed and as shown in an earlier example, the hatred of the hunter endured even after his death with succeeding generations often having to bear his disgrace. As historian James O'Laverty described it in his book *The History of Down and Connor*:

> *The wild justice of revenge even followed him after death and his body would not be allowed to rest in any of the churchyards.*

While the priests had been cast out into a life of hiding in the wilds, the priest hunter often found himself an outcast within his locale, sometimes shunned even by fellow Protestants, many of whom, as we've seen, viewed the profession with distaste:

> *The humble petition of Richard McElligott.*
> *Sheweth That your Petitioner discovered one Richard Pierce, Titular Bishop of Waterford and Lismore to have returned into this kingdom from France contrary to a late*

*Act of Parliament made here but the said Pierce being
harboured by one Collonel John Butler of the Castle of
Kilkenny and Collonel Thomas Butler of the County of
Tipperary soe that your Petitioner could not prosecute
him the said Pierce, as the law impowers. May it therefore please your Excellencies to grant your Order that a
fine may be levied on the Collonels aforesaid which they
are liable to by the Act above mentioned. And your Petitioner will pray etc. Your Excellencies may be sensible that
your Petitioner has lost the fame and friendshipp of all his
friends and Relations on this Account.*

When unable to vent their anger on the priest hunter himself,
eyes often turned to anyone perceived to be a party to the deed.
When a Fr Boyle was taken in the hamlet of Milford in east
Mayo and committed to Galway Gaol, a large crowd vented their
rage on the only available target – the unfortunate local Protestant clergyman's wife:

2 September 1712 [from Robert Millar]
*… I am told that soon after the priest was taken and
before I came to town that severall of the popish mob of
the town came to the house of Dr Falien, a Clergyman
in our Church and abused his wife by giving of severall
curses and ill landguage, alledgeing that her husband and
she were the occasion of Father Boyle's being taken.*

Mrs Falien got off lightly. Beatings, stonings and attacks on the properties of priest hunters were common. A priest hunter called Richard Huddy from Cork had his house burnt to the ground and a similar attack in Wicklow town almost had disastrous and tragic consequences when it spread from the intended victim's, a Mr Hamilton, and consumed seven other homes. In 1711, as was recorded in a proclamation by the Lord Mayor of Dublin seeking to identify Catholic rioters, a priest hunter called Henry Oxenard almost paid for his activities with his life,

> *Whereas on Saturday last being the 17th some hundreds of the popish inhabitants of this city in a riotous and tumultuous manner assembled in Fishamble Street and in other parts of the town in order to way-lay and insult one Henry Oxenard, on whose testimony several regulars and popish priests were lately convicted and brought to punishment in Her Majesty's Court of Queen's Bench. And whereas the aforesaid rioters or popish mob pursued the said Oxenard thro' several streets of this city crying out 'priest-catcher', and whereupon the said Oxenard took shelter in the main guard in St Werburgh's Street. Nevertheless the said rioters pursued him to the guard house and insulted the guards and afterwards wounded several constables and others, who were by the magistrates of this city sent to suppress the said tumult, and to secure the said Oxenard from the fury and insolence of the aforesaid papists.*

So seriously were incidents such this taken that on 24 March, a week after the riot, the Lord Mayor of Dublin issued a proclamation charging every single constable in the city to scour their individual wards for the perpetrators and to return within a week with the names of the guilty so that they could be 'prosecuted with the utmost severity of the law'.

Sixteen years later, little had changed. In 1727, the Protestant Archbishop of Dublin William King noted that the baiting of priest catchers had become a common occupation on the city streets:

> *The number of Papists is greater than of Protestant in most places ten to one and in some twenty to one, these have all a correspondence and mutual intelligence by means of the priests and they can at any time bring a mob together from very remote places, and when they have set their business, there is no more necessary but to cry a 'priest catcher' and immediately in the open streets of Dublin you shall have a mob of five or six hundred unknown faces to fall on him, and it is well if he escape with a severe beating, nay houses have been broke open to come at him.*

Spreading of fear did not always require such drastic measures. Digging of fake graves on people's property was a favourite practice as was the hanging of effigies from gateposts or trees. Threats would be called anonymously from across crowded village streets or men

229

would loiter at a safe distance at the boundaries of properties, but within plain view, so that the owner would live in a constant state of nervousness and always have to be on his guard. Nighttime visits were a regular occurrence, often deliberately unsubtle to ensure the household had sleepless nights. In the case below, John Bourke, the First Earl of Mayo, who evidently enjoyed a spot of priest hunting, was subject to such intimidation and even tried a little detective work to try and identify the culprits:

> *Castle Bourke 25 Feby. 1711-2.*
>
> *My Lord, According to your last resolution I have yesterday apprehended the priest of this parish and sent him to Castlebarr. About the dead hour of the night last night there came some people in their boots from the East Gate of my lane to my house doore where they stood for some time and from thence they walked to the West Gate towards my stable and soe back again to the East Gate. Whereto I went this morning as soon as I had the account from some of my servants, when I found the fresh tracks of men and horses. I tooke measure of boots, which I have tried with my own men and horses and finde they doe not agree any way.*
>
> *John Bourke, 1ˢᵗ Earl of Mayo.*

His Lordship goes on to request arms and ammunition be supplied to protect himself and his family forthwith.

The Penal Laws has shrouded the whole of Ireland in a cloud

of fear. For the Catholics it was the fear of losing their hallowed priest or of being arrested or fined an enormous sum for aiding a priest or participating in an illegal rite. For Protestants, and particularly the priest hunters and those who facilitated their profession, it was the fear of vengeance and intimidation and even murder. Yet the wind of change that would disperse that cloud would take over a century to rise. During which time span hundreds of priest hunters came and went, and a handful even achieved notoreity.

Part Five

THE INFAMOUS
PRIEST HUNTERS

JOHN GARZIA

THE PRIEST WHO BECAME A
PRIEST HUNTER WHO BECAME A MISSIONARY

What possesses a man to abandon his family, his faith, his homeland and his scruples, to travel a thousand miles into an inhospitable climate – both meteorologically and politically – and take up a profession that was not only despised by the masses but also, as he surely witnessed with his own eyes, extremely dangerous? In the case of one of the most notorious priest hunters, John Garzia, the answers are difficult to determine through the haze of history, although some part of his motivation can be guessed at through his own testimony and the politics of his country at the time.

Born in Cadiz, Spain, around the year 1690, Garzia was raised a Catholic and his mother seems to have been of sufficient means to provide him with a good education. There is no reference to his father in the surviving documentation, so he may have been deceased by the time Garzia arrived in Ireland. During his youth he entered the priesthood and some years later was officially ordained; while there are some references during the Penal Age to Catholic priests converting to Protestantism and informing on former brethren, Garzia is the only known priest who actually turned to priest catching. His mother was also wealthy enough to sponsor a journey he made to Civitavecchia in Italy, which likely formed part of his religious training, as at the time the town was the principal port of Rome and had many close links with the Vatican. Aged twenty at the time he visited Italy, Garzia is known to have become acquainted with Fr John Browne on his journey, an Irish priest who he would betray just a handful of years later.

Towards the end of the seventeenth century and the start of the eighteenth, the political situation in Spain was in turmoil. The country had seen its position as a leading world power decline greatly under the last Hapsburg King of Spain, Charles II, and the new century began with the Spanish War of Succession, which lasted for fourteen years and resulted in Spain losing much of its territory and influence and being relegated to a relatively minor player among the dominant global powers.

Socially the country was also enduring something of an upheaval. For two hundred years the Spanish Inquisition had sought to strictly regulate and control the morality of the masses and to expel or convert non-Catholics, often under threat of execution, its influence reaching right to the heart of the Spanish monarchy. Although its excesses are well documented, the minutiae of some of its laws give a sense of the extent to which it sought to guide the public mind. Women, for example, were forbidden to ride in a carriage with the curtains closed or to travel with any male who was not a close relative; having lucky charms such as a rabbit's foot could be deemed a heretical superstition and result in prosecution; smiling at the mention of the Virgin Mary could lead to denunciation; urinating against a church wall was considered grossly offensive. (Despite these strictures on people's personal behaviour, public morality had declined to the extent that in the latter half of the seventeenth century Madrid alone had over eight hundred brothels.) It was into this era of religious rigidity that John Garzia was born, but his chosen career of Catholic priest did not guarantee safety from the excesses of the Inquisition. Priests were regularly subject to denunciation, often by a person who simply had a grudge against them. Should an overworked priest yawn during a mass, he might suddenly find himself being flogged or worse.

In 1711, at the age of twenty-one, the young Garzia claims he made some slight transgression, the detail of which is unknown, but of which the Protestant Archbishop Synge of Tuam would later write:

> … *having (as it is said) been known to speak with some freedom concerning some points of the Romish faith.*

Whatever points of Catholicism he questioned, it was reported to the Inquisition who soon came in search of him. Leaving his mother behind, he fled his home and took a ship bound for England. No records of his life in England have survived, but it seems an odd destination for a Catholic priest at the time. Although the repression of Catholicism was much more severe in Ireland, it was no picnic in England either and while Garzia would later convert, it is possible he survived by pretending he was a Protestant. This would have been quite plausible, as many of the tiny population of Spanish Protestants had fled from the Inquisition to England and other northern European countries. How he earned his crust is a mystery, particularly as he never troubled to learn English and even in later life people had difficulty understanding his smattering of English words spoken through a heavy Spanish accent.

In 1717, Garzia decided to move to Ireland. As his activities as a priest hunter began almost as soon as his foot touched Irish soil, it is likely that while in London he'd learned of the recently-introduced bounties on Catholic clergy and realised he'd finally found a means of earning a very substantial, if not respectable, living.

Although Garzia is generally recorded as having been a 'priest catcher' or a 'priest hunter', a more accurate description would probably be 'Protestant deep-cover operative', as his *modus operandi* was not to dramatically seize priests and haul them before the law, but to use his position to spy on the Catholic clergy, whom he would then inform on to the authorities. Just a few months after landing in Ireland he converted to Protestantism and although not specifically referred to in the substantial correspondence about his financial affairs that exist, it is quite likely he was well paid for this as an earlier act of Queen Anne had stated:

*Every popish priest being approved of as a convert and
received into the church by the archbishop or bishop of the
diocese wherein they resided and conforming himself to
the Church of Ireland as by law established and having
taken the oaths and subscribed the declarations ... such
converted priests shall have twenty pounds yearly during
their residence in such county for their maintenance and
till they are otherwise provided for ...*

But twenty pounds, while a handsome sum of cash at the
time, was way short of the earnings Garzia had in mind. One
can only speculate if money was his primary motive, but as subsequent evidence would show, he could certainly get through it
quick enough. However it's quite likely that he also bore a grudge
against the Catholic Church. He said himself that he had queried
a number of points of the Catholic faith, so perhaps his com-
mitment to Catholicism wasn't as unquestioning and fanatical
as seems to have been prerequisite at the time. As a result of that
he'd been forced to abandon the only life he'd ever known and
flee into exile in a strange land, far from family and friends. As
he crossed the gangplank on to a Dublin dockside in the late
spring of 1717, John Garzia was probably driven equally by a
desire to earn large amounts of cash and by a simmering desire
for revenge.

Within weeks of his arrival, he had made his first contacts
with the Irish Catholic clergy, attending masses and confessionals

and secretly building up a file of names, places and illegal activities. He clearly ingratiated himself with members of the Irish Church as he was soon on sufficiently friendly terms that he was offered accommodation by one of them and he recorded that he had lodged with one Fr Francis Jones, who went by the alias 'Francis White'. Their residence was probably in the Franciscan Friary at Merchant's Quay, popularly known today as Adam and Eve's, which had taken its name from the Adam & Eve Tavern in nearby Cook Street. The fact that Garzia was a priest alone in a strange country undoubtedly won him considerable sympathy from the other young friars in Dublin, a situation he exploited to great effect, recording details of his fellow lodger's activities such as the particular Franciscan prayers Fr Jones recited in their candlelit room. He also accompanied his unsuspecting roommate to mass in 'Doctor Naries Chapel', where he witnessed the priest changing into Catholic robes and officiating at the service.

Over the coming months Garzia attended secret masses in Francis Street, St John's Lane chapel on Thomas Street, in the Duchess of Tyrconnell's house in Channel Row, now North Brunswick Street, in the Poor Clares' nunnery on North King Street and most frequently in the small, concealed chapel behind the Adam & Eve Tavern in Cook Street. He had soon earned sufficient respect to be entrusted with the means of entry into a mass. Posing as men out to enjoy a tankard of ale, Catholics would enter the pub, which was frequently crowded with visiting sailors and dock workers, seek out a man called Denis Ryan and simply say 'I'm going to the Adam and Eve'. The password uttered, Ryan would lead the man through the singing sailors and drunken dockers to a passageway at the back, where he'd unlock a door and admit the person to the mass. But Garzia's thoughts were far from worshipping God, as at each service he attended, his dossier of priests' names and particulars grew thicker.

His betrayal was surely all the more bitter for his fellow priests because of the closeness of the relationship he'd formed with them and the fact that he was probably accepting their charity and hospitality. Among these was a Jesuit called Fr Michael Murphy who, on being told by Garzia that he planned to visit Portugal in the near future (there is no record of him having any such intention), asked the Spaniard if he would personally deliver several letters to Jesuit friends of his that had been banished there. Naturally Garzia agreed and Fr Murphy unwittingly furnished him with even more information on priests abroad who might be planning to return, which he would subsequently hand over to the Duke of Bolton, the Lord Lieutenant of Ireland.

Garzia also became well acquainted with Fr Francis Moore, who went by the alias 'Francis Morry', who confided in him that he'd recently arrived back in Ireland from Bilbao, an admission that could have led to him being tried for high treason. He also by chance met up with Fr John Browne who he had encountered some years beforehand in Italy and doubtless they shared stories of the happy days they'd spent wandering the paths of Vatican City, information that Garzia would later use as evidence against the priest.

But the biggest coup for the Spaniard was witnessing the Titular Archbishop of Dublin, Dr Edmund Byrne, officiating at one or more masses. Byrne had been a thorn in the establishment's side for years, as they knew him to be administering many of the secret activities of the Catholic Church and ordaining innumerable priests. The authorities had been actively pursuing the Archbishop the length and breadth of the country and among those he'd eluded was another of the most notorious priest hunters, Edward Tyrrell.

Whether Garzia had already agreed to act clandestinely in identifying priests for the authorities or whether this was a purely private enterprise at this stage is not recorded. However what is known is that he had fully committed himself to betraying all of his friends and acquaintances by November of the year of his arrival in Ireland, as in that month he secretly converted to Protestantism, yet continued to attend all the normal Catholic services and meetings for months afterwards.

By the spring of the following year the Spaniard had amassed a considerable body of information on the city's Catholic clergy and duly presented it to the delighted authorities in Dublin Castle. Over the coming weeks plans were drawn up for a major swoop on a number of locations.

At 2am on Saturday 1 June 1718, sheriffs and constables descended on the clergys' residences around the city, bursting through doorways in the dead of night and startling the priests from their beds. The early hours of the morning had been chosen not only to take the clerics unawares, but also to avoid the real possibility of a riot springing up among the citizens. The Archbishop, Dr Byrne, was arrested along with six priests: James Dillon, Francis Moore, Francis Jones (Garzia's former roommate), Michael Murphy, John Brown and Anthony Bryan.

A fortnight later, at 4am on 15 June, the convent of the Poor Clares on North King Street was raided, constables surrounding the building. The Poor Clares had been taking in boarders and pensioners to support themselves and when the abbess heard the sheriff's men at the gate, she quickly ordered the other nuns to don peasant clothing and blend with their guests. Wary of the delay, the sheriff ordered his men to smash down the gates and minutes later they emerged with four women they'd arrested under suspicion of being nuns who had participated in Catholic services. The four were put in two separate coaches and, despite the early hour, were driven across the city to Judge Caulfield's home to be formally charged, the prompt action presumably arranged again to avoid a riot; they wanted the nuns locked up safely before the citizens of Dublin had risen from their beds.

Of the seven clergy arrested, five were unregistered, and trial for these was set for November of that year. Fr Bryan was charged as a registered priest officiating outside his allocated boundaries; he would be tried separately later that same month. The Archbishop's day in court would not happen for a year and the nuns would have to wait until February 1719.

Around the time of the arrests John Garzia married a woman known only by her Christian name of Mary, who was a Protestant. Their courtship was brief as he'd been in Ireland less than a year, but with the promise of an extremely healthy reward on the way, the Spaniard must have seemed like a good catch. Mrs Mary Garzia would prove to be no shrinking violet when it came to claiming every penny she could from the state. His subsequent letters concerning rewards were written in clear, well-composed English and as he spoke only a smattering of the language and had no other friends, she was almost certainly the writer, revealing her to be an educated and intelligent woman. During the course of their lives she would bear him five children, three of whom would survive into adulthood.

The trial of the five unregistered priests took place before a judge and jury in Dublin on 7 November, with Garzia appearing as the key witness against each man. A contemporary newspaper account of the event wrongly described him as an Italian, possibly due to his evidence of having seen one of the priests in Civitavecchia. One after the other, the priests were brought before the court and, using an interpreter, Garzia produced his evidence against them. The second trial, that of Fr Jones, alias White, is described by the correspondent, (probably working for a 'news pamphlet') who in the style of the time, was parsimonious to say the least with his use of full stops:

... the said Garsee being sworn, he said that about
12 or 13 Months ago he became acquainted with the
said Jones, alias White, and that he knew him to be a
Franciscan Fryar, the court ask'd him how they became
acquainted the Witness said that they Lodg'd in the same
House together for Four Months, the Court Examin'd the
said Garsee how he could tell that the said Jones was a
Franciscan Fryer who answer'd that the said Jones, alias
White himself told him so and besides that there was a
certain sort of a Prayer that belonged to that Order which
the said Jones, alias White frequently used, upon the said
Jones, alias White, having no defense to make for himself
and the Witness having sworn that he seen him Celebrate
mass in Doctor Naries Chappel in the usual Habit or
Robes, and at several other Places, the said Jones. Alias
White, was also found guilty immediately, having
remained in the Kingdom contrary to law.

One can only imagine the suppressed rage and hurt of the priests as they sat watching the man they had befriended, housed and fed as he stood in the witness box and betrayed them with every word that spilled from his lips.

A little drama arose during the third trial when one of the few witnesses for the defence was called. Garzia having sworn that he'd witnessed Fr Francis Moore celebrating mass in Cook Street, the priest was asked if he had anything to say in his defence and he duly claimed that Garzia was lying, that he had not been in the particular chapel for over a year and that the doorman, Denis Ryan, could testify to that effect. Ryan's evidence provided little help to the unfortunate priest as he apparently became agitated in some fashion, the detail of which the correspondent did not record, possibly because of its irreverence or disrespect to the court, and the doorman ended up on the wrong side of the law himself.

> ... the said Ryan being called, and Sworn in the behalf
> of the Traverser, he upon his Oath being Cross Examin'd
> and did not rightly behave himself, he was ordered by the
> court to be put into the Dock, and without any more ado,
> the Jury brought the said Moore alias Morry in Guilty ...

Although there is no detail as to what actually occurred to prompt the above, incidents such as this do give a sense of the verdict of the court being 'railroaded' through – no evidence the priests might bring was going to alter the outcome.

And so it continued with Garzia as essentially the only witness, the damning evidence tripping off his tongue as each of his victims was led into court.

> ... that he seen the said Dillon celebrating Mass in St.
> Francis Street Chappel ...
> ... he said that he became acquainted with the said Jones
> about fourteen Months ago, and that he very well knew

him to be a Franciscan Fryar …

… when Garsee told him he was going to Portugal,
that the said Murphy writ several letters by him to other
Jesuits there and said that the said Murphy kept School in
Dublin, taught Grammar and Philosophy …

… about Eight Years ago, since he had seen him at a
place called Civita Vecchia …

… the Court ask'd him how he could tell that Brown was
an Augustinian Fryar, Garzia answered that the Tra-
verser himself told him so.

Justice, or at least the court's version of it, was swift in those days and before the afternoon was out all five were tried, found guilty and sentenced to imprisonment followed by a lifetime's exile, and threatened with death if they returned. They were to be held in Newgate Prison until such time as transportation could be arranged.

Within weeks the priests were petitioning the Lords Justices for their sentence of transportation to be carried out, due no doubt to the appalling squalor in which they were confined, and although the petitions were accepted, it is not recorded how long the men languished in Newgate. According to Thomas De Burgo's *Hibernia Dominicana*, which provides a contemporary account of many of the events of the time, all five of the exiled priests eventually returned to Ireland despite the threat of a death sentence.

The registered priest, Fr Anthony Bryan, was tried later that month with a similar outcome, the only essential difference being that the priest reportedly gave a spirited defence and contemptuously called Garzia 'a Jew who merely pretended to be a priest', the term 'Jew' being one of abuse at the time. Many historical accounts of Garzia's time in Ireland (including the respected De Burgo's) inaccurately describe the Spaniard as a Jew, the error most likely springing from Fr Byran's 'insult'.

In February of 1719 the four nuns who had been arrested – Anne Crawford, Mary Smith, Jane Sexton and Mary Chivers – were brought before the court. Garzia was again the principal witness and he went into considerable detail in his efforts to prove their guilt.

> … *Garsee answered that he was sensible [aware] that every young Woman who took the Vow of Chastity, and became a Nunn, had in a Year's time a Ring bestowed upon her, and a knotted Cord, called a St Francis's Girdle and that he knew each of the Traversers to have the like. He likewise knew severally to have used a prayer that is not used by others but such as are Nunns and that they wore the Nunn's Habitt when at home but when they came abroad, they left the Black and White Habitt at Home for fear of being discovered. Garsee stated that Anne Crawford was an Abbiss and so Reputed and Respected by all the rest, and that all the*

rest of the Gentlewomen call'd her Mother.

In an apparent contradiction of their name, the four Poor Clares were of sufficient funds to employ a defence counsellor, who countered that a layperson might easily wear such as the ring and girdle and that Anne Crawford was in fact a married woman. Garzia's response, testimony to how closely he'd come to know the defendants, was that Crawford was a widow who had become a nun after her husband's death.

The next witness was Mrs Sergeant, wife of the appropriately named George Sergeant, High Constable of Dublin. After the nuns' arrest she had been employed to search the women and had found a ring in Smith's pocket and a knotted cord about her body. She'd also found rosary beads, a prayer book and a crucifix in Sexton's pocket, all of which items were brandished before the jury.

Various other witnesses for the prosecution were briefly trotted out; the High Constable, an arresting sheriff and a Mr Garvey, who claimed he knew Crawford for twenty years, had heard she was married but had never seen her husband or heard her referred to as anything but a nun or an abbess.

Offered the opportunity to speak, Crawford rounded on Garzia, calling him a liar and that he was 'as false as God is true' and stating that their only witness in their defence was God Almighty himself. And apparently God was listening, as Crawford and Chivers were acquitted. Smith and Sexton were found guilty and sentenced to exile, but as it happened they were all soon set free due to a technicality discovered by their counsel. It turned out that the laws as set down by Her Majesty's Government had in the discriminatory fashion of the day, omitted any mention of women. The anti-Catholic legislation referred only to 'clergymen' or to 'bishops, priests, friars etc', making no mention of nuns or clergywomen. The four nuns walked free from the courtroom. Garzia, on the other hand, had to be escorted out by a sergeant and ten soldiers who had stood guard about the Spaniard for the duration of the trial. If he hadn't realised the rage and venom he would evoke among the population of Dublin through his actions, it was surely beginning to dawn on him now.

Archbishop Byrne's trial took place the following summer; the only charge that could be mustered was that of officiating at a mass outside his designated parish. Garzia was to be the only witness, but curiously he didn't appear, and no apparent fuss was made of this by the court. It happened that Britain had recently entered the war of Quadruple Alliance against Spain, and among Britain's allies were its erstwhile enemies France and the Holy Roman Empire. It is likely that because of this alliance political representations were made on behalf of the prominent Archbishop and Garzia, who was of course a native of Spain, their now enemy, was ordered not to appear. With no other witnesses, the trial was abandoned and Dr Byrne released. He immediately resumed his illegal activities and managed to avoid arrest for the remaining five years of his life.

John Garzia and his wife may have been willing to suffer the slings and arrows of Dublin's Catholics because of the knowledge that they would now enjoy a comfortable life with so many rewards coming their way. Yet four months after the first five priests' conviction the only thing he'd received was the state's gratitude. On 3 March 1719, he wrote to the Lords Justices, his appeal containing the frequently employed priest hunter's tactic of presenting himself as being in a pitiful condition and in desperate need:

> ... that your Petitioner's reward according to Act of Parliament for the first five priests above mentioned was one hundred pounds of Which your Petitioner has not received a peny being a stranger to Such Demand, and knows not who to apply for the Same other than your Excellencies and honours.
>
> That your Petitioners has noe manner of Way of getting being an Actual Stranger in this Kingdome, Sometime in June last had the honour of Receiveing a present by theire Excellencie's orders off ffifty pounds, your Petitioner having a family to maintain and himself lyeing sick for a considerable time under the Doctor's hands which Misfortunes Consumed the said Present in a short time. That your Petitioner dare not walke the Streetes about his business being in Danger of his life by Romans.

Garzia's family at that stage consisted of himself and his wife,

Mary, and to have gotten through fifty pounds in nine months (remembering that a skilled tradesman's annual pay was about fifteen pounds), suggested that the Garzias were enjoying something of the high life. He was also in receipt of the annual allowance of twenty pounds for converting and as would later be revealed, had another regular income.

The Protestant Archbishop King of Dublin, fearful that the failure to reward the Spaniard would discourage other priest hunters and informers, took up his case.

> *March 16th 1719*
> *My Lord,*
> *There are due to the bearer Mr Garcia severall sums for*
> *the good service he hath done the Government but by the*
> *negligence of Collectors or some other impediment I find*
> *he has gotten nothing, my Lord this is a very great dis-*
> *couragement, and will have I fear very ill consequences,*
> *we ordered Mr Maddockes to write to your Lordship*
> *about this, which I hope he did, but I further hope that*
> *my sending it may have some influence and that we shall*
> *hear his mon'y paid, which will be very grateful to.*

For whatever reason, there seemed a reluctance to pay the reward and the Lord Mayor refused to accept responsibility, prompting Garzia to write to the Lords Justices yet again. In his letter he goes into a prolonged description of his conversion from Popish priest to Protestantism, his infiltration of the Catholic community, the arrests, the trials and his willingness to remain in the jurisdiction to testify, all in all painting a fairly heroic portrait of himself. He also suggests that the Papists of the city tried to bribe him not to testify, but that he was not to be corrupted. He begs an allowance to sustain him until the matter of the reward can be settled.

Whether they tried to bribe him or not, the 'Papists of the city' were going to have some satisfaction from the Spaniard one way or the other and early in March, just after the nuns' trial, he was walking down James's Street when the cries of 'priest catcher!' began to ring out. Easily recognised by his Mediterranean looks, a crowd quickly gathered, chased him down and beat him severely. Somehow Garzia escaped with his life, possibly through the intervention of constables.

The incident and the pleas from the Archbishop finally had the desired effect and the Grand Jury awarded Garzia his one hundred pounds along with apartments in Dublin Castle. Although the granting of the apartment has the appearance of a healthy bonus, in actuality John and Mary Garzia were moving into a life of virtual confinement and isolation as the man's infamy had spread so virulently throughout the city, the castle, with its garrison of soldiers was the only place he could be adequately protected. But as far as the authorities were concerned the payment of the reward and the granting of the apartment was the end of the matter and they promptly forgot about the Spaniard. He and his wife however, weren't finished with them yet.

Settled into his new, if rather restricted life, Garzia finally burned all his Catholic bridges in May of 1719, when he was confirmed as a priest in the Church of England. Not that he would have any immediate opportunity to openly hold services as every time he emerged from the Castle apartment it was under escort of a guard of soldiers. Despite this there were further attacks and Garzia was several times forced to flee a riotous, stone-hurling mob.

Notwithstanding their restricted circumstances, it seems the Garzias were well able to spend their recently acquired wealth, possibly through the purchase of fine furniture or expensive clothing, because by November, just seven months after being granted his one hundred pounds, he was again appealing for more cash. Citing his treatment at the hands of the mobs, Garzia sought the sympathy of the Lords Justices.

His appeal no doubt was met with many a disdainful frown and a muttering of 'not him again'. Likely wondering where all the cash they'd already forked out had gone in such a short time, Garzia's plea was ignored. He then wrote to Archbishop Wake of Canterbury outlining his situation and he duly wrote to the Protestant Archbishop Synge of Tuam for more background. Despite Synge's best efforts to paint the Spaniard in a sympathetic light, Wake was unconvinced and declined to intervene.

As the months passed, Mary Garzia bore the first of their children, Katherine, in May of that year. A second child, Jane, would be born the following year and the arrival of the infants can only have added to their penurious state. John Garzia now had renewed motivation for appealing to the state for financial help, prompted no doubt by his wife. His next approach to the Lords Justices appears to reveal a degree of mystification on his part as to why his actions had made him such a figure of opprobrium – he says he 'knows no other reason of his being so abused' except having informed on the Catholic clergy. He also reveals that he had up to this time been in receipt of an annual allowance from his mother in Spain, which has now ceased. Just how much this was is not recorded, but money certainly seemed to burn a hole in the pockets of the Garzia family. Besides his reward for the arrest of the priests, it seems he'd also somehow managed to negotiate an annual pension from the state of fifty pounds, which had not been forthcoming.

> *To their Excellencies the Lords Justices and the Lords of his Majesty's Privy Council.*
> *The humble Petition of John Garcia a converted popish priest. Sheweth That your Petitioner was a popish priest and that he made his publicke recantation in the church of Ireland and took the oaths in the King's Bench about three years ago. That the Irish papists did severall times endeavour to destroy your Petitioner by secret practices and open violence so that your Petitioner is in perfect fear of his life Seeing himself abused and sometimes assaulted in the streets by papists or persons disaffected to his Maj-*

esty. That your said Petitioner knows no other reason of his being so abused but because he is become a Protestant and has informed against and has convicted by due course of law six Irish popish priests and three nuns. That the popish clergy being incensed against your Petitioner for doing the duty of a true Protestant and faithfull subject did write to Spaine against him and have been the occasion of your Petitioner's mother and relatives having suffered persecution and that his own picture was burnt by sentence of the Inquisition who would burn him alsoe if he should fall into their unmercifull hands. So that your Petitioner is deprived of the yearly assistance he received from his said mother. That his Grace the Duke of Bolton being sensible of the good services done by your Petitioner to the Government and the Protestant religion in discovering and prosecuting the enemies of both at a very criticall juncture, did promise to settle on your Petitioner a pension of 50 per annum for his and his family subsistence and your Petitioner hopes that his Excellency my Lord Chancellor will remember the truth of this last allegation. That the said pension was not settled on your Petitioner who is actually in greate want and poverty with his wife and two children, and in danger of being arrested by those he was forced to borrow from to prevent starving. J. GARCIA.

The final sentence refers to the possibility of him being sent to the debtor's prison, which was common practice for anyone who fell behind in meeting their financial obligations. A committee was appointed to look at his case, but they largely remained unconvinced, agreeing finally to pay Garzia a pitiful – at least from his perspective – fifteen pounds. No mention of the pension he claims to have been promised by the Duke of Bolton was made, suggesting that they could find no evidence of such an arrangement or that Garzia had misinterpreted the Duke, which is quite possible given the language barrier.

Yet he wasn't completely without his allies and Archbishop King again took up his case later in the year when the fifteen pounds had been spent and the shadow of the debtor's prison loomed once more. Garzia was to appear before Judge Boat, who had presided over one of the priests' trials, where he provided the judge with a letter of recommendation from King claiming that he had 'not a groat', which was four pennies, and that the failure to take care of Garzia would seriously discourage other priest hunters. The letter had the desired effect and the Spaniard escaped prison.

He immediately began to pester the authorities again, who were evidently becoming weary of his presence and his repeated demands for money. But it was agreed that another committee should review his situation and luckily for Garzia two of its members were prominent Protestant clergymen. They calculated that in a three-year period Garzia had received two hundred and twenty-five pounds for his services, an enormous sum of money at the time and this didn't include the annual allowance from his mother or his annual payment for converting. Garzia claimed under oath that much of the money went to pay interest on other monies he'd borrowed and that as a result he'd barely been left with eighty pounds to live on. Despite the fact that the Garzias were apparently living well beyond their means, the committee was sympathetic to him, most probably because the bishops greatly valued his anti-Catholic activities. The committee recommended him for financial relief, which was granted.

Incredibly, a few months later he was once again pleading for more money, his opening lines hinting at the scepticism with which his repeated claims of penury were being viewed:

> *Your Excellency and Lordships may see that if he troubles*
> *with frequent petitions it is not bicause he is greedy or*
> *extravagent in his expenses but bicause he is really poor*
> *and unfortunate.*

His letter also claims that his mother has now disowned him and would happily throw sticks on to the bonfire if the Inquisition got their hands on him. The arrival of a new Lord Lieutenant in Dublin Castle had also meant that the Garzias were moved from their comfortable apartment and 'putt in a garrett that had been till then a passage'. Clearly the authorities were completely fed up with the man and wanted rid of him. His repeated appeals for an annual pension prompted the Lords Justices to refer the matter directly to the Duke of Bolton, who had allegedly promised Garzia the pension. He offloaded it to Lord Carteret, who was the Lord President of the Council, a position just subordinate to the Lord High Treasurer. (To put this in context, the current incumbent of this position is Nick Clegg, Britain's Deputy Prime Minister). Garzia's persistence had now brought him to the attention of the highest levels of British establishment. A recommendation was soon forthcoming that he be sent as a missionary to Minorca, which was briefly a British colony in the nineteenth century. For some reason, this offer was never taken up, perhaps because of the island's relative closeness to his former homeland and the possible clutches of the Inquisition.

By this time it seems the Spaniard had had enough of Ireland. Hated by the general population, a virtual prisoner in a tiny apartment, viewed with disdain by the authorities, he made one final plea to be provided with funds to travel to England. The establishment jumped at the chance to be rid of their embarrassing and expensive nuisance and sometime in mid-1723, John Garzia and his family finally fled Ireland, although he would have one further brief encounter with the country.

A few months later he was in contact with Bishop Edmund Gibson, in whom he likely found another sympathetic ear, as one of the renowned Bishop's later writings would be 'A Preservative against Popery'. Gibson suggested the notion to Garzia that he become a minister in one of the colonies in the new world, which apparently appealed to the Spaniard. The Bishop recommended that he receive 'the King's Bounty', which was a one-off payment of twenty pounds to a Protestant minister who was willing to move to America. His first ministry was intended to be the Bahamas, but he would never reach the Caribbean islands.

On 9 August 1723, the Garzia clan boarded the *Hanover* in London, bound for the Bahamas. However when it docked in Cork en route, they were thrown off for allegedly having stolen a chalice. Garzia was also accused of having taken a collection of books when he had disembarked which had been intended as a gift from Edmund Gibson to the library at Harbor Island in the Bahamas. Despite the charges, no legal action seems to have been taken against him, but he was forced to remain in Cork for several months until he could make some other arrangement. This he succeeded in doing by persuading the Protestant hierarchy to once again provide him with the King's Bounty – either he had some powerful skills of persuasion, which is unlikely given his paltry command of English, or they simply would do anything to be rid of him.

This time he was destined for the newly-established colony of Virginia, where he would serve as rector in the parish of Norfolk for just one year. No explanation for the brevity of his tenure survives. He then transferred to the town of Farnham where he would serve as rector for eight years until 1733 and during which time his wife would bear him a further three children, two of whom would die in infancy. It is interesting to note that the Garzias seemed to continue their spendthrift ways during their time in Virginia as he was brought to court eight times for non-payment of debt while resident in the state. This despite a healthy annual salary of fifty pounds from the Church and regular gifts of foodstuffs, furniture and so on from his parishioners. Garzia also had a case dismissed against him for overcharging for marriage fees, and he took a case against another man for assault, the motive for which is unknown.

It is also known that the Garzias kept indentured servants – these were little more than slaves who in exchange for transport to America and then accommodation and food, agreed to be bound to a master for three years. The case was recorded of one of his servants who had initially tried to run away and was recaptured and for reasons unknown had subsequently threatened to kill the Spaniard.

> Werrell, Thomas, servant to John Garzia, did threaten to
> kill his master, it is therefore ordered that for the offence
> the sherriff take him and carry him to the common whip-
> ping post and give him thirty-nine lashes on the bare back
> well laid on, also on the motion of John Garzia, liberty
> is hereby given him to put an iron collar about his legg
> with a wooden clogg at the end of it to hinder him from
> running away.

Some time later a female servant became pregnant out of wedlock, most likely by the aforementioned Werrell, much to Garzia's outrage. At the time this was a criminal offence and he hauled her before the court, where sympathy or even mercy for the pregnant girl was in short supply:

> *Elizabeth Parsons being brought to this court by her master, John Garzia for having a basterd child and she refusing to pay her fine it is therefore ordered that the sheriff take her and carry her to the common whipping post and give her twenty lashes on her bare back well laid on.*

Ironically, after his death, his own daughter Jane, who had been born in Dublin, would also become pregnant out of wedlock and be tried before the court for the offence.

After nine years in Farnham, the family moved to North Carolina where they would remain the rest of their days. If John Garzia never quite managed to shake off the shackles of debt that seemed to have accompanied him throughout his adult life, here at last he developed something of a reputation as a Christian devoted to the betterment of his community. Immediately upon his arrival in the town of Bath, he became the principal driving force behind the construction of St Thomas Episcopal Church, which was opened in 1734 and is still in use today – it is in fact the oldest surviving church building in North Carolina. He also set about improving the education of the local children, repeatedly applying for educational materials from the Society for the Propagation of the Gospel (SPG). His correspondence indicates that he was troubled greatly by the drunkenness and generally immoral behaviour he often witnessed. In one letter to a Mr Philip Bearcroft he outlines some of the obstacles he faced:

> *I do beg the favour of you to inform their Honours with my endeavours, to promote goodness, Christianity and the true Religion among the Inhabitants within my mission, but immorality is arrived to that head among so many, that it requires not only some time but great patience to conquer it; because upon my preaching upon any prevalent and predominant Sin, I must be prepared to stand the persecution of those who are guilty of it, especially in my resident Parish, in which adultery, Incest, Blasphemy, and all kinds of profaneness has got such deep root.*

It was as though Garzia had been reborn or experienced a 'road to Damascus' conversion. But it is impossible to know if he ever reflected on the morality of his own behaviour back in Ireland. It is possible that he genuinely believed he had committed no wrong whatsoever in betraying his former friends and clerical colleagues for money. But the contrast between his new life and that in Dublin could not have been greater – he had gone from being a man loathed by all those around him to one who would ultimately hold the respect of the entire community.

Unfortunately he hadn't left all of his old ways behind him and in an echo of his days as a priest-catcher, he exploited a law that forbade marriage by anyone other than a minister of the church by informing against a justice of the peace, for which he was granted a reward of five pounds.

Although he received a substantial salary and had been granted free of charge a large tract of land on which he'd built a house, the Garzias seemed to spend the remainder of their lives in debt. In a further reflection of his past life, a great many of his letters to the SPG and others are pleas for funding and support. In one he informs the SPG that he 'did Baptize and instruct severall Negroes' and asks that the Society 'be pleased to transmit for the said service and allowance as to you shall see fitt.'

But the debt incurred in his new life was of a totally different nature to that in Dublin. Running a ministry in an emerging colony, which was essentially in the wilderness at that time, undoubtedly placed a genuine financial burden on the Garzias, and his frequent requests for money were in all likelihood out of necessity for survival, rather than to support an opulent lifestyle. His life as a minister in Bath was more likely one of hardship, especially as his parish covered a vast, largely uninhabited landscape. He would frequently be required to travel great distances in all weathers to carry out his duties, sometimes being met with outright hostility by hardened, uneducated early settlers and his life could in no way be described as comfortable.

It was indeed a strange destiny for a man who had once been regarded by almost an entire city as lower than Judas himself. Garzia's efforts earned him such respect that he was invited to deliver a sermon to the Governor and Assembly at the annual opening of the State Parliament in Edenton. It was the highlight of his ministry in North Carolina.

In 1744, during one of his long treks across country to visit his far-flung parishioners, John Garzia was thrown from his horse and killed, ending a life that was nothing if not varied and had taken him from Spain to Italy to England to Ireland and finally to North Carolina in the New World. It had also taken him on the curious journey from Catholic priest to priest hunter to revered Anglican minister.

A sign near St Thomas Church honours the Spaniard's memory and the contribution he made to the parish in those difficult, early colonial days. But history is often a matter of perspective and from an Irish point of view the self same person was regarded as the most contemptible of all men during the dark penal age.

In Ireland, history would only remember him as John Garzia, Priest Hunter.

BARRY LOWE
OF NEWTOWN

THE FIEND OF WESTMEATH

W hile the vast majority of priest hunters were motivated by the acquisition of fast money, a substantial minority seemed to have been driven purely by a deep-felt
hatred of Catholicism. Combine this with someone who exhib-
its sadistic and ruthless traits and you've got Barry Lowe of the
parish of Newtown, County Westmeath. Or at least that's what
the few surviving accounts of the man's activities suggest.

Born Baracah or Barachia Lowe circa 1665, the most colourful
description of this individual is given by the nineteenth-century
historian and chronicler James Woods. In his book *The Annals
of Westmeath, Ancient and Modern*, written a century and a half
after Lowe's death, he described the man thus:

> *The priest hunter was a furious fanatic and in his features
> might be traced the malice of his mind. A fiend in human
> shape lost to every generous feeling and as insensible to*

pity and suffering as the lictor who lashed our Lord at the
pillar.

Very few documents survive to confirm the monstrous character of the individual described above, but Woods seems to have based his description on folklore he collected around the county and certainly the other accounts from the era paint Barry Lowe in a contemptible light. Factual historical documentation concerning his background would also seem to support the notion that Lowe was raised in an atmosphere of bigotry and with a sense of superiority over the huddled masses.

According to local folklore Lowe was responsible for the deaths of as many as ten priests, although none of their names or the circumstances of their capture and execution are recorded. Yet several tales have survived of other priests persecuted by Lowe, but who lived to tell the tale.

Even if Barry Lowe was the fanatical, merciless priest hunter he was reputed to be, it seems unlikely that he was responsible for the deaths of so many and the numbers are possibly the result of the exaggerations common to handed down folklore, each telling of the tale adding another layer of fiendishness. Although the authorities were often ruthless in their pursuit of clergy, it was usually with the intention of banishing them from Ireland or imprisoning them. They didn't advocate outright brutality and the wholesale murder of priests would surely have prompted the more moderate of the Protestant hierarchy to have raised objections to the likes of Barry Lowe, a member of the gentry, summarily executing his captives on a regular basis.

Having said that, the collective accounts of his activities suggest he was indeed quite brutal, possibly because he was motivated by something far more powerful than the acquisition of wealth – he was driven by hatred that had been bred into him from an early age.

Barry Lowe was the son of William Lowe and Joan Hawkins; William Lowe had served as a major in Cromwell's conquest of Ireland and was an Anabaptist – a Protestant of the Radical Reformation – a sect formed primarily in response to corruption in the Catholic Church. Catholics had heavily persecuted Anabaptists during the previous centuries, so it's safe to say that Barry Lowe's forefathers held no love for Ireland's priests. William's own father, John Lowe, seems to have had connections to Chapelizod in Dublin, and his family may have been involved in the jewelry or silversmith business. He was of sufficient means that upon his death he was buried in a tomb in St Laurence's Church in Chapelizod.

As a reward for his services to Cromwell, William Lowe was granted the manor of Newtown in County Westmeath with manorial powers, which consisted of five thousand acres of prime lands that had formerly been in the possession of the once powerful MacGeoghegan family, and which lies about three kilometers south west of Tyrrellspass. The granting of manorial powers required the ownership of a minimum of five thousand acres and the introduction of a colony of English settlers – he introduced about fifty English families to the neighbourhood, a few of whose descendants still reside in the area today. Earlier in his military career William Lowe had been cashiered from the army by Henry Cromwell, son of Oliver, for 'perverseness and peevishness', but had somehow managed to regain his command. The 'services' for which men such as he had been rewarded had included the wholesale plundering of the county and the murder and rape of numberless peasants by his troops. In his work *Cambrensis Eversus*, Dr John Lynch, Catholic Archbishop of Tuam at the time, painted his own grim picture of the behaviour of the invading forces:

> *All the cruelty inflicted on the city of Rome by Nero and Attila, by the Greeks on Troy or by Vespasian on Jerusalem – all has been inflicted on Ireland by the Puritans. With desolation is the whole land laid desolate; our adversaries are our lords, our enemies are enriched. Our persecutors are swifter than the eagles of the air; they pursue on the mountains, and lie in wait for us in the wildernesses; we have found no rest; our cities are captured, our gates broken down, our priests sigh, our virgins are in affliction. From Ireland all her beauty is departed; they that were fed delicately have died in the streets; they that were brought up in scarlet have embraced the dung; when her people fell there was no helper. All that has*

ever been devised by the ingenuity of most cruel tyrants,
either in unparalleled ignominy and degradation, or in
the savage and excruciating corporal torture, or in all
that could strike terror into the firmest soul – all has been
poured out on Ireland by the Puritans … Some of our
priests they put in chains and dungeons – that was the
most lenient punishment; others they tortured with stakes
and strapadoes; some were shot to death, others hanged or
strangled …

It may well be the case that some of the deeds of his father, like those described above, were ascribed to Barry Lowe thus embellishing his reputation as a monstrous individual. What *is* factually known about the family is that William had at least two sons – Barry and Ebenezer – and that both were heavily involved on King William's side in the Battle of the Boyne. Barry Lowe, who was the younger of the two, was a commissioner for raising supplies for King William's army. Ebenezer was killed on the muddy banks of the Boyne on 2 July 1690, leaving Barry as the sole heir to his father's estate and the large residence that had been built near to the ancient Newtown Castle. Only in his twenties, he was already an extremely wealthy individual and, with an annual rental income from his lands of almost one thousand pounds, he certainly had no need to hunt priests for what to him would have been a paltry twenty pounds.

One of the priests Barry Lowe was known to have persecuted was Fr James Dillon who had been ordained in Galway in 1688, spending some years in France before returning to Ireland, whereupon he began to illegally exercise his clerical duties. Although the bounty of twenty pounds had yet to be introduced, priests were still pursued with vigour by the authorities and their supporters, and a tale is recounted in the *Annals of Westmeath* of an incident involving Fr Dillon and a priest hunter who may have been a relation of Barry Lowe. On an August night in 1697, a trusted parishioner brought word to the farmhouse where the priest had been given shelter of a dying man in need of the final sacraments. Having reached the man's cabin safely he performed his duties, bade farewell to his hosts and set off into the night, which was said to be starlit and windless. As he ascended a small incline that was covered with furze bushes, the stillness of the night was broken by the sound of heavy panting and hastening footsteps and he turned to see the dark figure of a priest hunter rushing at him, a blood-hound on a leash straining to leap at the terrified cleric. He turned and fled towards his farmhouse sanctuary with man and beast in close pursuit. Running and stumbling through the wild countryside Fr Dillon enjoyed a touch of good fortune when the dog became entangled in a patch of briars; this not only halted it in its tracks, but its agonised yelps alerted the farmer in the cottage ahead that something was amiss. Abandoning the dog, the hunter continued his pursuit, and it is said that several times the priest felt the man's fingers grasping at his coat, but somehow managed to extricate himself. Within sight of the cottage he finally stumbled and the priest hunter was upon him in a moment, his hands clasping around the cleric's throat. But the priest hunter's success was short lived, for a moment later gunfire shattered the silence as a musket ball fired by the farmer ripped through the man's heart and he fell dead by the priest's side. The yelping animal was soon after put out of its misery and silence fell over the countryside once more. Fr Dillon had a lucky escape, but it wouldn't be his last brush with the hunters. It is difficult to know if the tale is apocryphal or based in fact, but it certainly wouldn't have been unheard of for a peasant to kill a member of the landed gentry in defence of his priest, or for patriotic reasons, especially in a remote country landscape far from the eyes of the authorities.

The entire Lowe family, who were spread throughout the county, had a reputation for hunting down priests and according to the *Annals of Westmeath* members of the Lowe house hanged several priests and persecuted and imprisoned many others. George Lowe, who was Barry's uncle, had been granted lands to the northwest of Newtown in the general area in which Fr Dillon had his narrow escape. Considering that Fr Dillion was said to have been persecuted for almost his entire life by the Lowes, it is possible that the dead priest hunter was a member of this branch of the Lowe family.

In 1704 Fr Dillon was registered at Mullingar as 'Popish priest of Ardnorcher and Kilbride' and was recorded as being forty-five years of age. Crucially though he had failed to take the Oath of

Abjuration which made him officially an outlaw. Yet he managed to remain at large for at least ten years, during which time Barry Lowe had made several unsuccessful attempts to track him down, posses of men trawling the woods and shallow glens of the county, yet repeatedly failing to outwit the network of lookouts and safe-houses that served the priest.

In 1714 Fr Dillon's name cropped up in official documents in relation to an enquiry by the High Sheriff of Westmeath about progress in tracing several outlaw priests.

> *17 June 1714*
> *In the barony of Moycashell there hath been diligent*
> *search made for one James Dillon a Popish priest who is*
> *registered but hath not taken the Oath. He cannot be yet*
> *found.*
> *J. WEST.*

But Barry Lowe was relentless in his pursuit and not long after the above report he finally got his man. Lowe's information led him to a place called Shureen near Kilbeggan where the priest was celebrating mass in a woodland. He and his party managed to outfox the lookouts and left the priest no opportunity to remove his vestments and vanish into the crowd. Some accounts state that Lowe, ignoring the pleas for mercy from the peasants, had the priest cuffed and marched to Mullingar Gaol, a distance of some twenty miles, others that he had Fr Dillon tied with ropes and he then proceeded to drag the man across the countryside. This version is probably an exaggeration, as it seems unlikely that Fr Dillon could have survived such an ordeal. Even so, aged almost sixty (which was considered quite old in the early eighteenth century), the march to Mullingar must have taken a huge toll on him. Folklore then recounts a colourful incident during the march, which led to a popular verse and phrase that was still in use in the county a century and a half later. The crowd who had followed Lowe and his gang continued to plead for the priest's release and at one point the priest hunter is said to have turned and yelled at them 'May the devil blind me if I do!' Whether it is pure invention on behalf of a local storyteller or by a striking coincidence, Barry Lowe was said to have become temporarily blind soon after, which was taken by the peasants as a Catholic God's retribution and led to the phrase 'You're as blind as Barry Lowe' becoming a common remark in Westmeath for subsequent generations. A short rhyme was also composed to recall the incident:

> *Barry Lowe you all do know,*
> *He was very ill inclined,*
> *He dirtied on the altar,*
> *And the devil knocked him blind*

In the meantime Fr Dillon had been incarcerated in Mullingar Gaol, but the forced twenty-mile march had taken a heavy toll and he became seriously ill. Surprisingly, the *Annals of Westmeath* suggest that such was his state of health that he may have been released on compassionate grounds, which although not at all common at the time, did occasionally happen because of the efforts of some of the more sympathetic Protestant magistrates. There is no record of Fr Dillon ever being arrested again, either by Lowe or anyone else and the year of his death is unknown. However it is known that upon his death he was succeeded as parish priest by a man who was just sixteen at the time of Fr Dillon's imprisonment, which suggests that he lived for many years after his release. He is said to be buried in the old churchyard at Kilbride.

Others were less successful in evading the clutches of Lowe and Westmeath's other priest hunters. Documents at the time reporting on the status quo of known priests in the area record the deaths of several priests including Fr Charles Deal of Ballintullagh and Fr Francis Fitzsimons of Rathconrath, and although the circumstances of their demise in not recounted, both officiated in parishes that were just a few miles away from Lowe's manor in Newtown. Local folklore also recalled the capture of an unnamed priest while he was celebrating mass at a place called Comagh. This is a mere stone's throw from Shureen, where Lowe had captured Fr Dillon. The priest was taken to a lane close to Lowe's manor that would subsequently earn the grim name of 'Murdering Boreen' and summarily hanged. This lane was said to be Lowe's favoured execution place.

Another who may have met his end at Lowe's hands is Fr James Dalton, who was the Parish Priest of Ballymore. His parish is a short ride from the Newtown estate and the mass rock he used may still be seen today close to the village, bearing the inscription – *Me fieri fecit Joannes Dalton, Sacerdos. 29 Aug., Anno Domini 1689* – which essentially gives the date of the mass rock's consecration. Fr Dalton was lambasted by some for swearing the Oath of Abjuration in 1709 when he was aged sixty and given the nickname 'Solomon' after the King of Israel who'd turned to idolatry, yet he continued to secretly carry out his duties and tradition holds that he was caught celebrating mass and executed. As no official executions of priests were recorded in Westmeath around that time, it is quite possible that Lowe, who was at his most active in those years, perpetrated the killing. A local GAA club, Fr Dalton's, is named in his memory.

Barry Lowe had taken some time out from his priest-hunting activities to get married in 1711 to a woman called Anne Pilkington, who came from another family of Westmeath's landed gentry. His wife would bear him five sons and four daughters, the first-born of whom, Ebenezer, rose to the position of High Sheriff of County Westmeath in 1739, but married contrary to his father's wishes and was disinherited. All the other sons would die without issue. According to Woods in *The Annals of Westmeath* Barry Lowe was of such a nasty disposition that he didn't reserve his cruelties for Catholics alone:

> [Lowe] ... *had a wife and children and such was the savageness of his nature that even on them he did not*

bestow ordinary affection.

And the lengths to which he was prepared to go are illustrated somewhat by an incident at a limestone cave, possibly Poll na gCat, which had been doubling as a secret Catholic chapel, at least until an informer led Barry Lowe and a bunch of hirelings to the location at dawn early one Sunday morning. The priest hunter concealed himself and his gang some distance from the cave entrance and waited and watched as the peasants filed into the cavern, the priest disguised as one of them. When the last of the worshippers had entered the cave Lowe and his men descended upon the entrance before any warning could be given, trapping those inside. He yelled for the priest to surrender but all he got in reply was the echo of his own voice from the dark hollow. Rather than risk entering, Lowe then decided to burn everyone out, and ordered his men to gather tinder and the abundant furze bushes that grew about the entrance. This was piled into the narrow mouth of the cave, which was then blocked by a wall of rubble to prevent anyone escaping – in other words he intended to suffocate everyone to death. A torch was then tossed over the rubble and the piled up brush was soon billowing with flames, thick choking smoke filling the cavern. Soon the blaze was so intense that lumps of rock about the cave entrance began to split and crumble, further blocking the entrance.

Yet after several minutes none of the anticipated screams for mercy or the gasping and coughing of the dying peasants could be heard. Frustrated, Lowe ordered one of his men to climb above the cave in case there was another means of escape and, sure enough, the man immediately spotted a plume of smoke rising from a field some distance away. He ran to the spot where he found only the multiple tracks of the congregation leading away in all directions, but not a soul was in sight.

Luckily for the priest and his parishioners, the limestone cave in which they were trapped had many of the characteristic channels created by water dissolving the limestone over the eons, and the moment Lowe's voice was heard demanding their surrender, most of the parishioners wasted no time in departing. The story, later recounted by the peasants, was that when the smoke began to billow about those remaining, they urged the priest to change into his disguise and flee, but the man refused as he was in the midst of the Consecration of the Eucharist (the Catholic belief in the transubstantiation of the bread and wine into the flesh and blood of Christ). Ignoring the pleas of his coughing and spluttering flock to run, he carried solemnly on until the rite was complete, at which point he also took to his heels and made his escape before Lowe's man arrived on the scene. His dedication to his faith won him even greater admiration in the locality.

Lowe, on the other hand, had cursed the news of their escape and in the hope that some had suffocated before they could flee, waited until the fire died down, cleared a path through the rubble and ventured into the cave with several men bearing torches. A long winding channel finally led them to a large hollow in which an altar had been constructed on a shelf of projecting limestone, decorated with a cross, a chalice, candles and flowers. All that remained of his prey were the countless footprints leading to the narrow escape route. He may not have earned his reward that day, but his action earned him the reputation of a pitiless brute who was willing to sacrifice the lives of men, women and children in his attempts to satisfy his hatred for the Catholic Church and its priests. The reputation would accompany him to his grave.

One further tale survives of Lowe's doings, that of the occasion when he used the common trap of summoning a priest under false pretences. He is said to have bribed a female servant to induce her husband to feign sickness, presumably by giving him some form of potion. Lowe would then secretly observe the disguised priest administering the sacraments and have the necessary evidence to seize him. For whatever reason the unfortunate husband, who had been in perfectly good health, actually died before the priest reached the house. This event is said to have shocked even Lowe, either because he believed he'd witnessed some form of divine retribution or possibly because he might find himself accused of being an accessory to murder.

Although many of the stories concerning Lowe were lost as the tradition of local storytelling began to die out, it can certainly be gleaned from the surviving accounts in books such as *The Annals of Westmeath* by James Woods and *The Diocese of Meath Ancient and Modern* by Rev. Anthony Cogan that the man was at the very least a bigot with a brutal temperament who showed little or no mercy to his victims. Mental instability was said to run in his family, the last of whom reputedly died in a mental asylum around the turn of the nineteenth century. It is possible that Barry Lowe was among those so afflicted as, if his reputation is only partially deserved, he would still be numbered among the most callous priest hunters of the era, particularly as he had no monetary need of the rewards on offer. The bounty on Catholic clergymen was merely a convenient excuse to indulge in a bigoted pastime.

Barry Lowe lived a relatively long life and when he died in 1735 he left over four thousand pounds to his offspring – wealth impossible to comprehend for the ordinary peasant. But as his children included no male heirs, his line became extinct at the end of the century and his manorial house fell into ruins.

All that remained of Barachia Lowe was a memory execrated by the people of Westmeath and tales of a fiend recounted on dark nights for generations to come.

EDWARD TYRRELL

A BOUNDER AND A CAD

T he kindest thing that can be said of Edward Tyrrell is that he never killed any priests or was personally violent towards his captives. Beyond that it is difficult to source material that suggests he ever displayed anything approaching compassion, honour or honesty, or even that he might have had an understanding of such concepts. His short life was a cocktail of greed, lying, betrayal, covetousness, lechery and crime. The introduction of a law that offered a bounty on the capture of priests was for Tyrrell merely a joyful happenstance, a calling that fell from heaven when his other career paths had failed.

The place and date of his birth are unknown, but his subsequent pursuit of women and the frequency and energy of his priest-hunting activities suggest a relatively young man, so he was likely born circa 1680, putting him around his thirties when his career in the pursuit of Catholic clergymen commenced, around 1710, or within months of the 'bounty' law appearing on the statute books. One description of him survives, which is hardly flattering:

> ... *a lusty man, well set and made, with the sign of the*
> *small pox in his face, hollow-ey'd, bigg-mouth'd, round*
> *nos'd, thick-legg'd.*

Given his apparent ability to win the hearts of a substantial number of women during his lifetime, one might assume that Tyrrell possessed some degree of charm, as it was hardly because of his Adonis-like looks.

Unlike most other priest hunters who tended to limit their activities to their immediate county or area, Tyrrell's travels encompassed Dublin, Louth, Monaghan, King's County (Offaly), Wexford, Wicklow, Tipperary and Cork, not to mention his foray into the Irish Catholic refuge in Louvain in Belgium and his visits to England. The information he frequently supplied on the numbers of Catholic clergy in Ireland was often wildly exaggerated, as were his reports on priestly plots of rebellion and attempts to place the Pretender on the throne. He also somehow found time to marry at least four times and his weakness for women would ultimately prove his undoing, and in the grimmest possible fashion.

When he married first is unknown, but in 1708 he was wed to a Miss O'Flaherty, who happened to be the daughter of the renowned historian Roderick O'Flaherty, the last recognised head of the O'Flaherty clan, who had lost most of their large estates after the Cromwellian invasion. Tyrrell, like his father-in-law, was a member of the *déclassé* gentry, a Catholic whose formerly-wealthy family had lost most of their possessions. Previous generations of this class of Catholic would have enjoyed a substantial income from leasing large estates to tenants, much like the upcoming Protestant Ascendancy who followed them. They would also have been well represented in the professional classes as barristers, doctors, accountants and so on. After the introduction of the Penal Laws, many of these people were forced to survive on a greatly reduced income from a smaller land holding. And a great number of professionals were forced to flee to continental Europe to earn a decent living, as although a Catholic who was, for example, a qualified barrister before the introduction of the Penal Laws, could still legally practise, few of the Protestant community would deal with him, and there was little business to be had from the impoverished Catholics. Among those who still managed to remain in Ireland and retain some of their wealth either through stealth or with the sympathetic assistance of a local Protestant, it was common to send children abroad for an education. Edward Tyrrell was one who benefitted so, and his family had provided him with a good education in Europe. Despite his learning, it seems that Tyrrell was unable or unwilling to provide for himself and his wife as sometime in 1708, O'Flaherty wrote to his friend, the influential scholar and future MP Samuel Molyneux telling of his son-in-law's distressed condition and asking if he could use his influence to secure Tyrrell 'the place of a boatman in her Majesty's boat in Gallway.'

Strangely, he also included the necessary qualification that Tyrrell was a Protestant, which suggested that by this point Tyrrell had decided his interests would be best served by converting, or more likely by pretending he had converted.

For unknown reasons, Tyrrell's career on the high seas foundered. Within a year of him embarking on a seafaring occupation, the substantial bounty on priests was introduced and six months later he'd decided on his true calling. If his subsequent tales were to be believed, he had spent the previous months engaged in an elaborate clandestine operation that had uncovered a mammoth plot involving both Catholics and prominent Protestants to usurp Queen Anne and replace her with James Francis Edward Stuart, 'The Old Pretender'. Early in January 1710, he took a ship to England, his life in such peril, he claimed, that he had to disguise himself as a woman during the journey. Arriving in Chester, he managed to gain an audience with Governor Brook, who was so alarmed at Tyrrell's news that he furnished him with a letter of introduction to Lord Cholmondeley in London, who had commanded the Horse Guards at the Battle of the Boyne and would no doubt provide a sympathetic ear. A week later, Tyrrell had managed to travel as far as Coventry where he wrote to Edward Hopkins, the city's MP who at that time was resident in London, asking him to direct Coventry's Lord Mayor to ensure he was given safe conduct to the capital, as apparently the conspiratorial forces of evil were hiding around every corner and were intent on doing away with him before he could deliver his revelations. His letter was suitably dramatic to convince Hopkins:

> *Honoured Sir,*
>
> *Though a stranger I made bould to trust you with those following lines. That I have left Dublin the 4th of this instant in Women's aparell and … that I have come out of Ireland in order to make a full discovery to the Queen and Parliament of Great Britain in Relation of a Private Rebellion Intended and upon footing now in our kingdom and a great number of disaffected persons to our Government hath lately landed in the Remoat parts of our kingdom. They are harboured and entertained and supported by men of very great Interest and Quality in our Country Prodestands as well as papists. I desire the favour of you as you are a Member of Parliament for this town where I now am at present that you may please to order the Mayor of this city to manage some way to send me safe to St. James or else to your lodgings in London. Sir without your directions I dare not travell further than this citty of Coventry. I fear there is some evil design intended against me upon the Road. I rest your Honors humble servant.*
>
> *EDWARD TYRRELL.*
>
> *14th of January 1710.*

Arriving in London about a week later, Tyrrell managed to stir sufficient alarm that he was introduced to Secretary of State,

Henry Boyle, who immediately instructed him to draw up a memoir to be presented to the Queen-in-Council, which effectively meant the government.

Given Tyrrell's apparent skill at gaining access to such prominent figures and his apparent credibility, it can be speculated that whatever else can be said about the man, he surely had the gift of the gab and could present himself as a serious-minded gentleman with only Britain's interest at heart. We can glean a first hint of his underlying motives in a letter he sent to Boyle a few days later in which he informed the secretary that he had put the details of the supposed popish plot to paper as commanded, but signs off with the following plea:

> *I am ready to attend your Honor as soon as you shall*
> *think fit though not in a condition, for want of cloathes*
> *and humbly beggs your Honor to grant me some present*
> *reliefe in order to cover my nakedness.*

The next day he forwarded his 'intelligence' to Secretary Boyle and once again begged 'a smile of his favours'. Among the information he supplied was the revelation that one Edmund Kennedy, the son of the late Baronet Sir Richard Kennedy of Dublin (a Protestant) was a practising Catholic priest.

> *He [Tyrrell] knows Edmund Kennedy the Son of Sir*
> *Richard Kennedy late of the County of Dublin, baronet.*
> *The said Edmund Kennedy goes under the name of Joseph*

Reeves. He is a frier of the Order of St Francis and titular
Bishop of Dublin. The said Edmund goes disguised in
a lay habit with a sword by his side and daily frequents
various public places. This Informant saw the said Ken-
nedy in Ireland in July last disguised as one Jones amongst
the Romish clergy.
March 21, 1710.

Tyrrell's 'evidence' in this matter is a mixture of blatant lies and error. For one, Sir Richard Kennedy, who had died recently, had no male heirs. (See panel – A Family at War). It is possible Tyrrell may have confused someone from Sir Richard's family with a member of the clan's other branch, but there are no records of an Edmund in this line either. Or else the entire thing was pure invention – something that would have been difficult to check from London at short notice. Whether this was a genuine error or not, Tyrrell's claim that 'Edmund Kennedy' was the Bishop of Dublin was an outright lie, as Edmund Byrne held the post at the time.

A FAMILY AT WAR

The Kennedy clan referenced by Edmund Tyrrell give us an interesting insight into how different strands of the same family fared during this repressive period of Irish history. During the Cromwellian era Sir Robert Kennedy converted to Protestantism and subsequently acquired a large estate at Kishoge in Wicklow. He was also MP for Kildare, and it was this man who gave his name to the town of Newtownmountkennedy in Wicklow.

Sir Robert had a brother however, Alderman Walter Kennedy, who had remained a Catholic and who at that time owned Finnstown Castle in County Dublin. Not surprisingly the brothers appear to have fallen out because of their alternate loyalties and religions. Walter's grandson, Thomas, would ultimately be forced to flee Ireland. He would serve as *aide-de-camp* to Richard Talbot, the Catholic Duke of Tyrconnell during the Williamite Wars, and then on to Spain where he would command a Spanish regiment under Philip V.

On the other hand, Sir Robert's great-grandson was the Fourth Baronet Sir Richard Kennedy – the man referenced by Tyrrell – and successive generations of his family had continued to enjoy the privileges of the successful and wealthy land-owning classes, along with prominent political offices such as Baron of the Irish Exchequer. This branch of the family was very loyal to the crown and it is highly unlikely any one of them would have become a Catholic priest. Upon Richard's death in 1709/10, this line of the Kennedy family ended. There is no record of his having a son called Edmund.

Tyrrell's great conspiracy theory – that rebels were massing in the remote corners of Ireland – seems to have been given little credence, but his evidence did create quite a stir and the matter would soon be before the House of Commons. The English Council was incensed at the notion of so many priests operating in Ireland and swaggering about armed with swords and over the coming year there were countless arrests, not to mention harsh reprimands to the authorities throughout Ireland for being so lax in their duties:

> *Resolved that it appears to this House that several popish titular Bishops and regular clergymen of the Church of Rome are lately come into this kingdom and continue the succession of the Romish priesthood by ordaining great numbers of popish clergymen. Resolved that the laws now in force against popish Bishops and regulars coming or returning into this kingdom are defective in the detection of such persons and their harbourers ...*
> *21 June 1710.*

> *To Wm Butler Esq. at Ennis.*
> *... in answer to which his Excellency and their Lordships are extreamely surprised to find there are so many popish priests in your County and no account from you of your having seized and committed any of them to Gaole in pursuance of his Excellencies and their Lordships express*

> *commands signified in my letter of the 26th of last month.*
> *I am again to repeat to you their former commands in*
> *causing all popish priests, whether they have taken the*
> *Oath of Abjuration or not or whether they are registered*
> *or not to be immediately seized and committed to Gaole.*
> *Dublin Castle 4 March 1711*
> *J. DAWSON.*

Tyrrell meantime was amply rewarded for his services and sent back to Dublin and within months he had been arrested for bigamy and sent for trial, having either married again while still married to Roderick O'Flaherty's daughter or it having been discovered that he already a wife at the time of the marriage, or both. The trial record has been lost, but it is possible that the O'Flahertys brought his bigamous behaviour to the attention of the law as Tyrrell would subsequently take a measure of revenge by naming O'Flaherty's son Edward as a leading instigator of another outlandish plot against the crown. Bigamy at the time was considered an offence against God and the state that greatly offended public morality and could result in harsh penalties up to and including the death penalty, depending on the precise nature and seriousness of the individual offence.

Tyrrell was found guilty sometime during 'Trinity Term' of 1710, which meant between April and June, and part of his punishment might seem barbaric to modern sensibilities as he was sentenced to be 'burnt in the hand', which involved using a red-hot branding iron to make a permanent scar on the back of his hand, a punishment that was extremely painful and also subjected the individual to public humiliation for life. However he also apparently was given some form of jail sentence, a fact we only know because on 25 July of that year, a notice was issued for his arrest as he had apparently escaped from Newgate Prison by knocking out the gaoler. The piece also reveals the man's fondness for going under false names, something he most likely used when marrying bigamously:

> *A man called Edward Tyrrell alias Captain Burke alias*
> *Fitzgerald, and goes by several other names; he is a*
> *lusty man, well set and made, with the sign of the small*
> *pox in his face, hollow-ey'd, bigg-mouth'd, round nos'd,*
> *thick-legg'd, burnt in the left hand last term and mark'd.*
> *He hath a black suit of English cloth, and speaks but*
> *indifferent English; he formerly went into all parts of this*
> *kingdom, and pretended he came out of France, so went*
> *by the name Mac-guier, and then followed priest-catch-*
> *ing: made his escape out of her majesty's gaol of Newgate*
> *on Thursday last being the 20th of this inst. July 1710. If*
> *any person apprehends the said Tyrrell, so as the keeper of*
> *the said gaol gets him into his custody, he shall have two*
> *guineas reward paid by the said keeper. The said Tyrrell*
> *knockt down the turn-key of the said gaol and is now*
> *languishing in his bed.*

There is a certain justice in the fact that for a brief period at least, Tyrrell would have been subjected to living his life in the shadows, out of sight of the law or potential bounty hunters and informers.

What happened to him in the intervening months is a mystery, but incredibly, by December of that year Tyrrell would be in the employ of the Privy Council in Dublin, with his conviction for bigamy just a memory. Testimony at a later hearing revealed that no less than Joshua Dawson, the Secretary for Ireland, had furnished Tyrrell with a pass permitting him to go under the name of Edward Fitzgerald (an alias he'd used before, as referred to in the escape notice), and travel back to London, from whence he would go on to France. One can only speculate that the authorities were aware of Tyrrell's Catholic background, his education in France and his enthusiasm for priest hunting, and decided to forget the fact that he was a convicted felon and employ him as a spy. Probably mindful of the recent criticism from London concerning the influx of priests into the country, the authorities had decided to try and infiltrate one of the key sources of returning priests – the Irish College in Louvain. His instructions were to obtain as much information as possible about Catholic clergy who were likely to return.

Tyrrell must have leapt at the chance to redeem himself in the eyes of the law and to potentially make some money, as within days he had travelled back to London from where he took a ship to Ghent. Although his intended destination was Louvain, Tyrrell managed to provide a bonus for the authorities before he even reached the town, claiming that he'd met one Fr Lynch with whom he'd formerly been acquainted and who, Tyrrell alleged, had often expressed his wish that the Pretender be returned to the throne. Having duly noted Fr Lynch's treasonous opinions, he continued on his way to Louvain where he made his way to the Irish College. Questioned by the guardian as to his identity (the Catholic Church was aware that Britain had a network of spies and informers operating on the continent), Tyrrell decided not to use the alias provided and instead passed himself off as Edward, the son of Roderick O'Flaherty, his estranged father-in-law. O'Flaherty's name would have been held in some regard as an eminent Catholic historian who had been robbed of his land and titles, and Tyrrell's skillful line of blarney (helped no doubt by his Catholic education) was accepted and he was admitted to the college.

Elements of Tyrrell's later report (a long rambling document of almost a thousand words that contains virtually no punctuation) no doubt contained some truth, but were it to be believed in its entirety, every member of the Irish Catholic clergy from lowliest curate to the cardinals were involved in a dastardly plot to raise a rebellion in Ireland and usurp Queen Anne.

> *... the whole management of the heads of those Cloysters and Colledges tended to the bringing in of the Pretender into the kingdom of Great Brettagne; and to forward*

the intreige they declared they had sent several Popish
Bishopps into Ireland in order to manage that design and
to incense the Popish inhabitants of that kingdom to a
rebellion ...

He also provides the names of over twenty curates, priests
and bishops, with whom he makes dubious claims to have had a
former personal acquaintance. Despite the fact that he'd passed
himself off as Edward O'Flaherty, he provided information that
the real Edward O'Flaherty was in the process of raising a rebellion and that his followers were those responsible for the agrarian attacks in Connaught. His intelligence may have been acted
upon, but a hint of scepticism on the part of the authorities back
in Dublin can be gleaned from the fact that they learned that
Tyrrell had returned to Ireland in December but had not been
seen for over three months and it was March of 1712 before he
came forward seeking his reward. Asked why he had not made
his report immediately, Tyrrell claimed to have been 'taken so ill
with a pleurisy and ague that he was not able to make his application' and had been forced to recover his health in the Wicklow
countryside. What he'd been up to for the intervening months
is anyone's guess, but at some time since his previous conviction
for bigamy, Tyrrell had married for a third or fourth time, to one
Miss Jane Moore. Astonishingly in 1712 he would also marry a
girl called Miss Margaret Clerk. His three-month absence was
possibly because he didn't wish to be in too close contact with the

highest law-making authorities in the land when he was involved in the extremely illicit and dangerous activity of bigamy. But the authorities did act on at least some of the information provided and upon learning of their return to Ireland, issued arrest warrants for Hugh McMahon, Bishop of Clogher and Fr Florence McNamara in Clare, two of those named by Tyrrell.

Yet some of those in positions of authority were beginning to smell a very large rat. A letter from Dublin Castle later that year would include the comment:

> ... *the only information we ever had of that kind was from Edward Tyrrell to whose credit you are no stranger and though he has often told us both priests and officers are lately come from France into Ireland yet we could never get the fact proved by any other testimony than his own ...*

It wouldn't be the first or last time doubt would be cast on the reliability of the priest hunter's information. Yet despite the scepticism that was being felt by some, clearly Tyrrell still enjoyed the trust of others of influence. He seems to have made some impression with persons of high office in England and very likely exploited their paranoia about invading Catholic hordes, which was rampant at the time in British society. For whatever reason, he continued to be granted the favour of the authorities in Dublin and the following year he would be commissioned to conduct major priest hunts in Offaly (then King's County),

Louth, Wicklow and Cork. Perhaps because he suspected that his intelligence was itself under suspicion, Tyrrell this time at least appears to have done his homework and met with partial success. Considering the nature and extent of the information he provided it seems likely he spent some time in each county disguised as either a priest or an ordinary Catholic worshipper, which would have been relatively easy for him given his education and his having spent so long in the Catholic college in Louvain. He also named several informers who provided him with information, purchased from the ample funds he was receiving from Dublin Castle. But as usual his subsequent claims were a mixture of fact and fiction; he did indeed capture several priests, but not content with that, exaggerated the numbers and importance of several of his captives. Later that year Tyrrell travelled to Louth where, with the assistance of a troop of soldiers, he arrested several priests around Ardee. But once again he provided greatly exaggerated reports of various other priests and their supposed harbourers. His information was embellished by the dropping of names such as that of Primate Hugh McMahon, about whom he gave vague information but an extensive search failed to lead to his capture. In one case he claimed to know for a fact that 'Dr Bardin, Bishop of Ferns' was present at an ordination – the man's name was actually 'Verdon'.

To Tyrrell, successes such as these were merely a means of lining his pockets so he could enjoy a philandering lifestyle among Dublin's finer taverns and inns, impressing gullible women with tall tales of his heroism and wealth and squandering his booty on wine and ale. To his victims, the priests he captured and the peasants he betrayed as helpers of the clergy, his actions meant the squalor of a long imprisonment followed by transportation or outright ruin for entire families.

Whatever his reputation at this point among the authorities, thanks to these miseries that he had brought upon the heads of numerous priests, he had clearly made a name for himself with the general Catholic populace, and a hated one at that. He was by now widely known as one of the most active priest hunters in the country, a hint of which can be seen when Tyrrell describes his attempt to have a letter delivered:

> … he was told that his letter would not be delivered
> to the Lord Chancellor for that his servants if they
> knew that the Letter came from this Examinate [Tyr-
> rell], would not deliver it. Saith that he went in person
> to the Lord Chancellor at his house who received this
> Examinate civilly and gave him half a guiney for his
> Encouradgement to proceed in his Discoveryes.

Another version of this story is given by a Symon Willoughby, a prosperous tallow chandler or candle maker with whom Tyrrell had acquainted himself. The priest hunter had asked Willoughby to take the letter to the Lord Chancellor on his behalf, which he did, but upon seeing Tyrrell's name, His Lordship declared the man to be 'a great rogue' and directed him to the Lord Mayor.

Tyrrell was eventually granted access to the Lord Mayor and presented 'evidence' of several priests recently arrived in Ireland, for which service he demanded money. The Lord Mayor refused and asked him to return when he knew the precise locations of the clergy, but he never saw the priest hunter again.

Tyrrell's expedition into King's County met with some success and besides his normal bounty, he was rewarded with a rare snippet of praise. Unfortunately for him his inquiries into the whereabouts of various priests seem to have fallen on the wrong ears and alerted many of his intended victims that they were about to be seized.

He first managed to discover the location of one Thomas Feaghny who he claimed was a bishop recently returned from the Court of the Pretender (Feaghny was certainly no bishop and later claimed he wasn't even a priest, but had merely been sent to Paris to study.) Tyrrell got short shrift when he approached the local magistrate John Moore Esq of Phillipstown (now Daingean), who was at first sceptical about the priest hunter's claims and said he 'did not care to concern himself with the matter'. Tyrrell naturally went directly to his employers who took the issue of a bishop who had been dispatched to Ireland by a possible usurper of the crown very seriously. Secretary Dawson immediately wrote to Moore and a fellow magistrate:

> *To John Moore, Esq. of Crochan and James Forth Esq. of Redwood near Phillipstown.*

Gentlemen Edward Tyrrell hath given an Examina-
tion on Oath that one Thomas Feaghny who is reputed
a Popish Bishop and came lately from St Germans now
lodges at the house of Mr Felix Coughlan neare Fairbane
and Tyrrell undertakes to have him apprehended there if
he may have sufficient assistance. The said Tyrrell likewise
informed the Justices and Council that there is a convent
of Fryers of the order of St. Dominicke at a place near
Fairbane called Fedan where a great number of them
constantly reside. Their Excellencies and Council hereby
signify their pleasure to you to go with the said Tyrrell
and require such assistance as you shall think necessary
and search the house of the said Felix Coughlan for the
said Thomas Feaghny and having apprehended him, to
secure him. Their Excellencies desire you will also endeav-
our to apprehend the Fryers said to be in said Convent
and commit them to Gaole. Tyrrell says he will make
further Discoveryes to you if you have but good assistance.
J. DAWSON. Dublin Castle 25 Oct. 1712.

In early November Tyrrell set off in the company of the magistrates and a troop of soldiers for Coughlan's house in Fairbane (Ferbane). It was a journey of almost thirty miles in foul
weather and through what was then wild, mostly uninhabited
countryside. Three miles from their destination Tyrrell seems to
have stopped off and spoken to one of his informers, learning

that Feaghny had since fled to a place called Cartron, which was fifteen miles back virtually in the direction they'd come. They located the large house late in the day with darkness closing around them, demanded entry and were met by servants who denied there were any priests in the house. A search gave the lie to their insistence, and Feaghny was indeed located and arrested. The owner, Felix Coghlan, was absent, but his wife, who was ill and near the point of death, pleaded with them not to take Feaghny, who she said was her physician. The tone of magistrate Moore's report suggests he felt some sympathy for her plight, but he was obliged to follow his orders and Feaghny was tied up, put on a horse and hauled away. The magistrate then led his troop off into the night towards Fedan, the alleged residence of numerous priests. When they came to the house they found that the clergy had apparently absconded, but they arrested two brothers, William and Redmund Kenny for harbouring the priests. As they were doing so, a drunken friend of the Kennys arrived on the scene and became incensed at the arrests, launching himself at the magistrates and troops. In the ensuing melee, Redmund Kenny managed to flee into the night. The exhausted troops' search continued, Tyrrell's intelligence directing them to the house of another man named Coughlan, who lived miles from anything resembling a road. There they did find ample evidence that a number of priests had been present, but all that remained were a few women. They would learn later that Coughlan had gotten word from his own informers of Tyrrell's designs and warned all the priests in the neighbourhood to make themselves absent. The search was abandoned in the early hours and a sense of the band's discomfort can be gleaned from Moore's subsequent report:

> *Our men and we rode from 5 o'clock on Monday morn-*
> *ing till 6 at night without any refreshment either to our*
> *selves or horses through as bad roads as I believe ever were*
> *Travelled and at night mett with very sadd entertainment*
> *and lodging at this place.*

Yet despite their meagre haul of two men, one a layman, Dublin Castle was well pleased and complimented Moore and his colleagues on a job well done. They directed that Feaghny be immediately conveyed to Dublin for trial, no doubt rubbing their hands at the capture of a prominent bishop. Moore for his part seems to have been impressed by Tyrrell's efforts and remarked in his report:

> *We think ourselves obliged to let you know that if Tyrrell*
> *had not been very vigilant and active, Feaghny had not*
> *been taken.*

But Dublin Castle's joy and Tyrrell's self-satisfaction was short lived as soon afterwards the case against 'Bishop' Feaghny collapsed and he was released.

Tyrrell's credibility was now stretched to breaking point. However, he did continue his efforts in King's County in early November and was involved in the arrest of several other priests, but once again his claims of success were greatly exaggerated. Only one of these was brought to court and the case against him also collapsed when the principal witness failed to appear.

During his time in the county it is also recorded – bizarrely, but perhaps unsurprisingly – that at one point Tyrrell was assaulted and beaten by an unnamed woman. The reason for the assault isn't given but considering that by this time he had at least four or possibly five Mrs Tyrrells around the country, one's imagination might easily fill in the blanks. The priest hunter's past – and his wives – were quickly catching up with him.

Later that same month he sought to redeem himself in the authorities' eyes by catching what was regarded as the biggest fish of all, the Archbishop of Dublin, Edward Byrne, who had long eluded their clutches. The current intelligence suggested that the Archbishop was hiding in Wicklow town, but searches led by several Justices of the Peace had proven fruitless. Enter the bold Tyrrell with certain information that Byrne was to be located in Drogheda, but an extensive hunt failed to locate the elusive clergyman. Whether his 'intelligence' was pure invention or based merely on loose gossip is a matter of speculation, but undaunted, Tyrrell now pronounced that Byrne had returned to Wicklow town and urged a fresh search of a house in the Wicklow mountains where they would find no less than fourteen 'officers and priests all lately come from abroad'. Not a sinner was captured and the manhunt leader's irritation at Tyrrell's unreliability is evident in his report:

I raised guards of both foot and horse with all privacy
imaginable and searched all suspected houses in our town
and found none, and Mr Allen and I Road [rode] to Red-
mond Byrnes in the Countrie and searched there also and
found none. All which gave us no small trouble. I am etc.
WILLIAM HAMILTON. Wicklow 20 Nov. 1712.

Tyrrell, not surprisingly, never succeeded in tracking down Archbishop Byrne, who would continue to evade capture for a further six years until John Garzia's information led to his arrest in Dublin. (Byrne's luck held even then as his trial collapsed and he remained free for the rest of his days.)

Yet the irrepressible Tyrrell was undaunted and made an excursion to Wexford the following month in search of more bounty. By now his reputation preceded him and he was met with a wall of scepticism. Clearly the Wexford magistrates weren't too keen on the prospect of spending long winter days and nights riding about the countryside on pointless searches. Tyrrell was incensed and wrote to Secretary Dawson:

To J. Dawson etc.
Most honord Sir, Send an order down in relation of
commanding assistance as it was to Mr Mone at Cap-
tain Starling. There is a management here to prevent my
Designe, which shall appear before the highest power. You
know my meaning. I doe not enlarge further till I see your
selfe. All their roguery again me shall not prevent what I

under took.

Your hons. most humble servt. E. TYRRELL.

Gory 22 Dec. 1712.

Not deterred by the uncooperative Wexford powers, he set off for Cork, stopping at Clonmel for a fortnight, during which brief time he reported to Dublin Castle several momentous discoveries; none less than a Cardinal, Thomas Ennis, was residing in the town, who 'has of late years been a great spy in the Court of England'; a bishop by the name of Bourk who he claimed he had seen officiating; a priest called Fr Adams who was supposedly building a private nunnery; several prominent Protestants who he alleged had accepted bribes to conceal the papists; information that nine hundred papists had lately landed in Ireland with 'no good design'.

His intelligence was considered by Dublin Castle, but Secretary Dawson had clearly had his fill by now and in a letter to a Justice of the Peace in Clonmel he remarked:

> *... I must inform you that the said Tyrrell has formerly given information of matters of this kind to the Lords Justices and Council, which he has not been able to make good, and that at this time has not any authority to go upon the service he pretends to do.*

In the meantime Tyrrell's situation was becoming increasingly perilous, and not just from the threat posed by outraged Catholic peasants. At one point he begs Dublin to provide him with protection, 'otherwise I shall be knockt in the head'. It wasn't forthcoming, possibly because Dublin Castle had been made aware that the priest hunter himself would soon be a target of the law and wished to dissociate itself from him. He was 'advised' to leave Clonmel by Mayor Wilkinson (who he had incensed by implying in a letter to Dublin that he could not be trusted), and he promptly continued on his way to Cork.

In February of 1713, Tyrrell adopted the *nom de plume* that he had employed with the approval of Secretary Dawson some years beforehand, that of Edward Fitzgerald. He used this to good effect, worming his way into Catholic society and garnering some useful information, which led to the arrest of two priests, Patrick Carthy and William Hennessy who were later sentenced to transportation. However he also claimed numerous other captures and indictments against various individuals he said were priests, which clearly raised the Cork Grand Juries' eyebrows as they allowed a small army of lawyers to cross-examine Tyrrell extensively, much to his annoyance, especially when, as he claimed, his only interest was in serving Her Majesty:

> *That your Petitioner (Tyrrell) has been for severall hours*
> *examined before the Grand Juries of the County and City*
> *of Cork when the said Grand Juries found severall other*
> *indictments against other disaffected persons, whereof*
> *your Petitioner gave the said Grand Juries an account*

> *(of) all this your Petitioner has done in her Maiesties*
> *behalf. Notwithstanding that Counsellor Patrick French*
> *of Dublin and Councellor French of Cork and Counsel-*
> *lor Charter with severall other Lawyers were feed (paid to*
> *act) against your Petitioner in order to stifle your Excel-*
> *lencye's Petitioner's evidence for her Maiestie.*

Before the end of the month Tyrrell was back in Dublin and although he didn't know it, his priest-hunting days were all but over. Several of his 'wives' had realised that their husband was already married and approached the authorities, and no sooner had Tyrrell set foot in the city than the sheriff arrived on his doorstep. He was carted off to Newgate Prison on 23 February 1713, from where he appealed to be bailed on the basis that the bigamy charge was a conspiracy of the papists, claiming:

> *It is only a trick putt upon him … I am a witness for the*
> *Queen, prevented from rendering service.*

Justice Nutley, who was asked to rule on the matter, was not impressed:

> *I humbly inform your Excellency that the petitioner*
> *stands indicted before me on Oath, for that he having a*
> *former wife living did in December last marry one Jane*
> *Moore. This crime is a felony, but it is certified to me by*
> *the Clerk of the Crown that the Petitioner was in Trinity*
> *Term 1710 tryed in her Maiesties Court of Queen's Bench*

for Bigamy and found guilty and burnt in the hand. So
that it is past all doubt that he is not bailable by law.
R. NUTLEY.

Confined within the squalid atmosphere of Dublin's Newgate Prison, Tyrrell resorted to writing long, self-glorifying testimonials to Dublin Castle in an effort to extract himself from his now perilous situation. In them he lists the innumerable captures of priests and documents he has made and stresses the value of his services in the fight against popery. Checking out the authenticity of every single one of the priest hunter's claims would have been hugely expensive and near-impossible on a practical level for the authorities, should they have been bothered to do so. But by this point it seems they were keen to cut the man adrift and no word of clemency reached Tyrrell's ears.

He was however due to appear in court in Cork and King's County to testify against a handful of priests he had successfully arrested and he seized upon this as a means of gaining at least a temporary release, embellishing his pleas with repeated claims that his confinement was entirely the result of a Catholic conspiracy and that his very life was in danger from other prisoners while he was held captive, which in all fairness, it surely was:

To their Excellencies the Lords Justices in Council.
I Edward Tyrrell have been bound over in five hundred
pounds bond to be in Cork the next assizes to prosecute

these affairs. I have been bound over by the Justices of Peace to be at the next Assizes at Phillipstown. I am able to do more service than is mentioned in this case notwithstanding I am confined by the management and spite of popery who spares no money to stifle my prosecution …

I am afraid every minute in this house to be destroyed by the management of the popish clergy and other convicted persons that do here reside. Even the very papishes come out of the street into the Gaol to abuse me in my confinement. I leave it to the Great God what misery I am in for serving her Majesty's government. I lye under no crime but what may be bailed by law according to the opinion of the recorder and others. If I be not bailed I should be very glad that your Excellency would give an order to have me transmitted as a prisoner as an evidence for the Queen to Phillipstown and Corke that all those prosecutions may not be stifled by the management of popery.

EDWARD TYRRELL.

Dublin Castle decided, in the interests of securing prosecutions, to agree to the priest hunter's request and ordered one Edward Shuldham, a councillor, to make the arrangements in March 1713.

Edward Tyrrell a prisoner in Newgate is to be sent to Phillipstown and Cork to prosecute Regulars at the next assizes. You are to attend at the said assizes to prosecute

> *in behalf of her Maiestie and you are to pay the expenses*
> *of Tyrrell, the sheriff's officer and messenger appointed to*
> *attend him and the horses of the two horsemen or Dra-*
> *goons ordered as a guard.*

The expedition to Cork and King's County was less than a resounding success and Shuldham later reported that the twenty or so indictments resulted in just a handful of convictions. Within a couple of weeks the cell door in Newgate was once again slammed in Tyrrell's face and any support he may have had among the influential in Dublin Castle was quickly evaporating. Despite his repeated claims of acting purely in the interests of Her Majesty, the authorities' correspondence gives us a sense of Tyrrell's true motives:

> *… we have done all in our power to encourage him in his*
> *discoverys and to endeavour upon his information to seize*
> *and apprehend such priests and officers. But we never*
> *could find any other effect from his service than to get*
> *money from us and you know he has given the very same*
> *information to some former governments.*

With his trial date rapidly approaching, the priest hunter realised he'd run out of friends and his desperation is evident in his continued letters listing the vast service he has given in the battle against popery and particularly in his suggestion that he has information of another great popish plot that will safeguard the future of the whole kingdom. It is also clear that he knows many of his claims are being met with outright scepticism and restates his belief that the bigamy charges are part of a great popish plot against him:

> ... *your Petitioner will further satisfie your Excellencies and lay before you severall matters of such weight and moment which shall be a wonderfull satisfaction to the whole Council and very much tend to the future safetie and welfare of her Majesty and all her good subjects. Your Petitioner would even now open the same but that he is sensible that some disaffected persons were of opinion that your Petitioner's late good services were but shams or lies. Sheweth That by the Invention and malice of severall Irish papists he is accused at present of marrying of two women and wrongfully impeached, and does protest upon the faith of a Christian that in the course of his life he had no manner of dealing with his prosecutor, but your Petitioner is informed that the said Irish papists as well clergy as laity all over the kingdom do unanimously joyne together towards his down fall...the said Irish papists will infallibly keep your Petitioner confined all the days of his life on pretence of some wicked practice or other if not prevented by your Excellencies.*
>
> *E. TYRRELL.*

His pleas fell on deaf ears. He now resorted to blackening

the character of the women – his wives – who had brought the charges of bigamy against him, claiming in a letter that Margaret Clerk is a 'common, lewd, debauched and disorderly woman', and that he can provide several witnesses to the fact. He goes on to assert that she had been bribed to appear against him and had received 'severall sumes of money and severall suits of Cloaths' and that she had previously been arrested herself and imprisoned in the Bridewell.

Of another of his accusers, Jane Moore, he lays the claim that she is part of the Catholic plot to destroy him and that she and her mother had been given fifty pounds to prosecute him and threatened by the Catholics that 'they would make her [Mrs Moore] fly the country and her daughter rott in gaol unless she prosecuted.'

But all his efforts were in vain as Tyrrell's mysterious witnesses were 'out of towne' and he was sent for trial on 9 May 1713, the record of which has unfortunately been lost. His sentence was much discussed however, and with particular satisfaction among Catholics. Tyrrell had indicated in an earlier letter a belief that he would be confined for the rest of his days, but his punishment would be far swifter. He was sentenced to be hanged the following day at Gallows' Hill (now Baggot Street).

COURTING DEATH

Although still a serious statutory offence in Ireland, in eighteenth century Britain and Ireland bigamy was among a long list of crimes that could carry a sentence of death. Among the principal reasons for this was that matrimonial practices in different countries were viewed as an indicator of the level of civilisation – those that practiced polygamy for example, were viewed as primitive or even savage. Bigamy therefore represented an attack on fundamental societal values. But although a harsh penalty, many other crimes that nowadays would be considered less than petty also carried the ultimate sentence. This was the phase in British legal history that came to be known as 'the bloody code' as by 1800, there were no less than two hundred and twenty crimes punishable by death. These included stealing a sheep, shoplifting of goods worth more than twelve pence (e.g. an embroidered handkerchief was one such item), cutting down a tree, being in the company of gypsies for one month, robbing a rabbit warren and 'strong evidence of malice' in a child aged seven to fourteen years. Most were introduced to prevent crimes against property, principally at the behest of the wealthy, but the number of actual executions did not reflect the myriad of offences carried out as often jurors took pity on the accused and found them guilty of a lesser crime. The introduction of transportation as an optional sentence further reduced the number of executions. The death penalty was officially abolished in Britain in 1965 and in Ireland in 1990. The last man executed in Ireland was Michael Manning, who was hanged for murder in Mountjoy Prison by the British executioner Albert Pierrepoint in 1954. Tom Pierrepoint, his uncle, had carried out the last execution of a woman – Annie Walsh, for murder – in 1925. At least their punishment would have been seen at the time as fitting the crime. In 1750 one Benjamin Beckonfield was hanged for stealing a hat.

In the desperate hope that his previous 'services' might earn him a reprieve he begged for a postponement, which was granted:

Upon application made to us by Edward Tyrrell a condemned prisoner in Newgate, we are pleased to grant a Reprieve to Saturday the 23rd day of May inst. and we hereby require the Sheriffs of the Citty of Dublin to forbeare execution to Saturday the 23rd day of May accordingly on which day the said Sheriffs are to cause the said sentence to be put in Execution.
Dublin Castle 13 May 1713.

But that was as clement as the Castle would become and no one rode to the priest hunter's rescue in the intervening fortnight. His final letter didn't beg a further reprieve however; he likely knew the game was up. Tyrrell is now reduced to begging that he will not be conveyed to his death in open disgrace, subject to the catcalls of a general populace who despised him:

> *To the Lords Justices Generall and General, Governors of Ireland.*
> *The humble petition of Edward Tyrrell.*
> *Sheweth That your Excellencies poore petitioner being convicted and sentenced to die on the 15th of May instant but being reprieved to the 23rd of same month and your Excellencies petitioner expecting nothing else but Death doth entreat your Excellencies for the tender mercy of almighty God to suffer your poor petitioner to be carried in a coach to the place of execution, your Excellencies petitioner being unwilling to be carried in a cart as Comonlye are thieves and Highway men. The premises tenderly considered may it therefore please your Excellencies to allow your poor petitioner to be caryed in a Coach to the place of execution and for soe doing your poor petitioner as in duty bound, will ever pray.*
> *EDWARD TYRRELL.*

There is no subsequent mention of his request being granted in the surviving documentation and it would seem that the priest hunter had to suffer the verbal slings and arrows of splenetic Dublin Catholics as the cart trundled its way over the cobbled streets to Gallows' Hill.

The report on his execution in the Dublin newspapers of the 23 May 1713, was brief, and did him the final indignity of misspelling his name:

> *This day, Terrel, the famous priest-catcher, who was condemned this term for having several wives, was executed.*

One can only imagine the cheers of the watching Dublin Catholics as the trapdoor opened beneath the priest hunter's feet and he was despatched to meet his maker.

SEAN NA SAGART

THE MAYO ASSASSIN

Unquestionably the most infamous of all priest hunters, Sean na Sagart's reputation was such that it spread all over Ireland and eventually became a generic term for men involved in this dubious trade. By the time of his death, every corner of the country had its own 'Sean na Sagart' and the lookout's warning cry on the approach of danger had become '*Sean na Sagart ag teacht!*' ('Sean na Sagart is coming!')

He inevitably became the stuff of dark legend, the central character of countless folk tales that soon became accepted as fact, and while there is no doubt about his existence in fact, it is likely the deeds of other hunters were wrongly ascribed to him. Many of these stories are even now still presented as reality and it is truly impossible to completely separate the actual truths of Sean's activities from the myths.

Among the wilder stories told are that he beheaded his victims and impaled their heads on the high gates at the entrance to the estate of his employer, a wealthy local landlord, as a warning to other priests. A different version claimed that the landlord paid him a bounty of twenty pounds for every priest's head he delivered, after which the heads were kept in the manor house's cellar like some sort of macabre trophy room. A third tale is told that Sean threw the heads into a small lough near his home and ever since the lough has been known as '*Lough na gCeann*' or 'The Lake of the Heads'. What is certain is that none of these stories have more than a slender thread linking them to the truth. Although times were often brutal in the early eighteenth century and the British crown was unquestionably ruthless and even violent in its suppression of Catholicism, to a large extent society had moved beyond such levels of barbarity by the time Sean na Sagart plied his trade; excepting times of war, when execution was carried out it was by hanging and performed by the state, and although atrocities did occur, they were the exception rather than the rule.

Unfortunately only one single lengthy document directly related to him survives, but it at least provides certain undisputed facts about his background and some insight into the extent of his priest-hunting activities. It is known that he was born John Mullowney or Mullowny around 1690 in Derrew in the townland of Skehanagh, County Mayo, about five miles directly to the north of Lough Mask. John Mullowney and his sister Nancy's parents died when they were in their childhood and they were left as orphans to fend for themselves. The brutal life he had been bequeathed almost inevitably made a brute of the growing man and in his teenage years he was seduced to join a band of rapparees. These were bandits or outlaws who took their name from a short-handled pike that was called a '*rapaire*' in Irish and who lived in the wilds of Ireland in the decades after the Jacobite defeat at the Battle of the Boyne. Originally the rapparees were guerrilla fighters who staged short, violent raids on English troops or the landed gentry, then vanished into the hills; the local community saw them as heroes. But as the years passed, many rapparees began to realise that raiding the properties of the Protestant landlords could be a profitable venture; stealing their horses, for example, was relatively easy and the beasts could be simply spirited away into the wilds for later sale. Having crossed the line from soldier to plunderer, many rapparee gangs even began to prey on the ordinary civilian population and were soon despised by all sides. The savage excitement of the banditry and the promise of easy money lured John Mullowney into a life beyond the law and alienated him from the people of his parish. He excelled as his new trade and early on in his life acquired a taste for strong drink. Said to be possessed of great physical strength, he had deep-set eyes and shaggy, dark-brown hair and probably appeared a fearsome figure to any of the gentry he encountered. Although utterly without education, he was gifted with a cunning that would serve him well in the years ahead and probably saved him from the hangman's noose.

Around the age of twenty his days as a rapparee and horse-thief came to their predictable end when he was captured by the authorities and brought to Castlebar for trial, where he was sentenced to be hanged.

It was fortunate for Mullowney that around the time of his arrest there was particular pressure to increase the numbers of priests seized as a result of a recently-passed edict from London that threatened severe penalties on the authorities who were negligent in this regard:

> *4 Anne, c. 2:*
> *All justices of the peace, sheriffs, high and petty constables*
> *and all other subjects are required to use their utmost*
> *diligence in apprehending clergymen of the popish reli-*
> *gion and other persons exercising the functions of a popish*
> *priest and not registered. If any mayor, justice of the peace*
> *or other officer, voluntarily shall neglect their duty in*
> *execution of this act every such mayor, justice of the peace*
> *and other officer, shall for every such neglect forfeit fifty*
> *pounds to be recovered by action of debt.*

Suddenly everyone was bending over backwards to show how active they were in pursuing Catholic clergymen and soon after the above edict was passed, Sir John Bingham, Fifth Baronet of Castlebar, convened a meeting of all Mayo magistrates to deal with the problem. Bingham would ultimately be John Mullowney's principal patron and was probably instrumental in saving his life. Another of those was John Vesey, the Protestant Archbishop of Tuam, Bingham's future father-in-law, who had recently complained of the laxity of the Connaught magistrates and about the influx of priests to the province:

> *There is a great resort of the Roman Catholic Gentlemen*
> *out of the other provinces to Galway to avoid the oath of*
> *abjuration. The Judges will find much opposition from*
> *the Roman Catholic Lawyers and the Gentry of this*
> *province.*
> *John Vesey, 22nd February 1712*

The High Sheriff of Galway was of the view that many of his own men were not to be relied upon:

> *Most of the Constables in this county are Papists and*
> *it is hard to trust them in this affair and especially [as*
> *regards] the priests who are in great numbers registered*
> *and unregistered. I have acquainted severall of the Justices*
> *of the Peace of the Lords Justices commands in relation to*
> *the priests and their meetings. It is a general rumour that*
> *there are several men with scarlet cloaks and that spake*
> *French go up and down the country by night. The Gentle-*
> *men in the county are in great feare and apprehension.*
> *David Power, High Sheriff, 26th February 1712*

Regarding the reference in Archbishop Vesey's letter to Catholic lawyers, although the Penal Laws denied Catholics education or entry into a profession, many lawyers and other professionals who had been educated prior to the laws of 1695 continued to practise. As for Sheriff Power reference to constables being Papists, Catholics were officially barred from the post, although some had converted or pretended to have converted to get employment.

Between the paranoia about Catholic constables, French-speaking cloaked figures stalking the land and threats from Dublin Castle, the magistrates became desperate to find a way to solve the problem. Sir John Bingham had his own solution – hire a bounty hunter.

Bingham, who was roughly the same age as Mullowney – a youthful twenty or so – clearly had no sympathy for the plight of Catholics, which had a certain irony as future generations of the family would be generous benefactors of the Catholic Church. He was a direct descendant of Sir Richard Bingham, the Governor of Connaught in the reign of Elizabeth, who had mercilessly suppressed dissent in the province. His father was Sir George Bingham who had actually fought on the side of James II in the Battle of Aughrim against the Williamite forces, but had deserted in the face of defeat and switched sides. John Bingham was an extremely wealthy and powerful man; his estates in Mayo totalled over twelve thousand acres and over five thousand in Galway. Ironically he was quite possibly a victim of John Mullowney's earlier career as a rapparee and horse-thief. His manor house, Newbrook, was just a few miles from Mullowney's birthplace and from the Partry Mountains, which had been the hiding place of many of the rapparees. It is quite likely that he was well aware of Mullowney's cunning and decided to turn it to his advantage.

As he sat in his prison cell in Castlebar Gaol, Gallows Hill visible a short distance away, John Mullowney, anticipating nothing but the long drop at the end of the rope, an official appeared with an offer he couldn't refuse. A full pardon would be granted on the basis that he renounce his criminal past and come to work for Sir John Bingham as his personal priest hunter.

In that moment John Mullowney ceased to exist and 'Sean na Sagart' – 'John of the Priests' – was born. (For simplicity's sake, this account will continue to use his real name). Sir John Bingham, anxious to be seen in Dublin as a zealous enforcer of the anti-Catholic laws, promised to personally pay him the bounty of twenty pounds for every priest he captured and put the local troops at his disposal to use in his hunts.

The extent of the priest hunter's activities in the years immediately after he gained his freedom is not known, although he did provide testimony some years later that in the year of his release he'd witnessed two of the most-sought after outlaw clergymen performing Catholic ceremonies. These were James Lynch, Titular Archbishop of Tuam, and Vicar General Francis Burke who engaged in a lengthy correspondence under the aliases of Dominic Deane and Miles Stanton:

> *The Examination of John O'Mullowny of Ballyheane ...*
> *saith that he (Mullowney) knows Francis Burke of the*
> *County of Gallway to be reputed Vicar Generall and*

James Lynch Titular Archbishop of Tuam, and that he
hath known the said Francis Burke to divorce severall
couples from the Bonds of Marriage particularly Thomas
Paddin and Mary Mannin att Ballheane in the County
of Mayo in the house of Edmund Costello parish priest of
Ballheane ...

As will be seen later, it is likely much of the priest hunter's testimony was fabricated. The authorities were desperate to catch Burke and Lynch who had evaded capture for years and they wanted firm proof that the pair were no mere priests, but clergymen of high standing. Mullowney provided the evidence that Burke and Lynch were a Vicar General and an Archbishop respectively, although it seems highly unlikely he would be privy to the appointments and titles secretly bestowed on outlaw clergymen by Rome. That said, it is probable that for several years the young Mullowney was acting as a paid informer on Bingham's behalf, returning to his own parish after he'd been freed and attending secret masses and other ceremonies and then reporting back to his patron, his fellow parishioners aware that he was a former rapparee but with no idea he had betrayed them and turned priest hunter.

In 1713, Mullowney is reputed to have killed his first priest, although here is where the past becomes particularly cloudy. Many of the stories concerning 'Sean na Sagart' that are now presented as fact actually come directly from a novel written in

1844 called *Shawn na Soggarth, The Priest Hunter* by Matthew Archdeacon. The successful novelist was born in Castlebar in 1800 and had grown up hearing the tales about Mullowney and other priest hunters of the penal era, a subject he'd studied and written about extensively in several other novels. In his preface to *Shawn* he says that his work is based on those oft-repeated stories and that he'd actually spoken to a farmer whose father had been present during one of the key episodes involving Mullowney, and that his description of the event is accurate. Another writer, R.J. Bennett, said he had encountered a local folklorist in 1949, who had recounted the priest hunter's final pursuit in great detail, much of which tallied with Archdeacon's version.

So with the qualification that the following is a version of a version of an account of a real life incident, John Mullowney made his first priestly kill sometime in 1713 at a place called Pulnathaeken, which was the name of a large sea cavern on the coast of Mayo. On a windy Sunday morning a crowd was gathered in the cave straining to hear a priest, Fr Terence Higgins, say mass over the crashing of the waves, when suddenly the shout of '*Sean na Sagart ag teacht!*' went up from the scout perched on the cliff top. The congregation immediately rushed for the entrance and began to disperse along the rocky shore or towards currachs that had conveyed them there from Mayo's islands. Fr Higgins meantime was scrambling to remove his vestments and secrete the prayer books and chalice in his cloak, delaying his escape from the cave.

Above his head, Mullowney approached, leading a band of troopers, several of whom fired shots at the fleeing crowd, but with little effect. Still mounted, they began to descend a steep track towards the shoreline where the priest hunter witnessed Fr Higgins running into the surf and clambering into a currach with the aid of a couple of fishermen. The oarsmen quickly turned the boat about and began to row for safety, but Sean was not to be denied his bounty and rode his horse out into the waves, bringing him within range of the priest. His reputed cry when trapping a priest was 'Now my year's rent is paid!'; this he exclaimed as he drew his pistol and fired, and Fr Higgins fell dead in the currach.

In November of the following year Mullowney claimed to have attended a series of masses and ordinations, presumably in disguise, all performed on the same day in a woodland near the village of Aughagower (see panel):

The Examination of John O'Mollowny of Ballyheane taken before James Macartney and William Caulfield Esquires Lords Justices of Assize for the Connaught Circuit the sixth day of April 1715.

… He this Examinat was present when the said Francis Burke did ordain Bryan Mulcroan and Peter Gibolane popish priests, who now officiate as popish priests in the County of Mayo and Peter Gibolane is popish priest of the parish of Cloghwell and the said Francis Burke now

dwelleth neare Slewboghteen … and that Patrick Duffy
Registered Popish parish priest of the parish of Ballinrobe
is reputed the other Vicar Generall of the said Diocese of
Tuam … and that the said Patrick Duffy and the said
Francis Burke together with Patrick Twohill, a regu-
lar, Bryan Mulcroon, Peter Gibolane, Edmund Nally,
Thomas Mulkeeran all popish priests and severall others
of the said function not known to this Examinat met at
Lane near Aghagower in the parish of Aghagower and
on or about the twentieth day of November last, the said
[priests] did celebrate seven masses from Dawn of Day till
12 of the Clock … and this Examinate's saw particularly
Francis Burke and Patrick Twohill elevate the wafer and
the same day the said Francis Burke and Patrick Duffy
ordained fifty popish priests…
Jurat coram nobis 7 die Aprilis 1715. John Mullowny
JA. MACARTNEY.
W. CAULFIELD.

WHIPPING PILGRIMS INTO SHAPE

The area around Aughagower, which lies five miles east
of Croagh Patrick, was an important stopping point on
the *Tochar Pádraig*, or the pilgrims' route to the mountain, as it boasted two holy wells. These were *Tobar na*
nDeochan (Well of the Deacons) and *Dabhach Pádraig*
(St Patrick's Vat). Pilgrimages such as these, which could

attract large numbers of people, came to be regarded by the authorities as a threat to peace and as undermining their attempts to eradicate Catholicism from Ireland. So in 1703, they came up with a solution: fine all the pilgrims and if they couldn't pay, have them whipped:

2 Anne, C. 6, S. 27.

Whereas the superstitions of popery are greatly increased and upheld by the pretended sanctity of places especially of a place called St. Patrick's Purgatory in the county of Donegal, and of wells to which pilgrimages are made by vast numbers at certain seasons. All such meetings and assemblies shall be adjudged riots and unlawful assemblies and punishable as such in all persons meeting at such places. All persons assembling at St. Patrick's Purgatory or any well or place contrary to this act shall forfeit ten shillings, the moiety thereof to be paid to such persons who shall give information, the other moiety to the poor of the parish where such offender shall be convicted. In default to pay the said sums such offender shall be committed to some constable or inferior officer where the offence was committed, to be publickly whipped. All magistrates are required to demolish all crosses, pictures and inscriptions that are anywhere publickly set up and are the occasion of any popish superstitions.

It is not known how frequently these punishments

were carried out, but such were the vast numbers that continued to flock to holy wells and other pilgrimage sites, it is likely the local authorities judged it too dangerous to attempt to intervene, lest they be beaten senseless by the devout pilgrims.

Some elements of his testimony stand up to scrutiny; several of the priests he named had been reported previously to be officiating in various parishes around Mayo. But other elements are at best exaggerations or outright fabrication, designed to provide evidence that would justify the issuing of warrants against the priests and to secure their transportation or possibly even their execution. The Fr Patrick Duffy of Ballinrobe that he refers to had been sent into exile several years beforehand. It is quite possible he had returned, but unlikely that with an automatic charge of treason hanging over his head he would participate so openly in such a large and prolonged ceremony. Celebrating seven masses, which the priest hunter himself said lasted 'from Dawn of Day till 12 of the Clock' was unheard of during the penal era. It would simply have been too risky, especially with the potential for so many priests to have been captured and the likelihood that they could count on there being at least one informer among seven congregations; as seen previously the clergy and their faithful flock went to great lengths to keep secret even one illegal mass, performing seven in succession would have been madness. As would ordaining fifty priests at the same time. This last claim was the most obvious falsification as Burke and Duffy were not bishops and therefore couldn't ordain priests.

The testimony did provide one other piece of information on Mullowney's background. His complete lack of education is signified by his signing his sworn statement with an 'X'.

The following year he reputedly captured a Fr Bernard Kilger, who was exiled to Portugal and who would in the future play a key role in the priest hunter's lore. But after that there is scant knowledge of his life for the following decade, other than one or two tales of priests having narrow escapes. One of the more amusing of these describes a waterfall, possibly Ashleigh waterfall at the eastern end of Killary Harbour, which was well known as a place to go for 'cures of the back'. According to the 1887 *Medical Mythology of Ireland*, the patient stands 'in his or her nakedness for about ten minutes under this waterfall' and a cure was supposedly effected. In his attempts to evade capture by Mullowney, a priest was reputedly forced to take refuge under the crashing white water for twenty-four hours.

Another story related in Matthew Archdeacon's book and one which is repeated in R.J. Bennett's 1949 non-fiction account of Sean na Sagart, tells of Mullowney's discovery of a secret mass on the upper floor of a Castlebar granary held at dawn one Sunday. The celebrant was Fr David Bourke who had eluded the authorities for years. But as Mullowney approached the building, look-outs shouted up a warning, which caused panic among the two hundred or so congregated above. As they tried to flee, the sudden shifting of two hundred bodies caused the aged wooden flooring to give way and a sizeable number went crashing into the downstairs room. An aged mendicant was killed, but luckily he was the only fatality, although many others suffered broken limbs. Fr Bourke, at the head of the room, had avoided falling through the floor, but had no time to help tending to the wounded, for he was still in mortal danger. He quickly threw off his vestments and clambered out of a window and dropped to the ground by the side of the granary. Mullowney appeared at the end of the laneway and was about to raise his gun when several of the men who had been on watch leapt on the priest hunter and pinned him to the ground. Fr Bourke fled towards Castlebar River and escaped with the help of a local boatman.

In 1726, Sir John Bingham received word from Dublin Castle that Fr Bernard Kilger (who was Fr David Bourke's uncle) was on a ship bound for Ireland. Bingham had since been appointed High Sheriff of Mayo, which gave him the ultimate responsibility for tracking down outlaw priests and rapparees. He'd been criticised for being lax in his efforts and particularly for not supplying enough troops to protect landlords, especially after rapparees had murdered a despised local landlord called J.P. Samper. Bingham believed that the Catholic clergy were in league with the outlaws and was determined to act on the new information concerning Kilger. According to folklore, he told Mullowney that if the priest was fool enough to return, to make sure his visit was short, to which he reputedly replied 'As short as this?' and

pulled a short dagger from his cloak. As previously seen, returning from banishment was a treasonable offence and could carry a
death sentence and some of the more ruthless priest hunters took
this as a licence to kill.

Some weeks later Fr Kilger was indeed secretly landed in Ireland, but was so well concealed by the locals that all attempts to
catch him proved fruitless, much to Mullowney's frustration.

The tale of Mullowney's, or Sean na Sagart's, dramatic demise
that follows was told by Mayo storytellers for centuries and most
accounts are reasonably consistent. As previously mentioned the
version in Archdeacon's novel was based on the stories that at
the time had only been filtered though a couple of generations'
telling, so it is reasonable to assume that this version is about the
most accurate to be found.

Mullowney had a reputation as a hard drinker and was known
to be overly generous with his rewards, lavishing free spirits on
the troops who often accompanied him on his hunts. Some time
after he'd been ordered to hunt down Fr Kilger he'd decided to
pay a visit to his sister, Nancy Loughnan, after a particularly
lengthy drinking session. She was said to be an attractive girl
in her twenties who had been widowed three years beforehand
and left with a pair of infant girls to look after. Although not
particularly bright, she was a devout Catholic and the shame of
her brother's activities weighed heavily on her shoulders. One of
the children was sick that evening and she had arranged for Fr
Kilger to visit the child. Much to her horror, her brother arrived

at her doorstep and her attempts to get rid of him failed. Luckily though, he was so much the worse for wear from the drink that he fell asleep.

The priest arrived soon after in the company of two men, both armed, who had accompanied him for protection. One of them, John McCann, a friend of the priest, wanted to kill Mullowney in his sleep, but the priest wouldn't countenance murder and they left without the priest hunter being any the wiser.

In the weeks after, McCann and his companion made the mistake of openly ridiculing Mullowney, telling how the very priest he'd been searching for had stood only an arm's length from his pursuer and how they'd all laughed at his incompetence. Now the butt of jokes throughout the neighbourhood, Mullowney was enraged, but had also been supplied with the crucial information that his own sister knew the means of summoning Fr Kilger.

After some time had passed he paid another visit to Nancy, this time completely sober, although he gave himself the appearance of being extremely feverish. He staggered into her cabin and collapsed by the fireplace, telling her he was near death and that he had bequeathed all his money to her. He pleaded with her that he needed absolution for all his misdeeds and begged her to fetch a priest before it was too late. Nancy helped him into her bed and covered him, but at first refused to do as asked. Eventually his continued exhortations got the better of her, and she naively accepted that he was telling the truth. She gathered up the two children and took off into the night.

She reached the cottage where she knew Fr Kilger was hiding and explained what had happened. His nephew, Fr David Bourke, had been visiting and knowing Mullowney's reputation and having personally tussled with him, warned the priest that it was likely to be a trap. But his uncle, who was now a man of sixty, was unable to deny a man final absolution and insisted on going. He told Nancy to leave the children there and accompany him back to her cottage.

When they entered, Nancy lit a candle and led him to Mullowney's bedside. The priest hunter was sweating and shivering under the blanket and did indeed appear to be at death's door, and the priest, bending over the bed, began to recite the prayers. At that moment Mullowney threw back the blanket and lunged at the priest with a knife. A brief struggle ensued, but the aged cleric was no match for the younger man, and after a few moments, Mullowney plunged the dagger into Fr Kilger's throat. Nancy's screams were silenced as she fainted and Mullowney took off into the night to report his success to Bingham. When Nancy eventually came to, still in shock, she ran back to the cottage to tell Fr Bourke that his uncle had been murdered and begged him to flee the area before the same fate befell him, but he refused and insisted that he had to attend to his uncle's mortal remains.

A sense of shock engulfed the community as word rapidly spread. There were dark murmurings that a massacre of Catholics was planned and talk of revenge. Sir John Bingham, delighted at the news of Kilger's killing, was tempered in his celebrations by the unrest he'd heard had spread over the entire area. He quickly ordered all the troops at his disposal to begin patrolling the roads to quell any possible unrest.

Having held a dawn mass in his uncle's name by a nearby lake-side mass rock, Fr Bourke insisted that he must attend the funeral later that day, if only to briefly bless the grave. John McCann and others warned him that the troops were everywhere and that it was too dangerous, but the priest wouldn't back down, so McCann insisted he take a dagger which might afford him some small measure of protection.

As the funeral procession approached the graveyard at Ball-intubber Abbey, Fr Bourke appeared dressed in a farmer's ragged greatcoat and took over the position of one of the coffin bearers. The mourners could hear troops approaching along the road behind them, but continued along the muddy road none-theless. Just before they reached the Abbey, Mullowney sprang from a ditch at the side of the road brandishing a pistol. He rec-ognised Bourke immediately having almost captured him pre-viously in Castlebar. The crowd swarmed around the priest and denied Mullowney a shot, and Fr Bourke, knowing that troops were approaching from the other direction, had no choice but to leap a wall and take off across the fields. Mullowney fired at him but his shot went wild and with no time to reload, he set off in pursuit of the cleric on foot.

Fr Bourke headed for the Partry Hills about four miles away. Although a relatively young man himself, he began to tire rapidly as he drew near to the village of Partry, and Mullowney had closed the gap almost to within a few yards by the time the priest entered a hillside woodland. But unknown to Mullowney, he had his own pursuer. John McCann had been late arriving to join the funeral procession and had witnessed the priest fleeing across the fields with Mullowney some distance behind. By this time he was still some fifty yards behind and was helpless to intervene when he saw the exhausted Fr Bourke trip over a fallen log. Mullowney was on him in an instant and tried to beat the priest with the butt of his pistol. McCann suddenly yelled out to Fr Bourke to use the knife he'd given him, his voice distracting Mullowney sufficiently to allow the priest to reach inside his cloak and withdraw the knife. He plunged wildly at his attacker and the blade sank into Mullowney's arm, causing him to scream and drop the gun. As he tried to wrench the blade from his arm, McCann finally caught up and, wielding his own knife, threw himself at Mullowney and drove the blade into his side. Sean na Sagart drew his final breath and the most feared of priest hunters in Ireland fell dead by Fr Bourke's side. A large rock is said to mark the spot where he was finally slain, which is just a stone's throw from the present-day Partry Garda Station.

In an alternate version of this final chase, McCann is not present. Mullowney catches up with the priest and throws his knife, missing his target. Fr Bourke seizes the knife and hurls it at the on-rushing priest hunter, striking him in the heart and killing him instantly. Which version is the more accurate will never be known, but it is possible McCann was introduced to deliver the final death-blow as it would not be fitting to have a priest take a man's life, no matter what his reputation or intention.

When the other parishioners arrived, Fr Bourke was spirited away to be cared for and folklore tells us that they carried Mullowney's body to Lough Carra, a mile away, weighted it with rocks and threw him into the depths. When Fr Bourke heard what they'd done he ordered them to retrieve the body and bring it to Ballintubber Abbey. There Sean na Sagart was given a Christian burial, albeit in unconsecrated ground. Legend has it that an ash tree grew over his grave, but the tree was struck by lightning and split down the centre. The tree can still be seen close to the abbey.

After his death in 1726, the figure of 'Sean na Sagart' became larger than life in the imaginations of people the length and breath of Ireland. His name conjured up images of a traitorous, merciless killer who preyed on the most revered figures among the Catholic peasants, and one who took pleasure in his work. He became the stuff of legend and myth and was the embodiment of evil, a symbol of the brutal repression of Ireland.

Separating the man from the myth when so little written documentation survives is almost impossible. But it can be said with some certainty that John Mullowney aka Sean na Sagart was one of the worst of his breed. His death in 1726 didn't mark the end of the era, but the apex had long been passed and within a generation, the day of the priest hunter would have drawn to a close.

Part Six

ENLIGHTENMENT

THE DEMISE OF THE
PRIEST HUNTER

As the century advanced, many Protestants increasingly saw the persecution of the Catholic Church in Ireland as unjust and even self-defeating. It had had the effect of rousing the beleaguered Catholic population to come to the protection of their clergy and no matter how many clerics were transported, or in some cases killed, there always seemed to be a ready supply to replace them. Vast resources were being expended in the pursuit of priests and, half a century after the introduction of the latest set of repressive laws, the forces of the crown were beginning to realise that their attempts to 'Protestantise' Ireland had utterly failed.

Across Europe the Age of Enlightenment had begun and leading philosophers and scientists like Isaac Newton and Voltaire sought to promote intellectual exchange and opposed religious intolerance. One of the United States' greatest Presidents, Thomas Jefferson, who was highly respected throughout Europe and had been influenced by the English philosopher John Locke, had long been a proponent of the separation of Church and State.

In Ireland, the obsession with hunting down and banishing priests waned sharply in the 1730s and in many communities Catholic ceremonies were openly practised, the authorities simply turning a blind eye.

> *Numerous chapels and Mass-houses had been built in which Mass was said without fear of interruption, the religious orders had settled down near the sites of most of their old convents, and had taken either houses in the towns or farms in the country.*
> *The Irish Ecclesiastical Record, Volume XIII.*

But in 1744, rumours of another Jacobite invasion were rife, this time led by Charles Edward Stewart or 'Bonnie Prince Charlie', who was the son of James, 'The Old Pretender', and naturally became known as 'The Young Pretender'. As it happens the rumours were this time correct and Charles would launch an abortive invasion through Scotland the following year. But after a decade of relative peace for the Irish Catholic Church, like the dying sting of a wasp, the powers-that-be decided to initiate a fresh series of round-ups in 1744 and orders were sent to magistrates. As a result many clergymen were forced to flee to Dublin, where it was believed they could hide more securely.

Early the following year a Meath-born priest, Fr Fitzgerald, was celebrating a mass in the upper floor of a derelict building in one of Dublin's back lanes. The room was crammed with people and just as the mass was coming to a close, the building collapsed. Fr Fitzgerald and nine of the congregation were killed instantly and as many died later. An outcry followed from all sections of society and the Privy Council quickly issued a proclamation permitting all Catholic places of worship to be opened from St Patrick's Day 1745. They remained open ever after.

Although the Penal Laws remained on the statute books until the end of the century, there was little appetite to enforce them. John Carpenter, for example, who was the Titular Catholic Archbishop of Dublin, which according to law made him an outlaw, was invited to join the Royal Dublin Society in 1773. The process of achieving complete Catholic Emancipation had begun, culminating in Daniel O'Connell becoming, in 1828, the first Catholic to sit at Westminster for over a century, and the Catholic Relief Act in 1829, marking the end of one of the darkest periods in Irish history.

The priest hunters had already become a symbol of ignominy long before the more tolerant period during the second half of the eighteenth century. Always hated by the Catholic community, Protestants soon began to view them at best as ruffians and scoundrels and at worst as violent mercenaries who preyed on the misery of others; because of the widely-known behaviour of men like Garzia, Lowe, Tyrrell and Mullowney, they came to be seen as sly, callous turncoats and intriguers and 'priest hunter' and 'priest catcher' gradually became terms of abuse. A civil action taken in Dublin in 1723 is demonstrative of the above:

> *THE EXAMINATION OF JOHN MOLLOY.*
> *Who being duly sworn and examined saith that one*
> *Samuel Dye a reputed Protestant on February 23rd 1722*
> *called this Deponent a Priest Catcher, a rogue, with*
> *many ignominious names, collaring this Deponent and*
> *most grossly treating him where there were many Romans,*
> *either to curry favour with them or to raise a Mobb about*
> *him as this Deponent verily believes by the often repeti-*
> *tions he made of the name of Priest Catcher. And this*
> *Deponent further saith that one Thomas Rearfoot on the*
> *3rd day of this instant April 1723 being taken on a War-*
> *rant of the Lord Mayor for a debt he owed this Depo-*
> *nent, he called this Deponent a Priest Catcher in the full*
> *market severall times.*
> *Jurat coram me 4 Aprilis Anno 1723.*
> *JOHN FIAGE.*

Reverend Adam Caulfield, a Protestant vicar in Sligo writing in the mid-eighteenth century, said:

> *To the honour of human nature be it told, that no persons*
> *were so infamous in the eyes both of Catholics and Protes-*
> *tants as those who pursued this abominable calling, if one*
> *can speak of such an occupation as a calling.*

A few men did profit from the clampdown in 1744, but with

the relaxation of the enforcement of the Penal Laws the following year, Catholic priests and bishops finally emerged from the their garrets, woodland hollows and caverns and began to practise their religion openly, erasing the priest hunter's *raison d'être*, and the profession quickly went the way of the steam train or the gramophone record, but would be far less fondly remembered.

The mass rocks too had outlived their original purpose. But they continue to serve another. They remain as monuments to the courage of a people determined to exercise their right to practise their faith in the face of intolerance and repression.

REFERENCES

GENERAL REFERENCES

Burke, Rev William P. (1914) *The Irish Priests in the Penal Times*,
Waterford: N. Harvey & Co.

Irish Ecclesiastical Record Volumes 6, 15, 20, 29, 30 (1864 -90),
Dublin: John F. Fowler

Woods, James (1907) *The Annals of Westmeath Ancient and Modern*,
Dublin: Sealy, Bryers & Walker.

His Eminence, Cardinal Moran, Archbishop of Sydney (1899) *The Catholics
of Ireland Under the Penal Laws,* London: Catholic Truth
Society

Cogan, Fr Anthony (1862) *The Diocese of Meath Volumes 1 & 2*
Dublin: John F. Fowler

Brady, Rev. John, (1951-57) *Catholics and Catholicism in the Eigh
teenth Century Press, Archivium Hibernicum, Vol. 16*, The Catholic
Historical Society of Ireland

Nicholson, Asenath, (1858) *Lights and Shades of Ireland*, London:
William Tweedie.

Mitchel, John (1869) *The History of Ireland: from the Treaty of Limerick
to the Present Day Vol 1-2*, London: Charles Griffin & Co.

Sullivan, Alexander Martin (1881) *New Ireland History*, New York: P.J.
Kennedy.

McCormack, W.J., Gillan, Patrick, (2001) *The Blackwell Companion to
Modern Irish Culture* (2001), Wiley-Blackwell

Sullivan, A.M., Member of Parliament for Louth (1878) *New Ireland*, New York: P.F.Collier

MacManus, Seamus (1921) *The Story of the Irish Race*, New York: The Irish Publishing Company

Websites:

http://library.law.umn.edu/Laws in Ireland for the Suppression of Popery

Introduction

de Burgo, Thomas, (1762) *Hibernia Dominicana*

PART ONE: A HISTORY OF VIOLENCE

The Spoils of War

Foster, R.F. (1988) *Modern Ireland 1600 – 1972*, Penguin Books

Ellis, Peter Beresford (1975) *To Hell or Connaught*, Blackstaff

Prendergast , John Patrick (1870) *The Cromwellian Settlement of Ire land*, Ireland: McGlashan & Gill

Kenyon, John, Ohlmeyer, Jane (1998) *The Civil Wars, A Military History of England, Scotland and Ireland 1638-1660*, Oxford University Press.

O'Flanagan, J. Roderick, (1870) *The Lives of the Lord Chancellors and Keepers of the Great Seal of Ireland - from the Earliest Times to the Reign of Queen Victoria*, London: Longmans & Green

Vallely, Paul (September 4th 2008) "Was Cromwell a Revolutionary Hero or a Genocidal War Criminal?" *The Independent*

Websites:

http://irelandsown.net/ - Mullin, James, "Out of Africa, Out of Ireland" Ireland's Own

http://www.historyireland.com/Cromwellian Campaign

http://en.wikipedia.org/wiki/Timeline_of_Irish_history

The Merrie Monarch

Oxford Dictionary of National Biography, *Charles II (1630–1685), King of England, Scotland, and Ireland*, Oxford University

Press

Encyclopaedia Britannica, Charles ll, Encyclopaedia Britannica Inc.

Storer, Jackie, (February 14th 2006) 'Samantha Cameron' BBC News Profile

Websites:

http://www.royal.gov.uk/The Official Website of the British Monarchy

http://en.wikipedia.org/wiki/Charles_II_of_England

Green, White and Orange

Oxford Dictionary of National Biography, *James II and VII (1633–1701), King of England, Scotland, and Ireland,* Oxford University Press

Cogan, Fr Anthony (1862) *The Diocese of Meath Volumes 2* Dublin: John F. Fowler

Gewertz, Ken & Sowerby, Scott (April 17th 2003) 'James ll' Harvard University Gazette

Moore, Malcolm (March 20th 2008) 'Pope funded William of Orange', The Telegraph

A Journal of the Waterford and South-East of Ireland Archaeological Society Vol X111 (1910), Bishop Brennan's Letter.

Seamus an Chaca

Wilson, Charles Townshend (1876) *James the Second,* London: H.S. King & Co.

Encyclopedia Britannica - *James II,* Encyclopaedia Britannica Inc.

Websites:

http://en.wikipedia.org/wiki/James_II_of_England

On the Wrong Side of the Law

Moore, Malcolm (20 March 2008) 'Pope funded William of Orange', *The Telegraph*

Lecky, William Edward (1892) *A History of Ireland in the Eighteenth Century,* London: Longmans Green

The Annals of Shrule (1700 -1710) *Extract of a Letter from Sir Richard Cox*

Websites:

http://library.law.umn.edu/Laws in Ireland for the Suppression of
Popery

http://en.wikipedia.org/wiki/Pope_Innocent_XI

http://en.wikipedia.org/wiki/Penal_laws

The Dawn of the Hunter

Burke, Rev William P. (1914) *The Irish Priests in the Penal Times*,
Waterford: N. Harvey & Co.

O'Fiaich, Tomas (1971) *The Registration of the Clergy in 1704* (1971)
Laws in Ireland for the Suppression of Popery Anne c.3. (1709)

Websites:

http://en.wikipedia.org/wiki/Registration_Act

http://en.wikipedia.org/wiki/Oath_of_abjuration

Tinker, Tailor, Soldier, Priest Hunter

Roud Folk Song Index No. 802

Burke, Rev William P. (1914) *The Irish Priests in the Penal Times*,
Waterford: N. Harvey & Co.

Irish Ecclesiastical Record Vol 30, (1864 -90), Dublin: John F. Fowler

Websites:

http://www.oldbaileyonline.org/Pounds, Shillings & Pence, and their
Purchasing Power, 1674-1913

http://armscollectors.com/The Queen's Arm

PART TWO: MANHUNTING

The Martyr of Inishowen

Harkin, Michael (Maghtochair) (1867) *Inishowen, Its History, Tradi
tions and Antiquities,* Derry: The Journal Office, Shipquay Street.

Irish Ecclesiastical Record Vol 15, (1864 -90), Dublin: John F. Fowler

Hart, Henry Travers (1907) *The Family History of Hart of Donegal*
London: Mitchell Hughes & Clarke, 140 Wardour Street.

(16 February 2010) 'Telling the Fr Hegarty Story' *The Irish Times*

Harvey Ros, *Painting and Stories from the land of Eoghan*, Cottage
Publications

McGrory, Linda & MacDermott, Eamonn (May 23rd-27th 2011) 'A Martyr Never Forgotten' & 'Bishop's Mass for Beheaded Martyr',
  Inishowen Independent
Websites:
www.genealogy.com/Vaughan Lineage/Descendants of Thomas Hart, Donegal Genealogy Resources
http://www.virtualtourist.com/Swilly Walk/Father Hegarty's Rock
http://www.discoverireland.com/Buncrana, County Donegal
http://www.uk-genealogy.org.uk/ireland/Donegal/towns/Buncrana
http://en.wikipedia.org/wiki/35th_(Royal_Sussex)_Regiment_of_Foot
http://en.wikipedia.org/wiki/Buncrana
http://www.buncranaparish.com/

The Most Dangerous Man in the County

O'Laverty, James (1878) *An Historical Account of the Diocese of Down and Connor, ancient and modern,* Dublin: James Duffy & Sons.
His Eminence Cardinal Moran Archbishop of Sydney (1899) *The Catholics of Ireland Under the Penal Laws,* London: Catholic Truth Society
Burke, Rev William P. (1914) *The Irish Priests in the Penal Times,* Waterford: N. Harvey & Co.
Lewis, Samuel (1837) *Kilclief, County Down, A Topographical Diction ary of Ireland,* London: S. Lewis & Co, Aldersgate Street.
Websites:
www.genealogy.com/Maxwell, Downpatrick Parish, County Down
http://www.devlin-family.com/Downpatrick Prisons

The Longford Fox

Irish Ecclesiastical Record Vol 30, (1864 -90), Dublin: John F. Fowler
Burke, Rev William P. (1914) *The Irish Priests in the Penal Times,* Waterford: N. Harvey & Co.
Collins, James (1913) *Newgate Prison - Life in Old Dublin, Historical Associations of Cook Street,* Dublin: James Duffy & Co.
Lewis, Samuel (1837) *A Topographical Dictionary of Ireland,* London: S. Lewis & Co, Aldersgate Street.

Lenihan, Maurice (1866) *Limerick; Its History and Antiquities*, Dublin: James Duffy & Sons

Websites:

http://www.longfordtourism.ie/History of Newtowncashel

http://www.longfordlibrary.ie/County Longford Graveyard Inventory

http://www.longford.ie/History of Kenagh/Mosstown House

Between the Devil and the Deep Blue Sea

Burke, Rev William P. (1914) *The Irish Priests in the Penal Times*, Waterford: N. Harvey & Co.

Irish Ecclesiastical Record Vol 20, (1864 -90), Dublin: John F. Fowler

Websites:

http://www.clarelibrary.ie/The Penal Laws in Clare by Pat O'Brien

Making a Killing

His Eminence Cardinal Moran Archbishop of Sydney (1899) *The Catholics of Ireland Under the Penal Laws*, London: Catholic Truth Society

Gallagher, The Most Reverend James (1877) *Sermons in Irish-Gaelic, with literal idiomatic English translation*, also *The Bishop and His Times*, Dublin: M.H. Gill & Son

Websites:

http://www.allenparish.ie/Penal Laws of the 17th and 18th Century/ James Gallagher

http://www.newadvent.org/Diocese of Raphoe

http://www.ricorso.net/Bishop] James Gallagher (1681-1751)

http://www.pdoherty.net/The Murder of Reverend Peter Hegarty

http://en.wikipedia.org/wiki/Lough_Swilly

PART THREE: SURVIVAL & RESISTANCE

Evading the Hunters

Lewis, Samuel (1837) *Shanrahan Civil Parish, Tipperary, A Topographical Dictionary of Ireland*, London: S. Lewis & Co, Aldersgate Street.

Cogan, Fr Anthony (1862) *The Diocese of Meath Ancient & Modern*, Dublin: John F. Fowler

His Eminence Cardinal Moran Archbishop of Sydney (1899) *The Catholics of Ireland Under the Penal Laws,* London: Catholic Truth Society

Irish Ecclesiastical Record Vol 30, (1864 -90), Dublin: John F. Fowler

Annals of Shrule (1700 – 1710)

Burke, Rev William P. (1914) *The Irish Priests in the Penal Times,* Waterford: N. Harvey & Co.

O'Reilly, Myles Patrick, (1869) *Memorials of those who suffered for the Catholic faith in Ireland in the 16th, 17th, and 18th centuries,* New York: The Catholic Publication Society

Moran, Patrick Francis (1878) Spicilegium Ossoriense , Dublin M.H. Gill & Sons, Sackville Street.

Comerfor, Michael (1883-86) *Comerford's Diocese of Kildare and Leighlin* Dublin: J. Duffy & Sons

Websites:

http://www.mohillparish.ie/The Place Names of Mohill by Michael Whelan

http://www.barberstowncastle.ie/Barberstown Castle 'Priest Hole' -

Protestant Resistance

Irish Ecclesiastical Record Vol 13, (1864 -90), Dublin: John F. Fowler

Cogan, Fr Anthony (1862) *The Diocese of Meath Ancient & Modern,* Dublin: John F. Fowler

Sullivan, Alexander Martin (1881) New Ireland History, New York: P.J. Kennedy.

A Protestant Spy at Court

Cogan, Fr Anthony (1862) *The Diocese of Meath Ancient & Modern,* Dublin: John F. Fowler

Burke, Sir Bernard (1879) *A Genealogical and Heraldic History of the Landed Gentry of Great Britain & Ireland (Waller lineage),* London: Pall Mall

House of Commons papers, Volume 4, *County of Meath Gaol.*

Websites;

www.ancestry.com/The Family of Barnewall In Ireland

http://www.turtlebunbury.com/The Plunketts of Crickstown/The
  Barnewall Connection
http://en.wikipedia.org/wiki/Allenstown_House

Sanctuary by the Boyne
Cogan, Fr Anthony (1862) *The Diocese of Meath Ancient & Modern,*
  Dublin: John F. Fowler
Massereene papers, D.207/19/25 Public Record Office for Northern
  Ireland
Burke, Rev William P. (1914) *The Irish Priests in the Penal Times,* Water
  ford: N. Harvey & Co.
Websites:
http://www.familyhistoryforum.co.uk/Peter Ludlow

The 'Haunted' Room
Cogan, Fr Anthony (1862) *The Diocese of Meath Ancient & Modern,* Dublin:
John F. Fowler
Lewis, Samuel (1837) *Ratoath, County Meath, A Topographical Dictionary
  of Ireland,* London: S. Lewis & Co, Aldersgate Street.
Burke, Rev William P. (1914) *The Irish Priests in the Penal Times,* Water
  ford: N. Harvey & Co.
Pulella, Philip (Fri Apr 20, 2007) 'Catholic Church buries limbo after
  centuries', Reuters News Agency
Websites:
http://www.buildingsofireland.ie/National Inventory of Architectural Herit-
age/The Manor House, Ratoath, Co. Meath
http://www.ashbournehistoricalsociety.com/archives/Ashbourne Histori
  cal Society/Killegland Old Cemetery -
http://www.ratoathparish.ie/history
http://en.wikipedia.org/wiki/Henry_Luttrell_(British_Army_officer)
http://en.wikipedia.org/wiki/Luttrellstown_Castle

Different Sides of the Coin
Croasdaile S.J., Fr. L.H. (1959) *A History of Rosenallis* Dublin: Dun
  Laoghaire Genealogical Society

Burke, Rev William P. (1914) *The Irish Priests in the Penal Times*, Water
    ford: N. Harvey & Co.

Larkin, David (2008) *Larkin of Silanchia; An Erenagh Family*

Websites:

http://www.discalcedcarmelites.ie/Discalced Carmelite Friars

http://landedestates.nuigalway.ie/Croasdaile Estate

http://www.thepeerage.com/Croasdaile lineage

Judicial Murder in Clonmel

Brennan, rev. Richard & O'Reilly, Myles (1878) *Lives of the Irish Martyrs
    and Confessors*, New York : James Sheehy, 1878

Conyngham, David Porter (2001) Lives of the Irish Martyrs, N. Ireland:
    Fredonia Books

Egan, P.M. (1893) *History of the City and County of Waterford*, Kilkenny:
    P.M. Egan

Irish Ecclesiastical Record Vol 30, (1864 -90), Dublin: John F. Fowler

Madden, Richard Robert (1897) *The United Irishmen, Their Lives and Times*,
London: J. Madden & Co.

Burke, Rev. William P. (1907) History of Clonmel, Waterford: N. Harvey & Co

Burke, Rev William P. (1914) *The Irish Priests in the Penal Times*,
    Waterford: N. Harvey & Co.

Websites:

http://newsfeed.rootsweb.com/Sir Edmund Burke on the "judicial murders" of
Fr. Nicholas Sheehy & Ned Meehan in 1766

Webster's Dictionary (1913) 'Abandoned Character'

http://www.ricorso.net/Nicholas Sheehy

http://en.wikipedia.org/wiki/Clonmel

http://en.wikipedia.org/wiki/Nicholas_Sheehy

The Four Corners of Ireland

O'Rourke, T. (1878) *History of the Parishes of Ballysadare and Kilvar
    net*, Dublin: G.T. Stokes

Rathdonnell Papers, Public Record Office of Northern Ireland
    D'Arcy of Hyde Park Papers, National Library of Ireland

Burke, Rev William P. (1914) *The Irish Priests in the Penal Times*,
    Waterford: N. Harvey & Co.

Cogan, Fr Anthony (1862) *The Diocese of Meath Ancient & Modern,*
    Dublin: John F. Fowler

His Eminence, Cardinal Moran, Archbishop of Sydney (1899) *The*
    Catholics of Ireland Under the Penal Laws, London: Catholic Truth
    Society

O'Laverty, James (1878) *An Historical Account of the Diocese of Down*
    and Connor, ancient and modern, Dublin: James Duffy & Sons.

Websites:

http://www.colganhall.com/The Story of John Colgan

PART FOUR: RETRIBUTION
Murder in the Name of God

Cogan, Fr Anthony (1862) *The Diocese of Meath Ancient & Modern,*
    Dublin: John F. Fowler

Burke, Rev William P. (1914) *The Irish Priests in the Penal Times,*
    Waterford: N. Harvey & Co.

Cutler, David & Deaton, Angus & Lleras-Muney, Adriana, (2006) 'The Determi-
nants of Mortality', The National Bureau of Economic
    Research, U.S.

Websites:

http://www.kilskyreballinlough.ie/history

Peasants to the Rescue

Irish Ecclesiastical Record Vol 30, (1864 -90), Dublin: John F. Fowler

Burke, Rev William P. (1914) *The Irish Priests in the Penal Times,*
    Waterford: N. Harvey & Co.

Beastly Vengeance

O'Laverty, James (1878) *An Historical Account of the Diocese of Down*
    and Connor, ancient and modern, Dublin: James Duffy & Sons.

His Eminence, Cardinal Moran, Archbishop of Sydney (1899) *The*
    Catholics of Ireland Under the Penal Laws, London: Catholic Truth
    Society

Burke, Rev William P. (1914) *The Irish Priests in the Penal Times,*
    Waterford: N. Harvey & Co.

An Intimidating Prospect

'Religion, The Penal Laws', Ulster Historical Foundation

Fagan, Patrick (1989), *The Dublin Catholic Mob 1700-1750*

O'Rourke, T. (1878) *History of the Parishes of Ballysadare and Kilvar
net*, Dublin: G.T. Stokes

Cogan, Fr Anthony (1862) *The Diocese of Meath Ancient & Modern,*
Dublin: John F. Fowler

O'Laverty, James (1878) *An Historical Account of the Diocese of Down
and Connor, ancient and modern,* Dublin: James Duffy & Sons.

Burke, Rev William P. (1914) *The Irish Priests in the Penal Times*,
Waterford: N. Harvey & Co.

PART FIVE: THE INFAMOUS PRIEST HUNTERS

John Garzia: The Priest who Became a Priest-Hunter who Became a Missionary

McGrath, Kevin (1949) 'John Garzia, A Noted Priest-Catcher and his
Activities, 1717-23', The Irish Book over, Vol XXXl

Irish Ecclesiastical Record Vol 30, (1864 -90), Dublin: John F. Fowler

Jones, Billy E. (2005) The Lives and Times of John Garzia, North
Carolina: Teach's Cove Publishers

McGee, John D'Arcy (1862) *A Popular History of Ireland From the
Earliest Period to the Emancipation of the Catholics*, Glasgow: Cam
eron & Ferguson

de Burgo, Thomas, (1762) *Hibernia Dominicana*

Burke, Rev William P. (1914) *The Irish Priests in the Penal Times*,
Waterford: N. Harvey & Co.

Letters of John Garzia, Colonial and State Records of North Carolina

*Minutes of the Lower House of the North Carolina General Assembly Volume 04,
Pages 115-155*, Colonial and State Records of North
Carolina

Hopkins, Frank (13 November 2008) 'Look Out! It's the Priest
Catcher …' *Evening Herald*

Websites:

www.sistersofclare.org/History of The Sisters of Clare

http://en.wikipedia.org/wiki/Spanish_Inquisition

http://en.wikipedia.org/wiki/Charles_Paulet,_2nd_Duke_of_Bolton

Barry Lowe of Newtown: The Fiend of Westmeath

Woods, James (1907) *The Annals of Westmeath Ancient and Modern*,
Dublin: Sealy, Bryers & Walker.

Cogan, Fr Anthony (1862) *The Diocese of Meath Ancient & Modern*,
Dublin: John F. Fowler

Egan, Oliver (1986) Tyrrellspass Past and Present, Ireland: Tyrrellspass
Town Development Committee

Sheridan, Jeremiah (1982) *Westmeath, As Others Saw It*

Sheridan, Jeremiah (1978) *South Westmeath: Farm and Folk*
Sunday's Well, Ballymore, County Westmeath/Dalton's Rock, National Inventory of Architectural Heritage

Index of Prerogative Wills 1536 -1810 – Sir Arthur Vicars

Lyons, John Charles (1853) *The Grand Juries of the County of West
meath 1727 – 1853*, Dublin: Hibernia Press Office

Lewis, Samuel (1837) *Newtown, County Westmeath, A Topographical Dictionary
of Ireland*, London: S. Lewis & Co, Aldersgate Street.

Websites:

http://www.offalyhistory.com/Kilbeggan in the 18th Century

http://www.bomford.net/IrishBomfords/The Low Family of Newtown
Low

http://ancestry.com The Westmeath Lowes

http://www.offalyhistory.com/Clara Parish

http://en.wikipedia.org/wiki/High_Sheriff_of_Westmeath

Edward Tyrrell: A Bounder and a Cad

Irish Ecclesiastical Record Vol 20, 30, (1864 -90), Dublin: John F.
Fowler

Burke, Rev William P. (1914) *The Irish Priests in the Penal Times*,
Waterford: N. Harvey & Co.

Brady, Rev. John, (1951-57) *Catholics and Catholicism in the Eigh
teenth Century Press, Archivium Hibernicum, Vol. 16*, The Catholic Historical Society of Ireland

Lecky, William (1878) A history of England in the Eighteenth Cen
tury Vol 2, London: Longmans Green & Co.

His Eminence, Cardinal Moran, Archbishop of Sydney (1899) *The Catholics of Ireland Under the Penal Laws,* London: Catholic Truth Society

Rafferty, Oliver (1994) *Catholicism in Ulster, 1603-1983: An Interpretative History,* South Carolina: University of South Carolina Press

No author credited (1912) *Parochial History of Waterford and Lismore During the 18th and 19th Centuries,* Waterford: N. Harvey & Co.

Lodge, John & Archdall, Mervin (1789) *The Peerage of Ireland* By John Lodge and Mervin Archdall Volume 5, Dublin: James Moore, College Green.

Websites:

http://www.donnybrook.biz/history.htm/A Short History of Some Dublin Parishes, The Parish of Lusk by M. Donnelly

http://www.clarelibrary.ie/The Penal Laws in Clare by Pat O'Brien

http://www.ricorso.net/Edward Tyrrell

http://en.wikipedia.org/wiki/Edward_Tyrrell

http://en.wikipedia.org/wiki/Hugh_MacMahon

http://en.wikipedia.org/wiki/Ruaidhri_Flaithbheartaigh

http://www.ricorso.net/rx/az-data/autjors/t/Tyrrell_E

Sean na Sagart: The Mayo Assassin

Archdeacon, Matthew (1844*) Shawn na Soggarth; The Priest Hunter,* Dublin: James Duffy, Anglesea Street

Bennett, R.J. (1949) *The Priest Hunter,* Dublin : Catholic Truth Society

Irish Ecclesiastical Record Vol 30, (1864 -90), Dublin: John F. Fowler

Sullivan, Alexander Martin (1881) New Ireland History, New York: P.J. Kennedy.

9 July 2010, 'Shaun na Soggarth', The Connaught Telegraph

25 June 2005, 'The Station Mass – A Tradition Steeped in History', *Castlebar News*

Fahey, F (1989) *Tochar Padraig, A Pilgrim's Progress* (1989) Ireland: Ballintubber Abbey Publication

Dalton, David, *Pilgrim Ways: Catholic Pilgrimage Sites in Britain & Ireland*

Burke, Rev William P. (1914) *The Irish Priests in the Penal Times*,
    Waterford: N. Harvey & Co.

Hyde, Douglas (1906) *'Mary's Well', A Religious Folk Tale From The
    Religious Songs of Connacht*, Dublin: Gill

Mooney, James (1887) *The Medical Mythology of Ireland* (1887) Phila
    delphia: Press of MacCalla & Company

Websites:

http://www.croaghpatrickheritagetrail.com/Killavally – Coill an Bhaile

http://towns.mayo-ireland.ie/Sean na Sagart - The Priest Hunter

http://www.mayoancestors.com/Sean na Sagart - The Priest Hunter

http://www.ballintubberabbey.ie/Sean na Sagart

www.tourmakeady.com/Sean Na Sagart

http://en.wikipedia.org/wiki/Sean_na_Sagart

PART SIX: ENLIGHTENMENT
The Demise of the Priest-Hunter

Irish Ecclesiastical Record Vol 13, (1864 -90), Dublin: John F. Fowler
    His Eminence, Cardinal Moran, Archbishop of Sydney (1899) *The Catho-
lics of Ireland Under the Penal Laws,* London: Catholic Truth
    Society

Burke, Rev William P. (1914) *The Irish Priests in the Penal Times*,
    Waterford: N. Harvey & Co.

O'Rourke, T. (1878) *History of the Parishes of Ballysadare and Kilvar
    net*, Dublin: G.T. Stokes

Phoenix, Eamon (1988) *Two Acres of Irish History: A Study Through
    Time of Friar's Bush and Belfast 1750-1918,* N. Ireland: Ulster His
    torical Foundation

Encyclopaedia Britannica, *Enlightenment*

Websites:

http://en.wikipedia.org/wiki/Age_of_Enlightenment

PANELS:
A Mass of Mass Rocks

McGinley, Paul (Jan 8th 2009) 'What 'The Liberator' said in Shan
    talla', Galway Advertiser

Websites:

http://en.wikipedia.org/wiki/Mass_rock

http://mcginleyclan.org/religion.htm/Mass Rocks 1609-1782

http://www.killenummery.com/Tullynascreena Mass Rock

http://www.lmi.utvinternet.com/massrock.htm/Ballymacpeake Mass
   Rock

Religion and The Battle of the Boyne

Moore, Malcolm (20 March 2008) 'Pope funded William of
   Orange' The Telegraph

Brown, Derek (12 July 2000) 'How the battle of the Boyne earned
   its place in history.' *The Guardian*

Encyclopedia Britannica, *The Battle of the Boyne*

Websites:

http://www.battleoftheboyne.ie/Office of Public Works

http://en.wikipedia.org/wiki/Battle_of_the_Boyne

What's in a Name?

Prendergast, John Patrick (1870) *The Cromwellian Settlement of Ire
   land,* London: Longmans, Green, Reader, and Dyer

Websites:

http://www.liberalhistory.org.uk/A Concise History of the Liberal
   Party

http://en.wikipedia.org/wiki/Tory

http://www.etymonline.com/Whig

A Vicious Circle

Lecky, William Edward (1892) *A History of Ireland in the Eighteenth
   Century*, Lecky London: Longmans, Green & Co.

Burke, Rev William P. (1914) *The Irish Priests in the Penal Times*,
   Waterford: N. Harvey & Co.

He Stoops to Conquer...

Burke, Rev William P. (1914) *The Irish Priests in the Penal Times*,
   Waterford: N. Harvey & Co.

Websites:

http://en.wikipedia.org/wiki/Oliver_Goldsmith

Bridewell – The Irish Connection

Bridewells of Ireland, House of Commons papers, Volume 4

Websites:

http://www.policehistory.com/The Bridewell, Cork City by Garda
   Leslie Rice

http://www.garda.ie/

http://www.worldwidewords.org/Bridewell

Right up his Street

Dictionary of Ulster Biography, *Joshua Dawson 1660 – 1725*

Lewis, Samuel (1837) *Castledawson, County Londonderry, A Topograph
   ical Dictionary of Ireland,* London: S. Lewis & Co, Aldersgate Street

Websites:

http://www.mansionhouse.ie/

http://en.wikipedia.org/wiki/Castledawson

Keeping the Irish Wolf from the Door

Hickey, Kieran R. *A Geographical Perspective on the Decline and
   Extermination of the Irish Wolf, Canis Lupus,* Galway: Department of
   Geography, National University of Ireland, Galway

Warner, Dick (15 November 2010) 'How the Irish Wolf Went to the
   Dogs' *Irish Examiner*

Websites:

http://en.wikipedia.org/wiki/Wolves_in_Ireland

A Family at War

Lodge, John & Archdall, Mervin (1789) *The Peerage of Ireland By John
   Lodge and Mervin Archdall Volume 5,* Dublin: James Moore, College
   Green.

Websites:

http://www.finnstown-hotel.ie http://en.wikipedia.org/wiki/Kennedy_baronets

Courting Death

Harrison, Kimberley & Fantina, Richard, *A Marriage of Inconvenience:*
   Bigamy and the Sensational Novel

http://www.oldbaileyonline.org/Punishments at the Old Bailey

Corless, Damien (21 Nov 2009) 'You Shall Hang by the Neck . . .'
   Irish Independent

Websites:

http://en.wikipedia.org/wiki/Bloody_Code

Whipping Pilgrims into Shape

Burke, Rev William P. (1914) *The Irish Priests in the Penal Times*,
   Waterford: N. Harvey & Co.

Websites:

http://library.law.umn.edu/Laws in Ireland for the Suppression of
   Popery .

OTHER BOOKS BY COLIN C. MURPHY

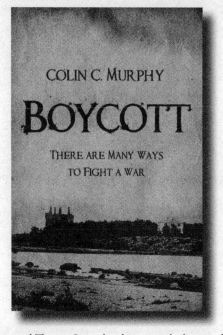

COLIN C. MURPHY

BOYCOTT

THERE ARE MANY WAYS
TO FIGHT A WAR

Two brothers, Owen and Thomas Joyce, barely survive the horror of the great famine that devastated Ireland in the 1840s. But it left a lasting effect on both of them. Three decades later they are thrown together during the Land War, when evictions and landlord cruelty reach an intolerable level. But Thomas places his trust in the gun, while Owen backs the passive resistance advocated by the Land League. Captain Charles Boycott, an English land agent in Mayo, becomes the first to suffer this new form of revolt, when he and his family are ostracised. It is a David versus Goliath situation, with Boycott supported by the military, the police, the press, the British Government. How can peasants stand against an empire? And how will the two brothers reconcile their differences and confront their troubled past?

A novel of brotherly love and brotherly conflict.

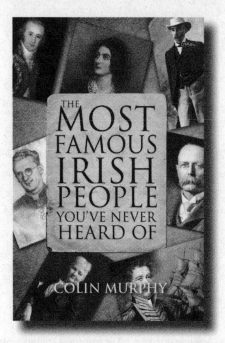

THE MOST FAMOUS IRISH PEOPLE YOU'VE NEVER HEARD OF

COLIN MURPHY

Irish people have left their mark on virtually every corner of the globe. This fascinating book tells the stories of the Irish who are justly celebrated in their adopted homelands, but virtually unknown in Ireland.

William Melville from Kerry, the First Head of MI5

Monsignor Hugh O'Flaherty from Cork, who rescued 4,000 Jews and Allied Servicemen from the Nazis

James Hoban from Kilkenny, who designed The White House

Jennie Hodgers from Louth, who served three years in Union Army during the American Civil War – as a man

George McElroy from Dublin, who became one of World war I's outstanding aerial aces

And many more …